Y0-BOJ-352

ASIAN ECONOMIC AND POLITICAL ISSUES

VOLUME V

ASIAN ECONOMIC AND POLITICAL ISSUES
Frank Columbus (Editor)

ASIAN ECONOMIC AND POLITICAL ISSUES

VOLUME V

FRANK COLUMBUS
EDITOR

WITHDRAWN

Nova Science Publishers, Inc.
New York

HIEBERT LIBRARY
FRESNO PACIFIC UNIV.-M. B. SEMINARY
FRESNO, CA 93702

Senior Editors: Susan Boriotti and Donna Dennis
Coordinating Editor: Tatiana Shohov
Office Manager: Annette Hellinger
Graphics: Wanda Serrano
Book Production: Jennifer Vogt, Matthew Kozlowski, and Maya Columbus
Circulation: Ave Maria Gonzalez, Indah Becker and Vladimir Klestov
Marketing: Cathy DeGregory

Library of Congress Cataloging-in-Publication Data
Available Upon Request

ISBN: 1-59033-302-0

Copyright © 2002 by Nova Science Publishers, Inc.
400 Oser Ave, Suite 1600
Hauppauge, New York 11743
Tele. 631-231-7269   Fax 631-231-8175
e-mail: Novascience@earthlink.net
Web Site: http://www.novapubishers.com

All rights reserved. No part of this book may be reproduced, stored in a retrieval system or transmitted in any form or by any means: electronic, electrostatic, magnetic, tape, mechanical photocopying, recording or otherwise without permission from the publishers.

The authors and publisher have taken care in preparation of this book, but make no expressed or implied warranty of any kind and assume no responsibility for any errors or omissions. No liability is assumed for incidental or consequential damages in connection with or arising out of information contained in this book.

This publication is designed to provide accurate and authoritative information with regard to the subject matter covered herein. It is sold with the clear understanding that the publisher is not engaged in rendering legal or any other professional services. If legal or any other expert assistance is required, the services of a competent person should be sought. FROM A DECLARATION OF PARTICIPANTS JOINTLY ADOPTED BY A COMMITTEE OF THE AMERICAN BAR ASSOCIATION AND A COMMITTEE OF PUBLISHERS.

Printed in the United States of America

CONTENTS

PREFACE

The articles presented in this book examine the current political and economic situations in nations across Asia, including to explore issues of global warming dealt with by Toshihiko Nakata and Japan's National Defense Industry by Andrew Hanami. China's economic development is examined by Xiao-Ming Li and UMTS by Robert Rickards. Important programs in East Timor, Cambodia, India and Indonesia are also analyzed.

Chapter 1

The "Inward and Westward" Shifts in the Strategic Emphases of China's Economic Development

Xiao-Ming Li[*]

Department of Commerce,
Massey University (Albany)
New Zealand

Introduction

While verging on becoming an economic superpower, China's economic growth has nevertheless slowed down in recent years and somewhat persistently. This worrying sign has catalysed topical studies on the causes and countermeasures of the slowdown by professional economists, policy researchers, and political advisers in China. On the one hand, short-run economic fluctuations are believed to be blameable, grounded on which were macroeconomic stabilisation programs pursued recently in China (See Li (2000) for more details). On the other hand, long-run factors are also considered unanimously as playing an increasingly important role. Consensus has thus been reached that, having enjoyed phenomenal growth for many years, China is now entering an inescapable period of large-scale adjustments of its economic development strategy.

China's economic development strategy adopted so far since the inauguration of economic reforms can be characterised as outward- and eastward-oriented in a sense, the former dominant in the 1990s while the latter in both the 1980s and 1990s. With little doubt, this strategy has been successful in retrospect. However, the growth thrust initially gained under the strategy is now fading out, and a new development strategy is being incubated and put in practice in a hope that it would help China to pick up its growth momentum. The new strategy may be characterised as inward- and westward-oriented. China's shifts in its strategic

[*] Address for correspondence: Dr. Xiao-Ming Li, Department of Commerce, Massey University (Albany), Private Bag 102904, North Shore MSC, Auckland, New Zealand. Tel: 64-9-4439799 ext 9471. Fax: 64-9-4418177. E-mail: *x.n.li@massey.ac.nz*

emphases of economic development will have far-reaching impacts not just on the Chinese economy *per se* but also on the world economy given the former's increasing integration into, and hence growing importance in, the latter. This article examines the long-run factors that underlie the strategic changes. It first reviews China's outward-oriented development strategy as concretised in the export-led model in the 1990s. The historical merits as well as the limitations of the model are discussed, to explain why China has now decided to mainly tap domestic instead of foreign markets for future long-run growth. This change may be labelled as an inward shift in the strategic emphasis of economic development. Building on different views of Chinese economists with regard to new growth sources in the domestic economy, there is a suggestion that urbanisation could act as an effective way of tapping such growth sources. A justification for this suggestion from both the demand and supply perspectives is given. The study next turns to China's shift from the eastward-oriented to the westward-oriented development strategy by looking at a question that immediately and logically follows: where to tap domestic growth sources, still in East China or in Middle and West China instead? In addressing this question, a section is devoted to investigating regional disparities and their historical causes, the need and favourable conditions for the great development of West China, and the policies promulgated and to be promulgated soon by the government to support such a westward shift in China's geographical emphasis of economic development. This is then followed by a section which offers conclusions of this article.

RECONSIDERING DOMESTIC MARKETS AS THE LONG-RUN GROWTH SOURCE

The Export-Led Growth Model of China in the 1990s

China's economic development since 1978 may be roughly divided into two phases. The first one covers mainly the 1980s. During the 1980s, growth of the Chinese economy was driven primarily by domestic demand. At that time, the planing system still dominated with its oft-accompanied "shortage state" prevailing in the economy. Li (1995) estimated excess investment and consumption demands over the 1980s to be something between 1.39% and 10.03% and between 0.1% and 6.9% of total investment and consumption respectively. Ironically, such a shortage state under economic reforms functioned as a growth engine that was fuelled by unsatisfied household consumption demand and infrastructure investment demand. As Tables 1 and 2 show, major farm and industrial products for consumption, infrastructure, residence and so on, had their production capacities and outputs expanded more rapidly in the 1980s than in the 1990s, thus creating the first wave of China's extraordinary growth in the reform era. It is remembered that the excessive consumption demand for the "Three Big Items" (colour TV, refrigerator, and washing machine, once referred to in China as the three "hot spots" of consumption), was one of the major thrusts of growth in the 1980s, as suggested by Table 1.

Table 1 Average Annual Growth Rates of Output of Selected Consumption Products

Major farm products	1979-89	1990-99	Major industrial products	1979-89	1990-97
Grain	2.67%	2.24%	Cloth	5.03%	2.83%
Cotton	5.21%	0.11%	Paper and Paperboards	10.62%	4.94%
Oil-bearing crops	8.62%	7.22%	Sugar	7.46%	5.56%
Sugar cane	7.91%	4.35%	Beer	28.72%	12.56%
Beet roots	11.83%	-0.67%	Refrigerators	64.56%	6.08%
Tea	6.48%	2.37%	Colour TV sets	103.46%	16.32%
Fruits	9.77%	13.03%	Washing machines	146.74%	4.98%
Meat	9.50%	8.51%	Electric fans	38.59%	2.12%
Aquatic products	8.59%	13.60%	Cameras	26.87%	34.73%

Source: Own calculations using the data from *China Statistical Yearbook* 2000.

**Table 2 Average Annual Growth Rates of
Selected Public Utilities and of Residential Building**

	1980-89	1990-99		1980-89	1990-99
Tap water supply	18.07%	1.73%	Sewer pipelines	10.69%	9.45%
Public transportation	7.13%	13.40%	Natural gas supply	29.20%	3.08%
Length of paved road	15.00%	7.15%	Passenger traffic	10.88%	5.83%
Public green areas	18.06%	7.40%	Residential building	5.99%	4.80%

Source: Own calculations using the data from *China Statistical Yearbook* 2000.

High growth rates of GDP in 1992 and 1993 (14.1% and 13.1%) may be attributable to sharp investment expansion (Investment growth contributed 52.68% and 82.22% to GDP growth in 1992 and 1993), since the aforementioned consumption demand for the "Three Big Items" had now reached a saturation point. However, investment alone could not sustain growth for long and consumption tended to become stable as its new "hot spots" were unlikely to appear soon. In this case, exports would have to become an alternative source of growth for the Chinese economy. Whether by design or accident, the second phase started from 1992 when the pace of shifting to an outward-oriented development strategy began to quicken. The southern and eastern coastal areas of China were the first beneficiaries of the experiment for the changeover, with their economic structures being quickly adjusted to meet the requirements of more economic opening. Coming along with this move had been a growing inflow of foreign capital, which provided China with a financial source for investment and an impetus for growth. Table 3 exhibits that, as a result of shifting to the outward-oriented development strategy, export growth picked up after 1994 till 1998 when the Asian crisis began to adversely affect China, and foreign-invested enterprises gradually became the main driving force of China's exports as they occupied an increasing share of total exports. For comparison, Table 4 calculates the average contribution of each component of GDP to its growth in the 1980s and 1990s. One can see that, compared with the 1980s, the combined contributions of consumption and investment to GDP growth in the 1990s declined by approximate 8 percentage points which were taken over by that of exports. So, if domestic consumption demand made the first wave of growth in the 1980s, then the export-led growth model (as well as the development of the non-state sector, which is not the focus of this article) allowed foreign demand to create the second wave of growth in the 1990s.

Table 3 Indicators of Outward-oriented Development Strategy in the 1990s

Year	Total exports (US$ bn) (Growth)	Primary goods (US$ bn) (Share in total)	Manufactured goods (US$) (Share in total)	Foreign-funded firms (US$) (Share in total)	Total investment (RMB bn)	Foreign investment (RMB bn) (Share in total)
1990	62.09 (18.2%)	15.89 (25.6%)	46.21 (74.4%)	—	444.93	27.83 (6.3%)
1991	71.84 (15.7%)	16.15 (22.5%)	55.70 (77.5%)	—	550.88	31.63 (5.7%)
1992	84.94 (18.2%)	16.99 (20.0%)	67.94 (80.0%)	17.36 (20.4%)	785.50	45.71 (5.7%)
1993	91.74 (8.0%)	16.67 (18.2%)	75.08 (81.8%)	25.24 (27.5%)	1245.79	90.73 (6.9%)
1994	121.01 (31.9%)	19.71 (16.3%)	101.30 (83.7%)	34.71 (28.7%)	1704.21	176.90 (10.4%)
1995	148.78 (22.9%)	21.49 (14.4%)	127.30 (85.6%)	46.88 (31.5%)	2001.93	229.59 (11.5%)
1996	151.05 (1.5%)	21.93 (14.5%)	129.12 (85.5%)	61.51 (40.7%)	2291.36	274.66 (12.0%)
1997	182.79 (20.9%)	23.95 (13.1%)	158.84 (86.9%)	74.90 (41.0%)	2494.11	268.39 (10.8%)
1998	183.81 (0.56%)	20.59 (11.2%)	163.22 (88.8%)	80.96 (44.0%)	2840.62	261.7 (9.2%)
1999	194.93 (6.05%)	19.94 (10.2%)	174.99 (89.8%)	88.63 (45.47%)	2985.47	200.7 (6.7%)

Source: *China Statistical Yearbook* 1994, 1996, and 2000.

Table 4 Average Contributions of GDP's Components to Its Growth

GDP components	1980-89	1990-99
Consumption	63.99%	57.75%
Investment	37.56%	36.98%
Exports	16.98%	24.68%
Imports	-18.53%	-19.41%

Source: Own calculations using the data from *China Statistical Yearbook* 2000.

Here, the issue of the role of exchange rate policy in promoting China's exports deserves special attention. China realised earlier that its currency had been overvalued. It then took action to correct the overvaluation and benefited from this proactive policy decision. Unlike China, however, the crisis-hit Southeast Asian countries were stubborn on not devaluing their already overvalued currencies until they were forced to by the crisis, and thus paid a great price. Some economists then went so far as to blame an almost 50% devaluation of RMB in 1994 for the Asian financial crisis that broke out three years later. They argued that the devaluation had enabled China to wrest a big share of world export markets from those crisis-hit Asian countries (Xu (1998)). In other words, China's export gains came mainly from the latter's mistakes in terms of their rigid exchange rate policies. One could refute such an argument by simply saying: "Don't blame others for your own fault. The market law is ruthless and only favours those who obey it". But these refutions do not sound very professional, and we need more in-depth and convincing analysis here.

It is true that, compared to 1993, the real exchange rate of the RMB rose by 25.5% in 1994, 8.64% in 1995, 4.64% in 1996, 6.73% in 1997 and 12.12% in 1998 (Calculated on the basis of Table 9 in Li (1999)). These improvements in China's international competitiveness stemmed not only from the 1994 currency devaluation but also from reductions in unit labour costs (ULCs). Since manufactured products accounted for more than 80% of exports in the 1990s, we computed unit labour costs in China's manufacturing industry for 1994-97. One can see from Table 5 that, while the overall trend of ULCs kept growing in newly industrialised Asian economies (NIAEs), China enjoyed nevertheless an overall decline of ULCs in its manufacturing sector. Three reasons may account for this: First, having experienced 10 years or so of "trial and error" since initially setting up businesses in China in the 1980s, foreign-funded firms and joint ventures enhanced the skill levels of their workers and managing staff in production and management, and thus labour productivity began to improve. Second, for those state owned manufacturing enterprises, deepened reforms including decisive decisions to lay off redundant workers and staff more or less improved their productivity. Third, owing to a huge pool of surplus labour force (about 0.1 billion) in the countryside, there was relatively low pressure of increasing wages and salaries in China. This last fact made China differ from the NIAEs. In a word, the rise in the real exchange rate (i.e., external competitiveness) of China should be attributed at least partly to its strengthening of comparative advantage in labour-intensive products. This comparative advantage was bestowed on China by its own built-in economic structure and characteristics. One should not be surprised by China's having been able to expand its shares in international markets, especially when the fading away of the initial momentum brought about by the 1994 devaluation is taken into account. It is likely that China will continue on this favourable trend for some time to come, if only the reforms of state-owned enterprises are to be smooth and successful.

The Limitations of Export-Led Growth Model for China

However, the fact that China still has room to raise labour productivity of manufacturing industry does not justify that it should continue to rely heavily or solely on the export-led growth model. Comparative advantage makes sense in "comparative" terms. After the crisis, many Asian nations started the process of economic adjustments, including substantially cutting labour costs. Table 6 shows that the wage levels in seven selected Asian countries fell by 15.2% to 69.1% in 1998. With the devaluation of their currencies between 60%-400% (Yu (1998)) even if net of inflation up to 70% in that year, these countries' international competitiveness rose greatly as compared to the pre-crisis period. Such a trend had begun to wipe out China's comparative advantage resulting from lowering unit labour costs, as witnessed by only 0.56% of its export growth in 1998.

Table 5 Annual Percentage Changes in Unit Labour Costs in China, Japan and NIAE's manufacturing industry (MI)

MI in China	1993	1994	1995	1996	1997
Annual wage/person in MI (RMB)	3348	4283	5169	5642	5933
Gross IOV of MI (RMB bn)	3540.35	4557.86	4842.11	5514.94	5973.07
No. of staff & workers in MI	52.30 m	54.32 m	54.39 m	52.93 m	50.82 m
Price index of products of MI	100	111.1	124.4	129.5	127.1
Consumer price index	100	124.1	145.3	157.3	161.8
China	-	-7.61%	8.78%	-10.32%	-11.05%
Japan	4.3%	-0.7%	-2.3%	-2.2%	-2.3%
NIAEs	1.3%	2.1%	-1.7%	1.1%	2.8%

Source: Figures relating to Japan and NIAEs are from the *World Economic Outlook* 1998, International Monetary Fund; and figures relating to China are own calculations using the data from *China Statistical Yearbook* 1994-98.

Table 6 Percentage Changes of Wages in Selected Asian Economies

Year	Indonesia	Malaysia	Philippines	Singapore	Korea	Thailand	Taiwan
01.97-11.98	-69.1	-33.5	-33.2	-15.2	-31.5	-29.0	-15.2

Source: *Singtao Daily* (05/11/98).

People often argue that China should further devalue the RMB to promote exports so as to restore high economic growth. However, the question missed here is whether exports will continue to be something on which China could bet its bottom dollar for that purpose. Let us address this question using the lessons as suggested by the Asian maelstrom. When talking about the financial chaos, many economists have focused on financial fragility (such as premature financial deregulation and capital-account liberalisation with weak supervision and prudential regulation), and on the nominal variables (such as foreign reserves, short-term capital flows, exchange rates, foreign debts). "Symbolic economy", if one may use this term to refer to these nominal economic variables, is surely important and should not be overlooked. But the root causes must be searched for in the real-economy sector or economic fundamentals. One of the main vulnerabilities of the troubled Asian economies was their heavy dependence on international markets. As can be seen from Table 7, in the two decades prior to the crisis, exports grew much faster than GDP and occupied an increasingly large share of GDP in these countries. Overseas markets provided them with a growth impetus as a merit of the pursued export-led growth model on the one hand, but the model also made them vulnerable to unforeseen and uncontrollable changes in the world demand on the other. In 1996, the growth of the world trade volume fell sharply to 6.65 from 9.5% a year earlier, with those Asian export-led economies bearing the brunt of the detrimental effects (See the figures on export growth for 1996 in Table 7). One explanation is that the sharp downturn in the world demand for semi-conductor/electronics products delivered a heavy blow to the Asian countries which had built excessive production capacity in the two decades 1975-1996.

Excessive production capability then inevitably led to an oversupply of the products and hence a rapid decline in the price (Lan (1999)).

Table 7 Growth of GDP, GNP Per Capita, and Exports of Selected Countries

Country	Year	GDP growth (%)	GNP per capita Growth (%)	Export growth (%)	Exports/GDP (%)
Indonesia	1975-85	7	4.3	-1	1975: 24
	1986-96	7.8	6.1	8.9	1986: 23
	1995	8.2	5.7	8.6	1995: 26.4
	1996	7.6	5.8	6.3	1996: 26.2
Malaysia	1975-85	7.1	4.1	8.2	1975: 43.7
	1986-96	8.7	6.1	14.6	1986: 54.9
	1995	9.5	6.8	19	1995: 95.5
	1996	8	5.8	10.7	1996: 92
Philippines	1975-85	2.9	0.3	7.6	1975: 19.3
	1986-96	3.2	1.3	8.8	1986: 26.3
	1995	4.8	2.6	12	1995: 40.5
	1996	5.7	4.5	20.3	1996: 49
South Korea	1975-85	7.5	5.6	11.7	1975: 27.8
	1986-96	8.1	7.1	10.8	1986: 34.1
	1995	9	7.4	24	1995: 33.1
	1996	7.1	5.6	14.1	1996: 32.4
Thailand	1975-85	6.4	3.8	9.5	1975: 18.4
	1986-96	9.6	7.9	15.4	1986: 23.2
	1995	9.2	8.2	14.8	1995: 41.7
	1996	6.4	4.4	2.4	1996: 36.8

Source: World Development Indicators 1998 CD-ROM, World Bank

Not only unpredictable changes in the world demand matter, but increasingly fierce competition also threaten export-led economies. Cheap labour costs and abundant labour resources have been frequently used as evidences of comparative advantages inherent in Southeast Asian countries. It should be noted that, as a global tendency towards trade and financial liberalisation, more and more economies with such comparative advantages have entered or are entering into the world market, in a belief that they have better advantages and can win a bigger share in the market than their competitors. The world market is thus getting packed with suppliers, which, in the face of limited growth of the world demand, ignites fierce competition among competitors in all aspects. As a result, the growth rates of trade prices fall relative to those of hourly earnings (see Table 8), profit margins become eroded, and few economies can remain in the top competitive position for long.

Latin American countries, such as Brazil, Argentina and Mexico, started industrialisation with labour-intensive industries in the 1960s and 1970s, and developed rapidly during that period. However, as Asian countries emerged in the world market during the 1970s and 1980s, Latin American countries lost competitiveness to them in labour-intensive products. Consequently, they ended up with a serious economic crisis in 1994-95. Then the emergence of China in the world market began to weaken the competitiveness of Southeast Asian countries, as China possesses still better advantages in labour-intensive industries. But again it is doubtful that China can continue to be the champion in the world market's competition, for the very same reason as stated above.

Table 8 World Trade Prices and Hourly Earnings (Annual Percentage Change)

	90-98	90	91	92	93	94	95	96	97	98
Trade prices in USD										
Manufactures	0.5	9.9	-0.3	3.5	-5.7	3.1	10.3	-3.2	-9.2	-2.1
Non-fuel primary goods	-0.2	-6.4	-5.7	0.1	1.8	13.6	8.2	-1.3	-3.7	-7.4
Hourly earnings										
NIAEs	10.7	18.9	15.2	13.5	9.8	10.9	7.5	9.3	8.5	9.6
Industrial countries	3.8	5.8	5.3	5.3	3.5	2.8	3.0	3.3	3.2	2.9

Source: *The World Economic Outlook* 1998, International Monetary Fund.

Economic development experiences of many developed and developing countries in the world have shown that, after potent growth for some time, foreign trade will need to undergo a period of adjustment and low growth. It is, therefore, unrealistic to attempt to keep a prolonged export boom, particularly when anti-dumping policy is nowadays increasingly appealing. In addition, the Asian crisis is, to a large extent, the result of too many countries adopting the export-led growth model. Oversupply in the world markets inhibits export growth, which in turn reduces the profitability of export-oriented enterprises. The lessons for China are clear: though exports will continue to make a contribution to the economy, its foothold for long-run growth now ought to be shifted to tapping domestic markets. The size of the Chinese economy cannot be matched by the five crisis-hit Asian countries even put together: with a population of over 1.2 billion, this is an enormous market potential. But how to turn the potential into reality? In what follows we consider the strategies that would help achieve this goal.

Urbanisation: An Effective Way of Tapping All Possible Growth Sources

Chinese authorities and economists have been engaged in searching for new growth sources in the domestic economy, and different views exist. A list of proposed growth sources include housing, information and telecommunication, high-tech industry, tourism, and finance industries. Although there are some plausible elements in these proposals, we still do not think that they have touched the crux.

China is now in a crucial period of the general adjustments of the economic structure comprising the consumption structure, the investment structure, the regional structure, the income distribution structure, the external trade structure, the industrial structure, the demand-supply structure, and so on. Successful structural adjustments would release huge growth energy, as cumulative problems in China's economic structure have not been seriously dealt with in the past two decades, and have begun to curb further economic development (Task Group, Institute of Economics, CASS (1998)). It can be argued that the general adjustments of the economic structure should be led by urbanisation, as it involves all the facets of the economic structure and thus will synthesise the effects of various structural adjustments. In other words, urbanisation is an effective way of tapping all possible growth sources mentioned above.

Table 9 Estimates of Income Elasticity of Consumption Demand 1996-2010

	Food	Clothing	Household appliances	Residence	Transportation and communications
Urban households	0.88	0.99	1.08	1.27	1.55
Rural households	0.87	1.20	1.30	1.13	1.49

Source: Fu, D Z (1998).

**Table 10 Number of Selected Durable Goods
Owned Per 100 Households at the End of 1999**

Items	Urban households	Rural households
Camera	38.11	2.69
Tape recorder	57.18	31.99
Colour TV set	111.57	38.24
Refrigerator	77.74	10.64
Washing machine	91.44	24.32
Electric fan	171.73	116.07
Motorcycle	15.12	16.49
Sofa	210.11	84.24
Composite furniture	57.36	Nil
Video recorder	21.73	Nil
Video disc player	24.71	Nil
Computer	5.91	Nil
Hi-Fi stereo component system	19.66	Nil

Source: China Statistical Yearbook 2000.

Urbanisation would greatly raise the consumption levels and inject energy into the economic growth engine. Table 9 illustrates that the fastest growing areas of consumption for the near future include, in an order of elasticity magnitudes, urban and rural transportation and communications, rural consumption of household appliances, and urban residence. These potential consumption areas are highly related to urbanisation. Also, according to Table 10, it seems that there exists a structural contradiction in rural and urban consumption demands. Whereas some durable goods (e.g., colour TV, washing machine and refrigerator) are close to a saturation point in urban areas, their possession rates are still quite low in rural areas. Apart from slowly growing income, a lack of necessary infrastructure in the countryside may be another important hindrance to consuming certain durable goods. Urbanisation, especially building and developing new towns and cities in rural areas, would not only facilitate absorbing the surplus rural labour force thus increasing rural income, but also create conditions for the rural consumption of those durable goods already saturated in the cities. This would have a great impact on the Chinese economy through the maximal utilisation of production capacity of the consumption-goods industries. Furthermore, residential developments, as a definite outcome of urbanisation, are likely to expand the budding consumer finance industry, stimulate a housing mortgage market, and foster other service industries such as insurance and underwriting.

In recent years, bank deposits of enterprises have risen dramatically, indicating that firms have lost investment directions. Urbanisation would generate massive and long-lasting investment demand in infrastructure construction, thus inducing investment demand of the private sector. As a matter of fact, in the eastern coastal areas, infrastructure construction for rural urbanisation has been financed mostly by non-governmentally-raised funds. This suggests that by allowing non-state investment in infrastructure development, the government would be able to mobilise sizeable social funds in addition to its own ones, and through the multiplier, to induce other investment demand and consumption demand so as to propel the growth of the economy as a whole.

The above discussion was centred on the demand side. From the perspective of the supply side, township and village enterprises (TVEs) have been among China's most dynamic sectors and played an important role in supporting rapid growth in output and income levels (See, for example, Li (1996)). However, as competition in domestic markets has become increasingly intensified, the dispersion of TVEs across the country has made their development more and more difficult, and their economic performance deteriorated sharply. One possible solution points to speeding up the process of urbanisation, in which TVEs could become more concentrated geographically, and could benefit from the special functions of towns and cities in adjusting their production structure and enhancing their competitiveness. It has been evidenced by the cases in the coastal regions that, only with help of urbanisation, can TVEs progress to a new development stage and resume their outstanding roles in China's economic growth.

From the perspective of regional development, pushing forward urbanisation would improve infrastructure in Middle and West China. This will attract more domestic and foreign entrepreneurs to invest in this vast and not yet fully tapped region, and bring out its potential comparative advantages (low labour costs, abundant resources and so on). Fuelled by massive investment in building towns and cities, the region is likely to become a new and powerful growth engine, which in turn would generate still greater demand for investment goods produced in East China. Such a virtuous circle would thus provide more room for the development of heavy industries.

Finally, urbanization would also conduce to the adjustment of China's industrial structure, in that tertiary industry will have a chance to develop further. According to international experience, the development of tertiary industry, particularly of service and information industries, must be accompanied by, or based on, urbanization. This is because urbanization drives the vigorous development of commodity trade which in turn begets, and provides opportunity for, service industry to emerge and thrive. As service and information industries prosper, so will commodity trade. In a word, the process of urbanization would bring China the development of tertiary industry, and maximize the growth effects stemming from the upgrading of its industrial structure.

THE GREAT DEVELOPMENT OF CHINA'S WESTERN REGION BEING UNDERWAY

But where, in a geographical sense, should China start with urbanisation or with tapping domestic sources of long-run, sustainable economic growth and development? In 1999, just before the turn of millennium, the Fourth Plenum of the Fifteenth Central Committee of CCP (Chinese Communist Party) put forward and discussed this question as its core of the economic agenda. After the meeting, the central government announced its decision to exploit and develop the western region of China on a large scale. This so-called "revive-the-west campaign" is now seen as the core of the general adjustment of long-run development strategy, and as a great cause for the whole nation to fight for throughout the 21st century. "The west, as a whole, shall complete the course of industrialisation to raise itself from an underdeveloped regional economy to a developed one", noted Chen Dongsheng, director of the Western Areas Research Centre under the China Social Science Academy (Shi (2000)).

The Backwardness of West China and its Historical Reasons

Since economic reform and opening were initiated in the late 1970s, China's regional economic development has been guided by the so-called "gradient theory" and "echelon strategy". Under such a strategy, the government laid special stress on developing the eastern coastal areas: Over half of the total investment of state-owned units has been directed to the east, 5 special economic zones (SEZs), the Pudong Development Zone (in Shanghai) and 14 open cities have been set up in the east. In tandem with the biased development strategy favouring East China, numerous preferential policies have also favoured the region for it to speed up the pace of economic reform and opening. Although the middle and western regions have not been totally forgotten, those favourable policies enjoyed by the eastern region have been applied to the hinterland to a much lesser degree. As a result, an echelon-like economic pattern has gradually taken shape with East, Middle, and West China being the most, less and least developed regional economies respectively.[1] The uneven development of the three regional economies over 20 years from 1978 to 1998 is clearly seen by looking at Table 11. The western region has gravely lagged behind, resulting in a huge gap between its economic development level and that of East China. Despite its area occupying 56% of the territory of the country and its population accounting for 23% of national population, West China only produced 15% of national GDP in 1998, even falling by 1% compared with 1978.

Some Chinese economists (e.g., Cai and Du, 2000; Lin *et al*, 1998) conducted analytical studies on regional economic growth of East, Middle and West China over the post-reform era. They found that the three regions can be classified as three discernibly different "growth clubs". Within each of them absolute convergence exists, while between them divergence (or conditional convergence) is present. Absolute convergence within the eastern region is reflected by backward provinces catching up with comparatively wealthy provinces, while absolute convergence within the middle and western regions is characterised as the reverse:

---

[1]   East China embraces Beijing, Tianjin, Hebei, Liaonin, Shanghai, Jiangsu, Zhejian, Fujian, Shandong, Guangdong, Guangxi and Hainan; Middle China consists of Shanxi, Inner Mongolia, Jilin, Heilongjiang, Anhui, Jiangxi, Hebei, Hubei and Hunan; and Chongqing, Sichuan, Guizhou, Yunnan, Tibet, Shaanxi, Gansu, Qinghai, Ninxia, and Xinjiang are grouped to form West China.

the relatively high-income provinces fall back to match the relatively poor ones. More importantly, what have impeded the middle and western regions from catching up with the east were identified as follows: (1) lack of human capital; (2) market distortion caused by heavy government interventions; and (3) low degree of openness.

Table 11. Uneven Development of Regional Economies in China

Regions	GDP per capita (*yuan*)		Increased by a factor of	Regional GDP/Average national GDP (%)	
	1978	1998		1978	1998
East China	460.6	11,466	23.9	121.63	179.04
Middle China	310.5	5,400	16.5	81.90	84.32
West China	255.0	4,231	16.6	67.28	66.07

Source: Own calculations using the data from *China Statistical Yearbook*, 1990 and 1999.

The uneven regional economic development has historical reasons. Letting the eastern region take the lead of economic development and growth was once considered to be a strategic step indispensable at the initial stages of China's economic reform and opening. The eastern region possessed several advantages over the middle and western regions, including better economic infrastructure, handier traffic, more developed communication facilities, and a larger number of various talents. It was thus the place more attractive to foreign capital and businesses where economic links with the world economy could be more easily established and strengthened and economic returns quicker. Based on these considerations, Deng Xiaopin once pointed out that policy-making at all levels on development strategy must take into account two successive general interests of the whole nation. The first is that the east is given the highest priority to prosper, and the middle and western regions should understand and support such a bias, in the general interest of the whole nation. The second is that, when on average the national economy reaches the level of *Xiaokang* (meaning comparatively well-off in terms of per capita GDP) by the end of the 20th century, emphasis will be shifted to the development of the middle and western regions, and the east should subordinate itself to this strategic change, again in the general interest of the whole nation.

The Need for Developing the West

Now seems to be the right time when China's regional economic development must and can make a shift from the first to the second step. Regarding "must", there are a number of reasons. First, compared with other regions, some advantages that used be enjoyed by the east have tended to lessen or to be counterbalanced by growing disadvantages. Due to upward movements in wage rates, land prices, rents for houses and so on, labour-intensive enterprises that were vigorously prospering in the eastern region can no longer continue like this and have to be relocated. As a good example, some Shanghai's textile companies and factories have recently moved westwards to Xinjiang. The east is in an urgent need for, and is currently experiencing, an upgrade in the industrial structure, due to China's impending WTO membership. Whether this upgrade will be successfully completed in a relatively short time period now depends crucially on the rapid development of such industries as high-tech and financial ones in the western region. Failure to achieve the latter may result in great difficulties in achieving the former, and hence the east may not be able to cope with the high international competition pressure brought about by joining the WTO.

Second, after a long period of exploitation and use, some of the east's natural resources are getting exhausted (e.g., coal), and some have started to produce a declining level of output (e.g., oil). Further economic growth of the east must then be supported by the resources from the interior of the country, and in particular from the western region. The middle and western regions possess 82.3% of hydropower potential, about 50% of 45 types of minerals, and some 70% of exploitable land resources in reserve. Exploiting abundant natural resources in the western region now demands immediate action. Otherwise, not just East China's but also the whole of China's economic development will be facing the constraint of insufficient resources.

Third, the demographic distribution of China is that 40% of the population resides in the east with 60% in the middle and west. This implies that the middle and western regions have a tremendous market potential. The preceding sections have shown that China will mainly count on domestic markets as the driving forces for prolonged economic growth in the 21st century. A rise in the development level of China's middle and western economies will certainly increase local residents' purchasing power, thereby releasing a strong effective demand for consumption and investment to spur national economic growth. If on the other hand the middle and western regions continue to grow slowly at the existing speed, both eastern and national economic developments will be shackled by the slow expansion of domestic markets.

Fourth, the widening of regional income disparities and investment gaps in human capital resulting from eastward-biased policies has led to the low quality of labour and the scarcity of talents (e.g., scientists, engineers and researchers) in the west. Tables 12 and 13 present some statistics as evidence. Moreover, by 1999 the eastern region alone had employed over 53% of all science-and-technology personnel in its R&D (research and development) institutions and departments. Looking at these statistics, people even with the best imagination would find it difficult to envisage a bright prospect of the "revive-the-west campaign". Such an eastward flow of talents, if not stopped or reversed soon, will preclude the economies in the middle and western regions from growing fast enough to catch up with the east because of their shortage of human capital. In fact, between 2000 and 2020 is probably a golden age for the whole as well as Middle and West China to enhance the level of education and accumulate human capital. Two accounts for this assertion are as follows. Number 1, the first twenty years of the 21st century are the period during which the whole of China's, and its middle and western regions' stock of labour force will grow relatively faster while their coefficients of supporting the elderly will be comparatively lower. This will not be the case beyond 2020. According to Yang and Yin (2000), in 2000, the whole country's labour resources accounted for 61% of the population, and this figure was 66% for the western region; and in terms of the whole country's and the western region's supporting coefficients, they were estimated to be 10% and 9.4% respectively for 2000. However, by 2020, China's population will become gravely ageing: Population over 60 years old will be approximately 0.25 billion, and the elderly's supporting coefficient will rise to some 28%. Number 2, right now China is at a peak in terms of its young labour force. Population born in 1962-1975 and in the subsequent peak periods of birth numbers is 0.36 billion, accounting for 50% of the total labour force. These people are at their best ages for education and training. Thus, it is of crucial importance for China to seize this golden period of 20 years and boost education and training especially in its middle and western regions.

Table 12 Some Basic Statistics of East, Middle and West China

Regions	Industrial and agricultural output per head (¥)	Population with middle and higher education/1000	Urban areas as percentage of the total	Birth rates (%0)
East China	4597	388	37.04	2.01
Middle China	2076	346	28.33	2.31
West China	1504	251	18.05	2.75

Sources: Own calculations using the data from the fourth national population census.

Table 13 Education of Employees in Selected Regions of China (%)

Regions	Illiteracy	Primary school	Junior secondary school	Senior secondary school	University and three-years college
Whole country	11.6	34.8	37.9	12.1	3.5
Beijing	1.8	8.2	40.9	31.1	18.0
Shanghai	4.1	13.3	42.9	28.1	11.6
Western region	25.79	36.53	25.52	9.11	3.05

Sources: Own calculations using the data from *China Statistical Yearbook*, 1998.

Finally, China is a country of multi-ethnic nations. The harmony between different ethnic nations always underpins its socio-political stability and hence economic development. It is well known that West China is populated by mass ethnic minorities while East China by the Han nation. The widening of regional income disparities in favour of the east has become one of the causes of tension between minority nationalities and the Han nationality, as evidenced by recently increasing terroristic activities and independent movements in Xinjiang and Tibet. Launching the 'revive-the-west campaign" is therefore not just out of economic considerations but also out of political considerations. A quick economic development of the western region is seen to be conducive to strengthening the solidarity between different nationalities and therefore the foundation and legitimacy of the regime.

In terms of political economy, three additional considerations might have been taken into account by the central government in modifying its regional economic policies: (1) The marginal costs of the eastern region's economic growth; (2) The marginal contribution of the eastern region to state finance; and (3) The social and political pressure. Regarding the first consideration, when such costs are rising rapidly so as to reduce the central government's marginal revenue from its biased policies towards the east, it will consider allocating resources to other regions. Zhang (2001) found that, since 1990 the marginal costs of factor inputs into the eastern provinces have kept rising and so has the external costs (such as environmental costs) of their economic growth. Both have exerted increasing financial pressures on the central government and now to the degree that the centre must reconsider its development strategy. As for the second consideration, at the beginning of regional decentralisation, the contribution was positively proportional to economic growth in the east.

However, growing regionalism has eventually threatened the central government's share in total fiscal revenue, as is the case in China's eastern and coastal provinces. The central government started to realise that its biased policies in favour of the east had fostered regionalism, and that the resources expended for pursuing such policies were getting harder and harder to bring fiscal returns as expected by the centre. Re-centralisation then occurred, which foretold the impending, comprehensive adjustments of the centre's regional economic policies in favour of non-eastern regions: a centralised system is always a "darling" of backward and poor regions due to its egalitarian nature. Turning to the third consideration, income disparities between households and regions used to act as driving forces for economic activities and hence growth during the early periods of reform and opening, but now have become strong resistances to further reform as the disparities have increased to reach an intolerable degree. Under this circumstance, the variable of interregional gaps began to enter the "utility function" of the central government, as it concerns deeply with further economic reform and growth as well as socio-political stability of the country.

To sum up, the disparities between the levels of economic development in East, Middle, and West China have become the cause of much concern to the whole country. The problem is regarded as having hindered the further improvement in the overall efficiency of the national economy, and having endangered the harmony and solidarity within the country. Therefore, China can no longer weather a further widening of such disparities, and a large-scale development of its western and middle regions is imperative.

The Mature Conditions for the Revive-The-West Campaign

"Must" does not necessarily imply "can". However, there are a few favourable conditions that have already begun to take shape, and they will help make possible the westwards shifts in the regional emphases of China's economic development. After 20 years' pursuing economic reform and opening, China's national economic power has increased considerably. In particular, the eastern region has laid a solid economic foundation and is able to further develop without having to rely on the financial support by the state. Accordingly, the state can now concentrate a huge amount of resources on fully exploiting and developing the middle and western regions. Furthermore, the west has also established an economic foundation good enough to accommodate the revive-the-west campaign, thanks to several large construction projects undertaken during the 1990s and especially during the period of the Ninth Five-Year Plan (1996-2000). These include the Lan-Xin multiple-track railway, the Southern Xinjiang railway, the Nan-Kun railway, and optical fibre cables built in some areas of the western region (Fu (2000)). In other words, some basic infrastructures have been laid on for the campaign. In addition, the system of market economy has been basically established in China, and the market forces are to be harnessed to quicken the speed of the west's development in that resources from both the state and non-state sectors can be mobilised. As a matter of fact, the existing "hardware and software" of the western region have already attracted an increasing number of overseas firms and businesses to pour their money into the region, suggesting that they are quite optimistic about the potential of economic development in the west (Dong (2000)).

An equally important factor to be mentioned here is the fiscal capability of the central government that will have to play a key part in the revive-the-west campaign. Indeed, during the Ninth Five-Year Plan that started in 1996, the bias of government policies towards the west had already shown an inkling. But why was this intent not turned to action taken by the central government until the Tenth Five-Year Plan started in 2000? Previous studies on the history of China's even and uneven regional development (e.g., Wang and Hu (1999); Zhang (2001)) have revealed that the pursuit of balanced regional development policies depend on both the central government's intention and its fiscal capability to do so. The former is a necessary condition while the latter a sufficient condition. It was found that the years when either or both of the two conditions were not met were the years during which inter-regional development gaps were widening. This historical experience suggests that, to be able to put into effect such an unprecedented development plan for the west, the central government needs a greater-than-ever fiscal capability. With hindsight, it becomes clear that, during the entire period of the Ninth Five-Year Plan, the central government actually already began its budgetary preparation: it launched the reform of the fiscal system as early as in 1994, and issued a growing number of government bonds from 1997 onwards. Fiscal restructuring aimed at converting the fiscal contract system into the tax-sharing system. As a result of the successful reforms, the annual increments of state fiscal revenue rose steadily (Liu and Zhao (1999)), and the year 2000 witnessed the greatest ever rise in state fiscal revenue of over 360 billion *yuans* (See Table 14). But in view of the limits to further increase tax rates, the state also resorted to the issuance of more debt. In a 3-year period between 1997 and 1999, the total amount of debt issuance was around 1,200 billion *yuans*, exceeding the sum of debt issuance during the previous 16 years from 1981 to 1996. In 2000 alone, the total value of borrowing was 465.7 billion *yuans*. See Chart 1. This fiscal preparation lasted the entire 5-year period of the Ninth Five-Year Plan, and considerably boosted the state's fiscal capability. As the aforementioned sufficient condition is now fulfilled, the state is then financially capable of adjusting its regional development policies and putting into action its premeditated intention to fully exploit and develop West China.

Table 14 State Fiscal Revenue under Different Systems (Billion *Yuan* and %)

Regimes	Under the fiscal contract system 88-93						Under the tax-sharing system 94-00						
Year	1988	1989	1990	1991	1992	1993	1994	1995	1996	1997	1998	1999	2000
Fiscal revenue	262.8	294.9	331.3	361.1	415.3	434.9	521.8	624.2	740.8	865.1	987.6	1137.7	1500.0
Growth rate	10.9	12.2	12.4	9	15	4.7	20	19.6	18.7	16.8	14.2	15.2	15

Source: People's Bank of China (2000); *Beijing Review*, No 1, Jan. 2001, p. 19.

Chart 1 State debts, 1981-2000

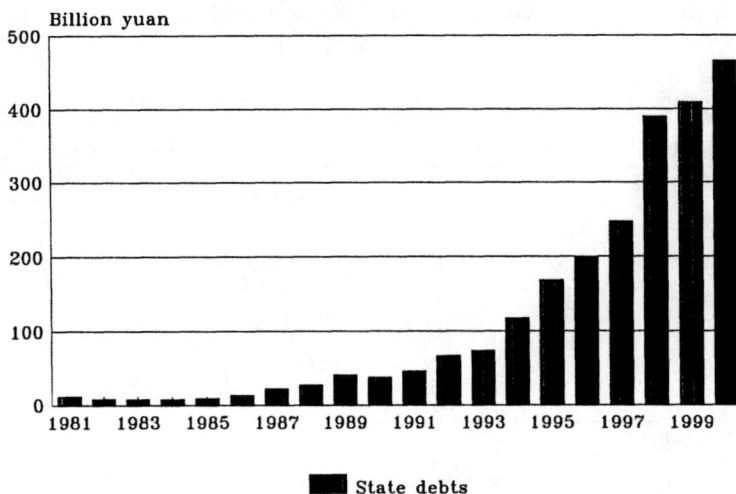

The Possible Difficulties at the Initial Stages of the West Campaign

People should, however, be aware that it is perhaps more difficult to develop the west today than to develop the east 20 years ago. The following problems are afflicting the west, which were largely absent in the east at its initial stages of development. One problem is that the basic installations of agriculture and animal husbandry are still backward and weak, giving rise to the region's low ability to withstand frequent natural disasters that have aggravated the already-fragile ecological environment. A more striking weakness of the west is the acute shortage of water resources, that is, the west's great development campaign is going to be unfolded in an increasingly desert area (He (2001)), although the region is where China's energy resources concentrate. Another problem results from inadequate infrastructure such as transportation and telecommunications. This is also a grave problem given that the inter-city distances in the west are much greater than in the east, and the distances between the west and the eastern coastal areas are even greater. The inadequate industrial structure in the west cannot be ignored either.

Pertaining to the existing economic system in the west, hindrances to the success of the campaign also require serious attention. The lowly competitive state sector predominates more in the west's regional economy than in other regional economies, as demonstrated in Table 15. In terms of fixed-asset investment in the state sector, the west exceeded the east by almost 16 percentage points, and in terms of employment this percentile is approximately 12. Concurrent with such a heavy and notoriously inefficient state sector has been the fact that the westerners relatively lack the mentality and sense that cater to constructing a market economy and pursuing openness. The old ways of thinking and doing things in the west may have stronger inertia than those in the east, and thus it is unrealistic to expect the same quick policy efficacy in the west as in the east 20 years ago. In sum, the revive-the-west campaign will be a marathon, not a sprint, if the development experience of the east can be likened to the latter.

Table 15 Comparisons in the Importance of the State Sector between Three Regions in 1998

Regions	State economy (%)		Collective economy (%)		Private economy (%)	
	Investment	Employment	Investment	Employment	Investment	Employment
Whole China	54.1	71.4	14.8	15.4	13.2	13.2
East China	50.8	66.4	17.0	18.3	11.7	15.3
Middle China	58.0	72.1	11.3	17.8	17.8	10.1
West China	66.6	78.2	7.6	13.2	12.6	8.6

Source: Li and Yu (2000).

Main Policies to be Adopted

In light of the favourable and unfavourable conditions listed above, hot and nation-wide discussions on policy choices and projects to be constructed in the west are currently being carried out among economists, politicians, and news media in China. The central government has promised to give full support to the development of the west, political, economic and financial, as exemplified by many preferential policies to be adopted.

It is widely recognised that infrastructure constructions must take the lead of the revive-the-west-campaign. Due to the bad natural conditions and weak financial capability of the west, the main projects of infrastructure and public utilities must be undertaken by state investment funds. These projects include railways, high/motor ways, airports, telecommunication, and harnessing of those large, cross-region rivers. Recently, the Ministry of Transportation has decided to build additional eight highways in the west, an investment of 120 billion *yuans*. During the period of the Tenth Five-Year Plan, construction projects of the railway system will be of a total value of 100 billion *yuans*, and by 2005 the newly-built railways will have reached a length of 18,000 kilometres. Investment in forestry and ecological environment is planned to be 200 billion *yuans* by 2010, with an emphasis on the protection of natural forest in the west. (See *http://west.middlewest.com.cn/policy*).

The purpose of infrastructure construction is to help develop potentially advantageous industries in the west such as basic industries of coal, oil, natural gas, and non-ferrous metal, high-tech industries, and tourism. To develop basic industries, the central government will adopt less-restrictive polities that allow foreign and private investments to exploit the resources of raw material and energy, and especially encourage them to take part in the development and construction of the energy and chemical-industry bases in the western region. To develop high-tech industries, policies to be adopted will include setting up risky investment funds to provide loan guarantee and interest payments for the production of high-tech products, increasing government subsidies to encourage enterprises of different ownership in their R&D activities, and raising funding for university academics and researchers in the west to pursue high-tech research projects that will directly benefit local economies. From now on, the Ministry of Science and Technology will implement the "Science-Technology Scheme of the West's Great Development". In 2001, as the first action taken for the campaign, the Ministry has appropriated 50 million *yuans* to fund the special science-technology projects in the west (See *http://west.middlewest.com.cn/policy)*. With respect to tourism, the west has extremely abundant resources. The central government will choose Shaanxi, Yunnan, Gansu, Sichuan, and Guizhou provinces to exploit new tourism resorts, so as to promote the rapid development of tourism in the region.

At the initial stages of development, the western provinces will have insufficient fiscal capability and their proportions of total expenditures on economic construction may not be able to rise. Thus to initiate the campaign, massive transfer payments of the central government are seen to be inevitable. The centre will enlarge the scope of subsidies, allowances, and financial aids in the following categories: poverty relief, public goods, ecological environment, investment from other regions, and enterprises run by ethnic minorities. In addition, state bonds under the name of "western prioritised enterprises" are to be issued, and the funds raised will be exclusively used for the development of energy and raw-material backbone enterprises in the west. At the same time, projects that are financed by foreign governments' loans, the World Bank's loans, the Asia Development Bank's loans, and other bilateral and multilateral aids are to be mainly located in the west (over 60%; See *http://west.middlewest.com.cn/policy*).

In order to protect the great zeal of the westerners in developing their homelands and to attract foreign investors, the centre shall apply preferential tax policies there. These include: (1) Exempting those resource-type enterprises from resource taxes or reverting most of the taxes to them. These exempted or reverted taxes will be treated as state investment in the further exploitation and protection of resources. (2) Applying a short-period zero tax rate to the projects that are badly needed and highly prioritised in the region. (3) After enjoying the existing preferential tax policies for three years (effective from January 1, 2000), those foreign businesses and firms in the west's economic sectors favoured by the state will be levied income taxes at a rate 15% less than the normal. (See *http://west.middlewest.com.cn/policy)*. And the re-investment projects in the west with foreign re-investment capital over 25% will be treated as foreign-funded firms for tax purposes.

Funds are the blood of a modern market economy. In addition to fiscal and FDI policies, macro-financial policies are also important in meeting the huge demand for funds in developing the west. The central government will consider the following policy measures: establishing two development banks and two stock exchanges in Xian and Chengdu respectively; lowering the requirements for setting up commercial banks, non-bank financial institutions, and various investment funds; creating favourable conditions to encourage foreign banks to open their branches in the west; developing future markets for coal, non-ferrous metal, agricultural products and staple foods; and giving the west's high-tech and non-state enterprises priority to be listed in domestic and overseas stock markets. Credit policies have already started their bias towards the west, as evidenced by the fact that the State Development Bank agreed, on February 17, 2001, to provide Sichuan Province with bank loans of 53 billion *yuans*.

As mentioned above, the dominance of SOEs in the west has become one of the main hindrances to its economic development. The centre has now become aware of this problem and is intent on greatly adjusting the ownership structure and allowing the proliferation of non-state enterprises and firms.

There are more preferential and favourable policies currently on the central government's agenda and to be promulgated soon. All of them will serve the only purpose: to best meet the needs of vigorously and comprehensively developing West China.

CONCLUSION

Expanding domestic demand is of crucial importance as China has parted from a shortage economy to a surplus economy. From 1998 onwards, the Chinese government began to pursue expansionary stabilisation programs to boost domestic demand, in a hope that such efforts could help the economy revert to its original high-growth path. However, such short-run policies have failed to show efficacy as strong and quick as expected on the basis of past experience. The difficulties encountered in the attempts to stimulate domestic demand have certain bearing on the long-adopted eastward- and outward-oriented development strategy that has over time accumulated adverse effects within the economy. In view of this, the government is intent on a new, inward- and westward-oriented development strategy as opposed to the old, outward- and eastward-oriented one. "Inward-oriented" is in the sense of relying mainly on domestic markets, and "westward-oriented" in the sense of being biased towards the development of West China. A caveat may be in order, however. The inward and westward strategic shifts in China's development emphases do not mean that China is going to close the economy and the eastern region is going to be disadvantaged. Rather, the Chinese economy will become more open as evidenced by its endeavours to join the WTO, and East China will gain greatly from West China's rapid development which was indeed an important consideration for launching the revive-the-west campaign.

The two changes in the development strategy have important implications for expanding domestic demand in the long run. Building on data, this article shows that the defects of the export-led growth model adopted in the Asian crisis countries may be blamed as one of the root causes of the financial turmoil. An important lesson for China to learn is that continuing to count on exports would be hopeless, if not disastrous, to its economic growth in the long run. The only way out or the only hope for the Chinese economy lies in creating and maintaining buoyant domestic demand. Urbanisation would be an effective way of exploiting and mobilising various new growth sources in domestic markets and thus would generate synthesised growth effects.

But urbanisation should be concentrated in the west of China. Data and their analyses suggest that, after 20 years of uneven regional development, China's inward shift of development emphasis must and can be accompanied by, or fulfilled through, the "go West" strategy. It is abundant resources and even the backwardness of interior and West China that are these regions' advantages for possible higher growth (and thus for catching up with East China). But such growth convergence is conditional on infrastructural, environmental, institutional and human capital improvements in the yet backward regions. To this end, favourable policies and measures have been and will continue to be promulgated and put in practice by the government.

REFERENCES

Cai, F. and Du, Y (2000): "Convergence and Divergence of Regional Economic Growth in China", *Economic Research Journal*, No. 10, pp. 30-37.

Dong F. R. (2000): "Preface", in Fu, T. S.: *Strategic Thinking on A Full-scale Development of the Western Region*, China Water Conservancy and Hydroelectricity Publishing House, Beijing.

Fu, D. Z. (1998): "Choosing and Fostering the New Growth Spots in the Development of the Chinese Economy", *Economics Information*, No. 9., pp. 21-24.

Fu, T. S. (2000): *Strategic Reflections on Pursuing the Great Development of the West of China*, the China Water Conservancy and Hydroelectricity Publishing House, Beijing.

He Q. L. (2001): "A Worry on the Environmental Consequences of the West China Development Campaign", *http://www.cnd.org/HXWZ/CM01/cm0108e.hz8.html#2*.

Lan, Y. (1999): *Foreign Exchange Rate Regimes and the Asian Currency Crisis*, MBS thesis, Massey University.

Li, X. and Yu, M. (2000): "Ownership Structure Adjustment Suited to Vigorous Development of Western China", *World Economy and China*, No. 6, pp. 46-53.

Li, X (2000): "China's Macroeconomic Stabilisation Policies Following the Asian Financial Crisis: Success or Failure?", *Asian Survey*, Vol. XL, No. 6, pp. 938-957.

Li. X. (1999): "China Being Buffeted from Within and Without: An Analysis of Its Macroeconomic Policies", the Department of Commerce's *Working Paper Series 99.09*, Massey University.

Li, X (1996): "China's Economic Reforms: Dual-track Transition", *EARC Research Papers 96.3*, School of East Asian Studies, University of Sheffield.

Li, X. (1995): *Disequilibrium, Economic Reforms and Economic Policies: A Theoretical and Empirical Investigation for China*, Avebury: Aldershot UK/ Brookfield USA.

Lin, Y., Cai, F. and Li, Z. (1998): "An Analysis of Regional Gaps in China's Economic Transition", *Economic Research Journal*, No. 6, pp. 3-10.

Liu R. C. and Zhao, Z. G. (1999): *The Frontier of China's Fiscal Theories*, The Social Science Literature Publishing House, Beijing.

People's Bank of China (2001): *The Prospects of China's Finance, 1994-2000*.

Shi, J. B. (2000): "West Faces Challenges, Opportunities", *World Economy and China*, No.2, p. 32.

Task Group, Institute of Economics, CASS (1998): General Adjustment: A Common Subject and A Necessary Choice: An Analysis of China's Macroeconomy", *Jingji Yanjiu (Economic Research Journal)*, No. 9, pp. 17-26.

Wang, S. G. and Hu, A. G. (1999): *The Political Economy of Uneven Development: the Case of China*, M. E. Sharpe, Inc.

Xu, D. Q. (1998): *The World Situation and China's Economic Development Strategy: Theoretical Thinking at the Century's Turning Point* (In Chinese), The Publishing House of Economics Science, Beijing.

Yang, J. Y. and Yin, Q. S. (2000): "Greatly Exploiting Human Resources: A Commanding Elevation of Implementing the "Stride-Across" Development Strategy in the West of China", *Economics Information*, No. 8, pp. 13-17.

Yu, Q. (1998): "The Asian Financial Crisis and China's Exchange Rate Policy", *Jingji Yanjiu* (*Economic Research Journal*), N0. 10, pp. 42-50.

Zhang, J. (2001): "The Wishes and Capability of the State and the Choice of Regional Development Policy", *Economic Research Journal*, No. 3, pp. 69-74.

Chapter 2

JAPAN'S EMERGING NATIONAL DEFENSE INDUSTRY

Andrew K. Hanami[*]
San Francisco State University

In the 21st century the world wonders whether modern Japan has a military industry or not. The assumption has been generally no, since defense industries are normally correlated with defense forces. Whether Japan even possesses a national-sized military has also gone unanswered. This question became acute in the wake of its burgeoning economy and the U.S. trade deficit, Japan's tardy response in the Persian Gulf war, and its limited peacekeeping deployments since then. The new 1997 Defense Guidelines, and the terrorist attacks from al Qaida on September 11, 2001, further placed this American ally on the map as the U.S. announced a global pursuit of international terrorists, including those in Asian states near Japan. The debate has created two extreme views. Half the world, primarily in the West, does not believe Japan has a military at all, since its Constitution forbids it. The other half, primarily throughout Asia, there is nervousness that Japan is again on the path to remilitarization. The truth is that a certain kind of military is growing in Japan, from the ground up. It has always been difficult to measure the extent of the slow and deliberate expansion of Japan's military forces from a small security force to a larger one. What can be concluded is that Japan is developing particular characteristics of a significant military force, one that resembles those of comparable GDP nations. But its acknowledgement has been particularly opaque because of both domestic and some international pressures to limit the military, and also because of the way Japan's military has grown. This is especially true of the building of the military, its infrastructure, or military keiretsu.

Because of the recent financial downturn, Japan's civilian keiretsu is by now well known: they are tightly interwoven groups of companies, banks, insurance firms and other linked firms who are interrelated to form both a vertically and horizontally integrated structure that

---

[*] Andrew K. Hanami is Associate Professor of International Relations at San Francisco State University. He received his Ph.D. from the University of California, Berkeley. He is the author of three books, *The Military Might of Modern Japan* (1995), *War, Peace and Power in the Post Cold War Era* (1997), and *Perspectives on Structural Realism* (2002). He has also written a number of articles on defense and economics, and was invited by the Gorbachev Foundation to deliver a lecture on Japanese defense to the Moscow Military Academy in 1993.

depend on each other for sharing resources and serving as a core market destination. They also share overlapping board of directorships. The most famous ones are Mitsubishi, Kawasaki, Sumitomo and Mitsui but there are also about a dozen major houses not as well known outside Japan. The Japanese, indeed the world, understands this arrangement to be perhaps unique and functional to Japan's recent economic miracle, thus they do not especially condemn it. Only in the deepest days of the trade deficit and again with Japan's banking crisis was the keiretsu made an agenda item for U.S. criticisms. What is less known is that these civilian keiretsu also house military production. The extent of the military aspect of all important keiretsu is surprising, but has a longer history than is commonly known.

As early as 1947 a team of Japanese defense industrial workers were organized through American guidance for the purpose of repairing American military systems from the war. In 1950 the U.S. created its policy of making Japan the "military-industrial linchpin of Asia", which soon led to rehabilitating 74 of Japan's previously dismantled defense industries, including aircraft and munitions. By 1955, the U.S. proposed the beginning of an arrangement in which Japan was to produce major U.S. weapons systems under license. The U.S. was interested, in part, in utilizing the Japanese as a market expansion point for U.S. arms. But Japanese industrialists quickly seized the American initiative and altered the objective to re-establish the American initiative and altered the objective to re-establish an indigenous, stand alone defense industry of their own. This instinct had deeper roots than WWII. Japan's defense was autonomous even as far back as the turn of the century with the fighting of the Russo-Japanese war of 1904-5.

The first major defense agreement, begun in 1952, sponsored jointly by the U.S. and Mitsubishi to produce a combat fighter scheduled the U.S. to finance 52% of the production costs. Japan's defense industrialists were soon supported and led by Prime Minister Kishi, who wished to cement an enhanced U.S.-Japan defense industry pact at the time of his visit to Washington,D.C. to meet President Eisenhower in June 1957. The new Japan offer to buildup and modernize its defense was to be a token of the Japanese prime minister's friendship with the U.S. Prime Minister Kishi also had a second agenda. He wished to "bring Japan back on the world stage through the U.S.-Japan alliance". Along with the leadership of Yasuhiro Nakasone, buying U.S. weapons, co-producing them, and building up a compatible defense industry was seen as a major method to realize this new policy.[1]

In 1954, as Japan's "Self-Defence Forces" emerged, the arms production operations became a permanent tier within the civilian industry. Because Japan has always sought self-reliance, it started to build all its own military ships, nearly all of its aircraft, and most of its firearms and ammunitions. Even during the 1950s Japanese defense companies were designing and producing virtually all of the main weapons systems that its own defense forces used. In 1962, a period when "only a handful of countries" made their own tanks, Mitsubishi introduced its tank. In military aircraft, however, only 21% were made in Japan. But only five countries maintained their own military aerospace capability in this period - the U.S., Soviet Union, United Kingdom, France and Sweden. Production of military fighters is regarded as the most expensive and complex of military systems. But the Japanese interest in building indigenous combat aircraft can be traced to the 1950s, seeing its continuation with the FS-X

---

[1]   Michael Green, *Arming Japan* (New York: Columbia University Press, 1995), pp. 8, 31, 34, 39-40, 44 and 54.

in 1988. The proportion of domestically produced arms has increased from 40% to 87% between 1950 and the early 1980s, higher today.[2]

American expediency also accelerated the growth of Japan's defense companies. Before and during the Korean War, the U.S. often by-passed the Japanese government completely and directed Japanese defense workers at 850 revived defense facilities in the production of military products, including rocket control systems, for the U.S. military.[3] The Korean War itself propelled Japan's production of war material, urged by the U.S. government, for U.S. forces in the region that amounted to 70% of Japan's total exports. Vietnam also caused an estimated $1 billion per year demand for Japanese military materials for that effort. What also helped the growth of the Japanese defense industry is Japan Defense Agency (JDA) argument that Japan's "exclusively defensive defense" policy requires purely defensive systems. But relying on importing U.S. military systems alone may be too offensive for Japan's military framework. Moreover, the JDA feels it is unpractical to send American purchased military blackboxed equipment back to the U.S. for repairs. This extra step adds to the inclination to make it at home.[4]

In 1970 Nakasone formally linked the military with the civilian production sector of the economy, calling for integrated development. In 1981, Ronald Reagan added to this shift by regularly pressuring Japan to increase its military spending. Reagan may not have only wanted Japan to be America's "unsinkable aircraft carrier", but also its unsinkable silicon chip maker. About 40% of America's weapons systems today depend on Japanese technology. The Pentagon in Washington, D.C. also changed its rules to call for foreign inclusion as military subcontractors to American defense firms.[5]

Due also to the traditional policy to "buy within Japan" today virtually all manufacturing firms are participating in defense production in some way. Unlike U.S. firms that specialize wholly or greatly in defense production, Japanese companies widely share that activity. Due to of the phenomenal expansion of Japan's postwar economy, defense has, in a sense, also automatically expanded, too. Unlike in America where key defense firms must outbid others, which creates defense "losers", in Japan, there is wide inclusion so that most major firms get a piece of each new defense contract. Though working with a limited budget, the Japanese have been creative. One study reports that a key way to keep the military budget down to within the 1% limit is to allow for "nothing down, five years to pay system". It has been estimated that perhaps as much as two thirds of the year's defense budgets are "forward expenditures".[6] When seen on a year-to-year basis, the rate of defense production typically grew 11%. Taking 1981 as a base year, in the decade that followed Japan's military arms production increased a total of 220%, compared with its civilian industrial growth of 143% in the same period. Of course the military base began from a much lower level, but it is interesting to see the emphasis while virtually no awareness of it has penetrated through Japan's national consciousness, or the world's.[7]

---

[2] Mark Lorell, *Troubled Partnership* (New Brunswick, N.J.: Transaction Publishers, 1996), pp. 52-3; also, Reinhard Drifte, *Arms Production in Japan* (Boulder: Westview Press, 1986), pp. 11, 13, 21 and 34.

[3] Masako Ikegami-Andersson, *The Military-Industrial Complex* (Aldershot, England: Dartmouth Press, 1992), p. 74.

[4] Green, op. cit., pp. 20 and 29.

[5] GAO, *U.S.-Japan Burden Sharing*, 1989, p. 3; and Roderick Vanter, *U.S. Industrial Base Dependence/ Vunerability* (Washington, D.C., National Defense University Press, 1986), p. 10.

[6] Richard Samuels, "*Rich Nation, Strong Army*" (Ithaca: Cornell University Press, 1994), p. 314.

[7] Calculations made from data in Defense of Japan, 1991 and 1992.

Major trading houses like Mitsubishi, Kawasaki, Mitsui, Sanwa and incorporated companies like Toshiba, Toyota, Nissan, NEC and hundreds of others form the front line of Japan's well known economy. But smaller defense operations also exist in each of those companies as part of an embedded second-line. While Japan's 20 largest defense firms manufacture three fourths of the nation's defense products, the big 3, and their subcontractors, account for nearly half of the total. In Japan's big 3 - Mitsubishi, Kawasaki and Ishikawajima-Harima - about 20% of their total production is dedicated to defense. This figure is small compared to American defense giants like Lockheed, but is similar to its European counterparts. If one counts subcontractors, some 800 Japanese companies produce defense products directly, while up to 49 million additional Japanese workers may be switched from their civilian to military operations on an ad hoc basis, if needed. Hitachi can quickly convert up to half of its 27 factories and 6 R&D facilities for defense purposes.[8]

One recent study observed that the Japanese defense industry generally operates "at only 50% of its real capacity". Mitsubishi, moreover, the dominant defense manufacture, has been described by one Japanese defense analyst as Japan's most "patriotic" company, aiming to "serve the country by the industry". More recently, Nissan Motors has joined Japan's top 10 defense companies principally through its manufacturing technology transfer from Martin-Marietta for munitions and rocket systems. The Nissan shift into military systems has been because of its flagging auto sales worldwide. Though Toyota makes armored personnel carriers (APCs), Honda started up a cooperative aerospace R&D project with Mississippi University. Mitsubishi produces the widest range of large military products, like ships, aircraft and missiles. Kawasaki and Ishikawajima-Harima and Sumitomo also manufacture similar major components, including engines for those systems. Many others tend to specialize. Toshiba, Oki, Hitachi, NEC and Fujitsu produce military electronics. Private company initiative is the key to understanding the Japanese defense industry. Typically, a private firm will draw up an in-house study on a new weapons systems using its own monies. Their engineers are then informally sent to "military R&D centers for further development, contracting and manufacture".[9]

According to Richard Samuels, "The Japanese commitment to defense research and development has never flagged...and has been more extensive than many acknowledge. Defense R&D typically accelerates each time the Japan-U.S. alliance is strained...". When the FS-X controversy erupted in 1989, the "JDA was authorized to build an indigenous surface-to-air missile". In 1990 the Japanese government began a system of further parceling out R&D to private firms. Though at very low levels, the rate of defense R&D spending has increased faster than other budget items since 1976. The Japanese have begun a process of building off defense products from civilian designs, including distant sensors, distant radar, robot and artificial intelligence, high energy lasers and electromagnetic pulse technologies. From smoother bearings of video tape recorders Japanese makers have developed a more reliable air-to-surface missile "than U.S. missiles because they have better gyrocompass technology".[10]

[8] Office of Technology Assessment, U.S. Congress, *Arming Our Allies* (Washington, D.C.: U.S. Government Printing Office, May 1990), pp. 64, 66 and 80; also, Tetsuya Kataoka and Ramon Myers, *Defending An Economic Superpower* (Boulder: Westview Press, 1989), pp. 58-60, 62, 64-5 and 68-9.
[9] Ikegami-Andersson, op. cit., pp. 79, 82-3, 85 and 112.
[10] Samuels, op. cit., pp. 189-90, 192 and 195.

Generally, the private sector in Japan accounts for 80% of Japan's total R&D, while in the U.S. the government itself pays for the majority of R&D costs. Thus it is difficult to estimate the extent of Japan's military R&D. American military R&D is around 13%, Japan's only 2.35%. It should be noted, in addition, that Japan has relied on follow-on work from U.S. military R&D monies. But the Japanese do specialize in their military R&D. It has been calculated that Japan's R&D ratio of military-specific electronics as a percentage of Japan's total equipment R&D expenditures was approximately 38%. That same figure for the U.S. is reported to be 39%, "the highest level in the world".[11]

The increasingly "dual use" nature of Japanese products has hastened this process. Japanese companies have a talent for switching back and forth. During WWII, Yamaha switched from making pianos to aircraft parts and back to pianos after the war. Today, Mitsubishi, TDK, Toshiba, Sony and others have developed military products from systems manufactured originally for civilian applications in computer, hi-fi and T.V. Even the vital military chips, gallium arsenide along with silicon-on-sapphire were first developed for big screen TVs, but were found to resist radiation and could function even under extreme battlefield conditions. The nature of modern weapons demands increasing reliance on dual use electronics. Nearly a quarter of Japan's modern T-74 tank is made up of electronics. In today's world civilian products can have military applications since the end-user customer determine how Japanese products are utilized. Between 1976 and 1990, military R&D grew on average by nearly 15% per year, though its total is still regarded as smaller than Germany and the U.K. Kawasaki helicopters have been converted by Sweden, Burma and Saudi Arabia for military purposes. U.S. smart bombs rely on Sony and Sanyo video camera technology. About half of Japan's electronics goes abroad, some of it for defense.[12]

The Japanese government keeps no records of products that are subsequently converted to military applications. This is no surprise since by law Japan is not permitted to sell weapons abroad, except to America. However, during the Korean War, Japan arms makers, though under a general export ban, exported small military munitions, or parts thereof: pistols to the U.S., plants for bullets to the Philippines, machine gun components to Indonesia, guns and bullets to Thailand. Since that period Japan has exported military-usable items to Yugoslavia, Sweden and certain Middle East countries. The U.S., by treaty as an "exclusively friendly partner", is the exception. NEC sells fiber optics to the U.S. military, Kikusui delivered oscilloscopes and Kyoto Ceramics provides ceramic parts for America's Tomahawk missiles. Since the 1980s, owing to the high quality of Japanese defense technology, increasingly more Japanese industrialists have questioned Japan's ban on military exports to foreign countries. An American study showed in 1986 that Japan exported over $210 billion abroad in military-applicable products.[13]

Moreover, Japan, as well as Italy, ranks number one in the world in licensing the production of major U.S. weapons systems. Japan is building close to 30 major weapons systems from the Americans, South Korea only half that number, with England and Germany ranked third and fourth. The Bush administration actively promoted the sale of arms to Japan

[11] Ikegami-Andersson, op. cit., pp. 56-7 and 66.

[12] Lorell, op. cit., p74; also, Drifte, op. cit., pp. 40, 67-8 and 74-5; and Malcolm McIntosh, *Japan Re-armed* (London: Frances Pinter, 1986), pp. 51-3.

[13] Ikegami-Andersson, op. cit., pp. 90-3; also, Lorell, op. cit., p. 425; and, Dong Joon Hwang, "Regional Arms Production Cooperation and Pacific Security", in Dora Alves, ed., *Change, Interdependence and Security in the Pacific Basin* (Washington, D.C., National Defense University Press, 1991, p. 128.

via loans calling it a "defense GATT". Clinton has continued that pattern of arms purchases. In the previous decade alone Japan signed 100 military co-production projects with the U.S. Such projects include the very expensive Aegis system, the FS-X and the new stars wars for Japan - a perimeter, multi-layer anti-missile defense system aimed ostensibly against a possible North Korean, or even Chinese missile attack. Licensing has produced some advantages. The FS-X project allowed the Japanese to further advance their own development capability of hitherto unattained capabilities like software for complex flight-control circuitry. Though originally agreed as a U.S. black-boxed technology transfer, the Japanese pulled back from the "sanitized" U.S. system in 1993 and developed their own, which the Americans originally though they could not do.[14]

Slowly, the Japanese arms makers have evolved from small munitions to repair and maintenance of U.S. and Japanese systems, the making of small systems, to licensing, codevelopment and production of large projects to stand-alone development of its own major systems. Even with the cold war over, in 1992 Bill Clinton asked Japan to cooperate with the U.S. in theater missile defense, which would require access to the now advanced Japanese military technology. Clinton's aim was not only to continue the defense of Japan and to new defense projects for American firms, but to put in place an early warning tactical weapons system that protects American soldiers deployed around Japan. President George W. Bush will likely accelerate those systems.

In 1994 Kawasaki developed a helicopter that was to replace its older American counterpart. Mitsubishi and Toshiba co-developed an anti-missile air defense system that was to replace the American Hawk missile. Japan's companies have also begun developing satellite systems for what it calls its defensive militarization of space, emphasizing launch and surveillance functions. The "Perry Initiative" further called on Japan to provide the U.S. with leading edge military technologies, as flat panel displays, new composites and semiconductors. In 1994, the U.S. called on Japan to develop a long range mid-air refueling capability in order to fulfill its alliance obligations.[15]

Though the Japanese aircraft industry is seeking to be on par with Western leaders, "the space sector is considerably stronger". Japan manufactures its own communications satellites, rockets and monitoring ground systems. Until 1993, Japanese rockets were based on U.S. technologies, but its newest launcher, the H-II, is wholly indigenous. Japan's "military-industrial strategy", according to a leading international defense expert, "is to produce a broad range of major weapons at very low production rates, developing the technological know-how and industrial infrastructure that would have to precede a decision to rearm".[16]

The low but steady military production output figures for 1997 bear this strategy out. There were 18 new tanks, 10 artillery, 36 APCs, 4 surface-to-ship missiles, 2 destroyers, 1 submarine and 8 F-2s produced. These numbers approximately reflect the production output from previous years. This suggests an incremental or pre-surge capability in waiting. Though as recently as 1995 it was widely believed that the Japanese could not develop the most critical aspects of missile and aviation technology, by 1998 Japan is completing the

---

[14] Lorell, op. cit., pp. 411-2; also, William Keller, "Global Defense Business", in Ethan Kapstein (ed.), *Global Arms Production* (Lanham, MD: University Press of America, 1992), pp. 66, 80-2, 89.

[15] Green, op. cit., pp. 125, 129-31, 140 and 147; also, Ikegami-Andersson, op. cit., p. 112.

[16] William Keller, *Arm in Arm* (New York: Basic Books, 1995), p. 176; also, Keith Hartley and Stephen Martin, "International Arms Collaboration: Euro-Japanese Collaboration in Aerospace", in Ron Matthews and Keisuke Matsuyama (eds.), *Japan's Military Renaisance?* (London: Macmillan Press, 1993), pp. 175-6.

construction of a full fledge jet propulsion laboratory in Sapporo where they expect to "improve" the performance of their high speed vehicles. There are some new and continuing joint U.S.-Japan research projects as well. Chief among them include a ducted rocket engine that boosts combustion in its second-stage, which both extends the range and delivery speed of future missiles. The U.S. and Japan are also developing an advanced extra high tension steel to be used in larger submarines in ultra-deep waters. In addition, both countries are cooperating in the development of eye-safe laser technology that will enable operators to calibrate distance measurements more safely and precisely.[17]

One incentive for Japanese companies to join in arms productions is that defense products earn on average 50% more profits than civilian products, including automobiles. In addition, arms production can act as a "cushion" in recession, since the government-as-customer is a steady and reliable buyer for defense items and not as subject to civilian market fluctuations. The newest push has come from American defense companies who have lost whole military research labs with downsizing. American makers now need to rely on foreign labs, including the Japanese. Costs to develop state-of-the-art defense technologies have dramatically increased in recent years. An investment of $1-2 billion is required simply to develop a new advanced jet engine.[18] The prevailing consensus inside Washington, D.C. is that America can no longer develop its weapons system on its own, it needs its allies, and that includes Japan. Japan's companies are still too hemmed-in to do much expanding within their parent company. But they can expand through tie-ups with American firms, now reaching out to them. Thus today a strange kind of courtship is taking place between the military-industrial complex of the United States, and that of Japan. Instead of shrinking in isolation, they are growing in concert, at least in certain domains. Heretofore, national defense companies may have been thought of as being somehow a part of a state's structure. But defense companies may resemble their purely civilian counterparts in more ways than we have seen. They are tied to their governments but they also seek to survive as corporate entities, and to maximize profits. If this leads them to form strategic business alliances abroad then defense companies may be interdependent in that way. Moreover, by linking with Japanese companies, U.S. makers can continue the nation's hegemony in global security production. In 2000, the U.S. remained the world's number one defense arms seller, capturing an average of 55-60% of global sales after 1994. Clinton even created a defense loan program for foreign sales to 39 states in 1995.[19] The U.S. can continue its dominance not only because Japanese companies supplement them, but also because Tokyo does not act as direct arms export competitors.

An important consequence to understand is that even as defense industries lose their support base from downsizing in their own countries, it has not proven fatal. They are able to look to one another for stability and growth even in an increasingly austere environment. Therefore, as long as great defense companies exist in more than one setting, they can form their own logic. Thus they will be always be one industry that cannot die, and may indeed evolve in ways that are not predictable or desirable by those whose national interests they were originally designed to serve.

---

[17] Defense of Japan, 1997.

[18] Keller, "Global Defense Business", op. cit., pp. 50-2.

[19] Richard F. Grimmett, Excess Defense Articles: Grants and Sales to Allies and Friendly Countries, CRS, January 10, 2000, p. 17.

Chapter 3

UMTS IN JAPAN: HAS THE FUTURE *REALLY* BEGUN?

Robert C. Rickards
The Leipzig Graduate School of Management
Handelshochschule Leipzig
Leipzig, Germany and
Harz University of Applied Sciences
Wernigerode, Germany
email: rrickards@hs-harz.de

ABSTRACT

Long an industrial powerhouse, Japan has been playing a relatively smaller role in the digital world. In closing the resultant tech-gap, UMTS likely will play a crucial role. Both in making frequency available and in distributing licenses to use it, Japan appears to have learned important lessons from America's and Europe's mistakes. Assuming world leadership, NTT DoCoMo has begun both a limited rollout of 3G technology and export of its popular i-mode applications. This article sketches NTT's business strategy, strengths, and weaknesses. It also reports on progress in deregulating the Japanese telecommunications industry, price effects resulting from increased competition, new cooperative agreements in China, and foreign firms' efforts to gain a foothold in the Japanese mobile telephone market. The article concludes with brief observations about the current state of the Japanese telecommunications industry in general and of the role NTT plays in particular.

INTRODUCTION

Although poised to make significant gains, Japan is not now a leader of the wired world's economy. To illustrate that fact, this article begins with a brief examination of the country's relative ranking in the information technology and telecommunications standings. Next, it explains what 3G technology is. The article then describes major mistakes made by American and European firms in trying to implement 3G technology and how Japanese companies have profited from them. Thereafter, it turns to Japan's small-scale introduction of 3G wireless telecommunications as well as the different situations confronting NTT and its mobile telephone subsidiary, NTT DoCoMo. After elucidating NTT DoCoMo's business model, the article gives an overview of some Internet services currently accessible by handset in Japan, together with a preview of new services soon to be available there. It also summarizes accounts about software glitches and manufacturing snafus that have delayed service expansion at home. The article goes on to discuss NTT DoCoMo's efforts to export its handset applications to Europe and the United States, cooperative agreements with Chinese mobile telephone operators, and efforts by foreign competitors to establish themselves in the Japanese market. Finally, it concludes with a few brief observations about the present state of the Japanese telecommunications industry in general and of the role NTT plays in particular.

JAPAN ADRIFT IN A WIRED WORLD

That their economy is the world's second largest is a point of pride for many Japanese. Japan, they can brag, is Asia's financial kingpin, its industrial powerhouse, and the country with the largest export surplus. It also seems determined to flex the same kind of muscle in competing for prowess in the digital world.

Studies say leading in this tech-age race will strengthen the Japanese economy and society over the long run. The economy will benefit measurably, both in term of growth rates and competitiveness, as it employs more and more workers with skills in databases and information services.[1]

Yet according to a study by Merrill Lynch, Japan's information-technology sector does not even make the charts when it comes to contributing significantly to overall economic growth. As Table 1 shows, the leaders are the United States, Great Britain, Sweden, Switzerland, Finland, and Ireland. Japan lags in part due to restrictive labor regulations, which limit its ability to draw skilled labor into the country. In addition, until recently, the Japanese have not had unmetered, flatrate Internet access. Experts deem such access essential to developing a public view of the Internet as an everyday medium like radio or television.

The overshadowing presence of NTT, the former telephone monopoly, is a mixed blessing in this regard. On one hand, its continuing dominance of the telecommunications industry discourages new entrants to the marketplace. On the other hand, its ability to harness and channel e-commerce through its pervasive infrastructure is a force that could help the country improve its standing in the tech rankings quickly.

The Organization for Economic Cooperation and Development last year did not rank Japan at the top of the 29 member countries in terms of the importance of information technology in its economy. That ranking was based on employment in the information-technology sector as well as research-and-development outlays. Furthermore, Table 2 shows Japan well behind Switzerland, the United States, Sweden, Denmark, and Norway in terms of per capita expenditures for information technology and telecommunications in 2000.

---

[1]   Schmid, John, "In a Wired World, Germany's Economy Loses Its Way," *International Herald Tribune*, March 22, 2001, pp. 13-14.

Table 1: New Economy Leaders

Country	Rank
United States	1
Great Britain	2
Sweden	3
Switzerland	4
Finland	5
Ireland	6
Netherlands	7
Denmark	8
Europe	9
Belgium	10
Germany	11
Japan	12
Austria	13
France	14
Greece	15
Spain	16
Portugal	17
Italy	18

Source: Merrill Lynch/*International Herald Tribune*

Table 2: Expenditures for Information-Technology and Telecommunications in 2000[2]

Country	Expenditure (in DM)/Capita
Switzerland	5292
USA	5090
Sweden	4028
Denmark	3915
Norway	3737
Japan	3406
Great Britain	3343
Netherlands	3241
Finland	3001
Austria	2898
France	2828
Germany	2737
Belgium/Luxemburg	2702
Ireland	2522
Italy	2083
Spain	1904
Portugal	1461
Greece	1352

Source: BITKOM/*DieZeit*/Globus

---

[2] N.a., "In Zahlen," *Die Zeit*, 22. März 2001, p. 25.

Given its size, it is little surprise that Asia's biggest economy also generates the highest volume of online sales in that part of the world. In absolute numbers, Japan is the second-place Internet country, lagging only the United States. But the low rate of Internet penetration has put Japan behind Britain, the Netherlands, Sweden, and Switzerland in e-commerce sales as a percentage of gross domestic product.

Is there a way for Japan to recover? The country's digital advocates want to goad more Japanese online to hasten the transition to an Internet-age society without getting into a critical development lag behind the United States, Scandinavia, Great Britain, and other countries. Along the way, UMTS seems likely to play a crucial role.

WHAT IS UMTS?

The "Universal Mobile Telecommunications System" (UMTS) should come into general use in Europe and Japan as the third-generation (3G) handset-standard by 2002.[3] It will allow quick transmission of up to two megabits of information per second and will replace mobile telephone standards like GSM that currently are in use.

With UMTS-handsets, one still will be able to make voice telephone calls. More importantly, though, these handsets also will have the capability of data transmission via new networks. Hence, one will gain quick access to the Internet even while underway. In addition, one will be able to send and receive pictures and videos or remotely control the heating, security devices, and other appliances in a wireless networked house.

UMTS, however, likewise spells sizable investments for a mobile telephone system's operator because the number of base stations necessary for complete coverage in a medium-size country lies between 8,000 and 10,000 per network, about 50 percent higher than with the current handy-networks. Moreover, before an operator can start building a network anywhere, it has to acquire frequency spectrum and a UMTS-license from the country's government.

FREQUENCY AVAILABILITY: A LESSON
LEARNED FROM THE AMERICANS

Asian governments have learned from the United States' mistakes. In the world according to the wireless phone industry, the future of the U.S. economy and American technological leadership also rests on its ability to roll out the next generation of services, including high-speed Internet connections on mobile devices. Yet the American government still has to deliver what the industry needs most to help it attain its future goals: new rights to transmit through the airwaves.

In the autumn of 2000, President Bill Clinton signed an executive order directing federal agencies to identify and make available additional spectrum the industry can use for such sophisticated new services. But the most attractive slices of the frequency spectrum remain under the control of the Defense Department, which is loath to surrender its claims.

---

[3]   Zdf.msnbc.de, "Stichwort: Was ist UMTS?," 6. März 2001.

An auction of airwaves, initially planned for October of that year, has been postponed three times by the Federal Communications Commission (FCC). Bidders had requested the postponements in order to sort out the spectrum's value, a process complicated by overlapping claims from television broadcasters.

So, the major U.S. wireless carriers now are in the midst of a fierce lobbying campaign for more frequencies, while calling for lifting federal limits on how much spectrum they may own in a single market. That is a question the FCC is studying in a formal proceeding. Industry executives and analysts accuse the government of imperiling innovation, consumer choice, and economic growth by failing to open the airwaves.

"The market is going to deliver tremendous competition," Reed Hundt, a former FCC chairman, has said. "Investment is going to pour in here. Big bets will be made. The only fundamental obstacle is bad government policy."[4]

Perceptions of a spectrum drought and its potentially dire economic consequences clearly have taken hold in powerful offices. When, amid great fanfare, President Clinton signed the executive order in the autumn of 2000, the Council of Economic Advisers simultaneously released a report showing that wireless carriers employ 150,000 people and generate $44 billion in annual revenue. The study portrayed the advent of 3G as a key driver for future economic growth.

"These benefits are likely to be substantial, on the order of tens of billions of dollars per year," the study said. "Greater delay in providing additional spectrum licenses for high-speed applications reduces the likelihood that U.S. industry will take the lead in developing wireless technology and applications."[5]

Tom Wheeler, president of the Cellular Telecommunications & Internet Association, a trade group representing major U.S. carriers, notes that federal authorities have made available only about half as much spectrum as their counterparts have in France, Britain, and Japan. As a result, he said, carriers across Europe and Asia have gained a two-year lead in deploying 3G services. Among these carriers, NTT DoCoMo has emerged as the clear leader.

UMTS-LICENSE DISTRIBUTION: A
LESSON LEARNED FROM THE EUROPEANS

After Europe's telecommunications industry financially exhausted itself with bids in UMTS-license auctions totaling €140 billion,[6] Asia's governments have begun distributing their licenses for mobile telephones. Apparently, they have learned lessons from Europe's bad experiences too.[7]

Game theorists among the European economists had asserted, that an auction's costs, however high they might be, represent only "one-time" outlays. In the long-run, therefore, such costs would not hurt the industry, but spur its further development. The outgo

---

[4] Goodman, Peter S., "Wireless Carriers Plead With U.S. for More Frequencies," *International Herald Tribune*, March 1, 2001, p. 15.

[5] *Ibid.*

[6] Rickards, Robert C., "€140 Billion Out of Thin Air: Europe's UMTS-Auctions," in Frank Columbus, (ed.), *European Economic and Political Issues*, III, (Huntington, NY: Nova Science; 2001), pp. 19-43.

[7] Dodwell, David, "Teures Spiel: Asien profitiert von Europas UMTS-Debakel," *Die Zeit*, 15. Februar 2001, p. 29.

meanwhile certainly has proved to be "unique." Auction costs have left all "winners" mired deeply in financial muck. Their debts are enormous and their stock prices have nosedived.[8]

These developments led Singapore, Taiwan, and Hong Kong to experiment with mixed auctions in 2001. The resulting revenues, though, have proved disappointing for the governments involved. In contrast, both Japan and Korea have conducted no auctions at all. Instead, they have remained true to their proven, performance-based license distribution methods.

What are the results of the different European and Asian license distribution procedures? First, Europe's financially strapped telephone giants had to skip the Asian auctions altogether. That made license acquisition easier and cheaper for operators in the Far East, East Asia, and Southeast Asia. Second, it left the larger Asian telecommunications firms in an excellent financial starting position. NTT DoCoMo, Hutchison, Telstra, and Singapore Telecom are all enviously debt-free. The most important result, though, is that Asian businesses accordingly will continue to have cheap telecommunication costs. Furthermore, Asian telecoms generally and Japanese ones in particular now find themselves with extra cash for takeovers, participations, and joint ventures in Europe, Latin America, and elsewhere.

SMALL-SCALE BEGINNINGS

In April 2001, the Munich-based technology concern Siemens started taking into service the first commercial 3G UMTS-mobile telephone network in Europe. In doing so, Siemens supplied 400 handset users on the Isle of Man with UMTS-mobile telephones.

Besides voice telephone service, this pilot project for British Telecom (BT) also tests the technical and commercial possibilities of faster data transfers. The data services at first will offer a transmission speed of 390 kilobit per second, which is equivalent to five times faster speed than the ISDN-standard.

The timing of the Siemens/BT initiative suggested an effort to upstage developments in Japan, the acknowledged current leader in 3G technology. There, construction of full-coverage networks for the country already is well underway. In Europe, full-coverage network construction will not begin until early 2002.[9]

Amid much ballyhoo in the media, NTT DoCoMo and Japan Telecom had been vying against one another to be the first company to offer 3G service on a large scale. Although both firms had announced rollouts for May 2001, only the former was able to meet the deadline. Even then it was limited to 3,300 users in a test run. Fans chosen from among 147,000 applicants lined up in Tokyo to get free handsets directly from the mobile carrier. NTT DoCoMo furthermore warned users there might be problems with service. It was those problems, which had prompted the company to postpone a wider 3G debut. At any rate, the "lucky" customers now pay transmission fees of ¥100 (80 cents) to ¥150 ($1.25) for three minutes.[10]

According to Keiji Tachikawa, President & CEO, NTT DoCoMo, Inc., the future nevertheless has begun. In his view, this test run in the Tokyo area marked a milestone in the

---

[8] Rickards, Robert C., "UMTS2: A Game For Europe's Big Gorillas?," in Frank Columbus, (ed.), *European Economic and Political Issues*, IV, (Huntington, NY: Nova Science; 2001), pp. 105-140.

[9] Zdf.msnbc.de, "Siemens startet erstes UMTS-Netz," 22. April 2001.

[10] Connell, James, "Tech Brief: 3G Sneak Preview," *International Herald Tribune*, May 31, 2001, p. 18.

development of mobile telecommunications. The company calls its 3G service "FOMA" (Freedom of Mobile Multimedia Access). It makes use of W-CDMA (Wideband Code Division Multiple Access), an IMT-2000, 3G mobile communications international standard. Via the Internet, FOMA one day supposedly will support multimedia content, thereby transforming cellular terminals into powerful interactive tools.[11]

Although Internet service already has been available by mobile telephone via the so-called WAP-technology for several years, the service thus far has been commercially successful only in Japan, and even there chiefly with teenagers. Industry management, however, believes that limited success justifies further pursuit of the (ad)venture. A closer look at NTT's situation will explain the reasons why.

NTT'S SITUATION

The overall business strategy of Junichiro Miyazu is simple: the boss of Nippon Telegraph & Telephone Corp. (NTT) promises his customers the best service for the lowest price. With it, NTT up until now has been successful against the competition. Above all, though, its past as Japan's telephone monopolist has helped the concern. Although the government in Tokyo began privatizing NTT in 1985 (currently 46.7 percent) and deregulating the market step by step, the firm's dominant position scarcely has changed. The world's largest telecommunications service provider controls more than 90 percent of the domestic Internet traffic and around 60 percent of the voice connections overseas.

For the year ended March 31, 2000, Nippon Telegraph & Telephone returned to profit thanks to a stellar performance by its mobile telephone subsidiary NTT DoCoMo, which offset a weak fixed-line business.[12] But the parent company said net profit for the current financial year would drop by about 70 percent because of growing competition in the local call market and losses on investments.

For the year through March, group net profit at NTT was ¥464.07 billion ($3.59 billion), wiping out a ¥67.81 billion loss the previous year caused by a onetime charge to replenish dwindling retirement funds. Revenue rose 9.5 percent to ¥11.41 trillion. The result was below NTT's own target for a ¥503 billion net profit, but within analysts' wide range of forecasts of ¥230 billion to ¥540 billion.

NTT's core traditional fixed-line operations are broken into geographical units, NTT East Corp. and NTT West Corp. NTT East had a ¥20 billion net profit, but NTT West reported a ¥44.6 billion net loss. Analysts have raised concerns about losses from investments made by NTT Communications, particularly its $5.5 billion purchase of the U.S. Web hosting firm Verio Inc. last September. NTT Communications said Verio's loss would swell to $1.29 billion in 2001 after a $777 million loss in 2000.

NTT's forecast for a drop in net profit this year to ¥128 billion mainly reflects the introduction in May of its "Myline" services. Reductions in its local call rates stemming from the Myline services likely will weigh heavily on the company. Furthermore, many analysts doubt that NTT management can handle the problem of Verio's bleeding.

---

[11] Tachikawa, Keiji, President & CEO, NTT DoCoMo, Inc., "The Future is about to Begin," *International Herald Tribune*, February 7, 2001, p. 5.
[12] Reuters, "NTT Swings Back to Profit for Year," *International Herald Tribune*, May 18, 2001, p. 15.

Downward pressure on prices for other services is growing too. By the spring of 2002, NTT must lower the access fees for use of its cable network, initially by one-fifth, then within the coming three years by 40 percent. In addition, the number of fixed-line network connections is falling. For many people their handy now is enough.

So, despite its technological lead over competitors like KDDI and Japan Telecom, continuing business as usual unlikely would increase NTT's profit growth. To improve profitability, the firm therefore has adopted three measures. First, as part of a three-year restructuring plan announced earlier in 2001, NTT has begun transferring as many as 30,000 workers to other group companies in an effort to cut costs. The firm declined to say whether it would eliminate any jobs altogether.

Second, through its mobile telephone subsidiary, NTT currently is building a broadband, 3G mobile telephone service in the Tokyo region.[13] Third, again through NTT DoCoMo, it plans further expansion abroad.

NTT DoCoMo's SITUATION

In contrast to its parent company, NTT DoCoMo, which has been riding a sustained boom for mobile communication services, reported strong earnings that exceeded many analysts' projections. Moreover, the report yielded evidence that data services, rather than voice communications, could drive the company's future growth.[14]

For the year ended March 31, 2001, the cellular phone service provider posted a group net profit of ¥365.5 billion ($3.01 billion), as revenue shot up 26 percent to ¥4.69 trillion. The profit figure is 45 percent more than in the prior year and constitutes almost 84 percent of parent-company NTT's overall profit. However, as the Japanese cell-phone market nears a saturation point, NTT DoCoMo forecasts slower growth for the current year. It projects net earnings will gain just 6.7 percent to ¥390 billion on a sales increase of 13 percent to ¥5.3 trillion.

Yet, while demand for mobile telephone services generally is growing more slowly, wireless data service, based on the company's intensely popular wireless i-mode applications, is increasing much faster than anticipated. One reason for i-mode's rapid growth appears to have been the launching of similar services by NTT DoCoMo's competitors, which expanded the market overall.

Like European WAP-services, NTT DoCoMo transmits Internet-contents to handset display screens. But, in contrast to the Europeans, NTT DoCoMo has had great success with customers, thanks to its i-mode applications. Two and one-half years after starting, more than 24 million Japanese users surf through their own Internet pages, download music onto their handsets, or send photographs. By the end of the year, NTT DoCoMo wants to offer these services in Europe too.

Subscribers to NTT DoCoMo's mobile phone service rose 22.7 percent to 36 million by the end of March from a year ago, while i-mode saw its users nearly triple to 21.7 million. The percentage of mobile phone subscribers surfing the Internet via i-mode therefore grew

[13] Böcker, Birga, "Weltpremiere in Japan," *Die Zeit*, 11. April 2001, p. 26.
[14] Tanikawa, Miki, "Popular I-Mode Helps DoCoMo's Net Profit Rise 45%," *International Herald Tribune*, May 10, 2001, p. 20.

from nearly 19 percent to more than 60 percent of its mobile phone customer base during that period.

Data services accounted for approximately 10 percent of the total revenue for the past year, company executives said. Moreover, NTT DoCoMo's boss Tachikawa expects equal volumes of voice and data transmissions by 2005. The implicit fast growth in data use will result, in part, from the advanced, 3G mobile phone services, which NTT DoCoMo is pioneering. Despite its having to delay large-scale launch of 3G commercial services until October 2001, most analysts foresee little impact on the firm's earnings because it had expected only 150,000 subscribers this year.

The cellular giant expects to invest ¥1 trillion in 3G over the next three years and that it will be profitable in four years. As for investment with strategic partners, Tachikawa has said he would focus on cultivating alliances with Asian companies this year after cutting a series of deals with Western operators such as AT&T Wireless in 2000.

Analysts believe improvements in the ratio of data to voice business will prove pivotal to both NTT DoCoMo's and the parent company's future earnings. That is because cellular carriers will have to slash voice call rates repeatedly to retain customers in an increasingly saturated market, while luring consumers to increase usage of data transmission services. Accordingly, NTT DoCoMo has developed a business model to harness its profit potential.

NTT DoCoMo's Technology and Business Model

NTT DoCoMo introduced FOMA (Freedom of Mobile Multimedia Access) – its 3G mobile communications service in May 2001 in Japan. Via compact cellular terminals, this revolutionary 3G service allows effortless high-speed transmission of multimedia content, including high-resolution video images. Already it is transforming the way people communicate, bringing unprecedented convenience into business and personal lives.[15]

FOMA is based on W-CDMA (Wideband Code Division Multiple Access), which satisfies all requirements of the IMT-2000 international standard. Developed through collaborative research at NTT DoCoMo's R&D center in Yokosuka Research Park (YRP), it incorporates advanced technology that minimizes the effects of interference and noise, ensuring highly stable multimedia communications. Moreover, FOMA provides data transmission speeds far surpassing the speeds of conventional systems.

Just as important as leading technology is the business model behind FOMA. That model is similar to the one NTT DoCoMo successfully executed for its phenomenally popular i-mode applications. As depicted in Table 3, just one year after i-mode's introduction in February 1999 in Japan, it had attracted over 20 million subscribers! Moreover, the age distribution of i-mode users in Table 4 shows it enjoying wide acceptance by the general population. Clearly, it is not merely a teenage fad as some critics have suggested.[16]

---

[15] "FOMA," *International Herald Tribune*, March 22, 2001, p. 5.
[16] Fischermann, Thomas and Matthias Naß, "Die Welt im Handy," *Die Zeit*, 15. Februar 2001, p. 27.

Table 3: I-Mode Subscriber Growth 1999-2000

Date	Number of Subscribers
Feb 1999	0
Jun 1999	523,000
Oct 1999	2,235,000
Feb 2000	4,456,000
Jun 2000	8,290,000
Oct 2000	14,037,000
Feb 2000	20,000,000

Source: NTT DoCoMo

Table 4: I-Mode Users By Age Group

Age Group	Percent
Unknown	2
Under 20	7
20-24	24
25-29	20
30-34	12
35-39	8
Over 39	27
Total	100

Source: NTT DoCoMo

NTT DoCoMo's formula for this broad success includes services that are attractive and exceptionally convenient. With the touch of a cellular phone button, users of i-mode already can access over 40,000 sites, as well as such specialized services as e-mail, online shopping, banking, and ticket reservations. Since FOMA's arrival in May, the firm's focus has been on further expanding the range of services offered, providing higher quality content that attracts people of all ages and all walks of life. Soon stock trading and Internet transactions will be much more secure and quicker, developments that should enable NTT DoCoMo to increase its sales revenue per user still further. Whether the new services actually are well-received by the Japanese will not become apparent for several months. How great customer acceptance will be is somewhat questionable because consumers already regard i-mode as a very good service.

In any event, economy is another key component of NTT DoCoMo's strategy. Through an advanced packet transmission system, the company charges i-mode users by volume of data received, rather than time spent online. Doing so encourages longer, more frequent visits. In fact, over 90% of i-mode subscribers are everyday users, accessing an average of 11 sites per day. FOMA's dynamic multimedia content and speedier service likely will encourage even more frequent use as well as more varied content and services.

Accordingly, NTT DoCoMo is now applying lessons learned from its spectacularly popular i-mode applications, which attract providers by offering a huge user base, a straightforward system of payment, and a simple solution for converting Internet content into i-mode content. I-mode is based on a subset of HTML, the world's *de facto* scripting language, making conversion a breeze.

Finally, NTT DoCoMo's approach to the provision and development of technology is contributing to a host of win-win relationships with content providers and phone vendors. These partnerships, together with NTT DoCoMo's technological leadership and clarity of vision, no doubt will help ensure progress in the ongoing development of FOMA. Through FOMA's high-speed, multimedia capabilities, NTT DoCoMo intends to transform compact cellular terminals (handsets) into formidable business tools.

CURRENT I-MODE APPLICATIONS PROVIDE GLIMPSE OF FUTURE

Present cellular applications from NTT DoCoMo provide a tantalizing glimpse of what is to come. I appli, for example, is a Java-based service launched in January 2001. Made possible by new technological advances and cooperation with Sun Microsystems, i appli allows extremely small, Java-compatible i-mode terminals to download applets and other advanced content from over 30 new sites. Furthermore, users can utilize the downloaded content at any time without re-connecting to the respective websites.

In addition, i appli enables more productive business scheduling through automatic notification whenever one changes appointments on corporate groupware. From remote locations, users can monitor staff members, check the availability of meeting rooms, and so forth.

I appli also supports two versions of Secure Sockets Layer encryption, both the 40-bit version common to e-commerce and the 128-bit version favored by financial institutions. They add a high level of data security and thus likely will fuel a dramatic surge in the popularity of cellular-based e-commerce. For example, Amazon.co.jp, which started in Japan in November 2000, now offers a selection of 2 million books in English and Japanese via this mode of service.[17]

Users furthermore can download maps to assist them in reaching their business destination, or display charts of daily stock price fluctuations for accurate tracking of the market. With Java-based agent applications, users easily can set their terminals to receive automatically periodical updates on weather, traffic, and other types of information affecting business efficiency.

All i appli content is both high-resolution and, due to its reliance on Java, easy to use. Given Java's open specifications, combining its power with FOMA's high-speed multimedia capabilities thus sets the stage for creation of thousands of additional business applications in the future.

Moreover, once FOMA begins delivering high-quality, high-speed multimedia services in the palm of a user's hand, the world of entertainment never will be the same again. NTT DoCoMo is paving the way with the world's first mobile entertainment service, M-stage. It allows users in Japan to enjoy music and images on demand through compact mobile terminals and a speedy 64 kbps PHS network.

---

[17] Shannon, Victoria, "Tech Brief: Amazon on I-Mode," *International Herald Tribune*, April 19, 2001, p. 12.

M-stage allows instant downloading of a wide range of music, as well as information on artists and hit rankings. Japanese record companies already are providing over 3,000 music titles for purchase and sample streaming.

M-stage also smoothly delivers high-definition video and still image content at low bit rates, thanks to state-of-the-art NTT DoCoMo technology and MPEG-4 compression. Numerous content providers are collaborating to provide wide-ranging services through roughly 50 different channels and 130 submenus.

Although the varied services above even now comprise a broad assortment, FOMA's higher speed capabilities likely will expand it much further. Together with its global partners, NTT DoCoMo is determined to realize the full business and entertainment potential of FOMA.

RELATED DEVELOPMENTS

Omron Corp., a Japanese electronic company, recently announced development of a microprocessor for cell phones that is 10 times faster than existing processors. The chip, designed to process the flexible Java programming language, was created for 3G mobile phones, which can download data and software from the Internet at transmission speeds six to 40 times faster than currently possible.[18] The increased speed will make existing and future services even more attractive to users.

In this regard, the worldwide leader in business software, Germany's SAP, and NTT DoCoMo are cooperating in the area of mobile data transmission systems for business customers.[19] Both firms signed a corresponding declaration of intent in April 2001. Feasibility studies now will explore how to combine SAP's business software with NTT's mobile telephone technology. One goal is to develop existing applications further so customers can access data from SAP-systems via mobile telephone more readily. As yet, however, there still are no concrete product plans. The partners also must clarify remaining financial details.

NTT DoCoMo already had made the proposed cooperation public in Japan. According to its announcement, both firms also want to explore possibilities of developing new products jointly and distributing them in Japan as well as on the world market. In a first step, the firms plan to target their existing customers in their respective markets.

Another related development involves major European and Japanese players too. Sony's games division has gained worldwide sales success with its Playstation 2 console. Recently, though, it concluded an agreement with the British mobile telephone operator Vodafone. The firms have decided to connect Vodafone handsets to Playstations and per SMS deliver tips and tricks to players running games on the console. Once players have accustomed themselves to using both devices simultaneously, Sony and Vodafone then want to build a common mobile game apparatus for the fast UMTS-network. European mobile service operators, who have invested billions in licenses and networks, are looking desperately for such UMTS-applications. Apparently, Vodafone has found one.[20]

---

[18] Connell, James, "Tech Brief: Omron Speeds Dialing," *International Herald Tribune*, June 6, 2001, p. 17.

[19] Zdf.msnbc.de, "SAP und NTT wollen kooperieren," 12. April 2001.

[20] Borchers, Detlef, "Online," *Die Zeit*, 15. Februar 2001, P. 35.

Consequently, four major equipment manufacturers (LM Ericsson AB, Nokia Oyj, Motorola Inc., and Siemens AG) have set up the Mobile Games Interoperability Forum. Its purpose is to define a mobile games standard for network operators. Standardization would permit game developers to produce mobile games for distribution across various servers and networks and for play on different devices.[21]

SOFTWARE GLITCHES AND MANUFACTURING SNAFUS

From the outset, NTT DoCoMo had aimed to become the world's first wireless operator to offer services using 3G technology. As mentioned above, NTT DoCoMo met its rollout deadline, but on a much smaller scale than originally announced. Moreover, it delayed a full-scale trial run until October 2001 because of software problems. On account of these glitches, the company now says it will not cover all of Japan with third-generation mobile phone services for at least three years.[22]

KDDI Corp., Japan's second largest cellular company by user numbers, has not given a start date for its 3G offerings. For its part, the country's third largest mobile phone operator, Japan Telecom Co., has postponed starting mobile phone services based on 3G cellular technology until June 2002.

The six-month postponement was caused by delays in the development of networks and communication equipment that resulted from changing technical standards. According to Haruo Murakami, president of Japan Telecom, the postponement thus was "unavoidable." Murakami went on to say that the drawback of creating confusion among consumers was much bigger than postponing the start of service. Japan Telecom now plans to start service in the Tokyo metropolitan area in June 2002.[23]

Also reflecting the mood of many telecoms worldwide, Japan Telecom's Murakami said the firm planned to invest less than initially projected in its 3G services, although he did not disclose the actual amount it intended to spend. In any event, the delay will allow the company to adopt the latest 3G cellular technology standards, which were revised in December 2000.

Japan Telecom's delay puts the company in the same situation as many European phone companies, which have postponed their rollout of 3G technology due to the heavy investment required. Qualcomm Inc., a developer of widely used mobile phone technology, has said the introduction of 3G phones in Europe may be put off for at least two years. The company furthermore has said 3G services likely will not be commercially viable until late 2004 or early 2005.

Slower than anticipated growth in handset usage has had a dramatic impact on equipment manufacturers. For this reason, Mitsubishi Electric Corp. said its mobile phone shipments to Europe would be about a third less than expected for the year ending March 31, 2001.[24] The company had targeted a tripling of shipments for the year. The firm now thinks it's likely to

---

[21] Shannon, Victoria, "Tech Brief: Mobile Games Mobility," *International Herald Tribune*, July 4, 2001, p. 11.

[22] Connell, James, "Tech Brief: 3G Not There Yet," *International Herald Tribune*, May 23, 2001, p. 13.

[23] Bloomberg News, "Japan Telecom To Delay Start of 3G Service," *International Herald Tribune*, March 7, 2001, p. 21.

[24] Staszewski, Barbara, "Tech Brief: Phone Shipments Disappoint," *International Herald Tribune*, March 1, 2001, p. 15.

be about double. Mitsubishi had shipped 5 million handsets to Europe in the prior year. Other major producers including Nokia, Ericsson, Motorola, Lucent Technologies, and Cable and Wireless also have reported slowdowns, plant closings, and layoffs.

Manufacturing problems have plagued the industry too. For example, KDDI Corp. recently announced it would recall 560,000 mobile phones built by Sony Corp., the latest in a string of phone recalls in Japan.[25] The recall of the phones, sold under KDDI's wireless unit "au" brand and by subsidiary Okinawa Cellular Telephone Co., is the largest thus far in 2001 and would replace the handset's battery pack. In addition, KDDI had recalled 126,000 units of another Sony model, the C101S, in May 2001 due to a similar manufacturing snafu.

This year, software glitches also have struck two advanced phone models built by Sony and Matsushita Communication Industrial Co. under the Panasonic brand for NTT DoCoMo. NTT DoCoMo had disregarded a warning in April from Sony Corp. about flawed software, leading to a handset recall that one analyst said may cost as much as $183 million.[26] However, NTT DoCoMo waited more than a month to order the recall of 420,000 of the Sony-made SO503i phones, said Kanji Ohnishi, head of product planning at Sony's handset division. Sony shares posted their biggest one-day decline in five weeks on the first trading day after the recall was announced May 11.

In acknowledging the delay for the first time, spokesman, Toru Hinata admitted NTT DoCoMo had been slack. According to him, if the firm had checked when it first received reports about data leaks, the recall probably would have happened earlier. In Japan, Sony and other handset makers such as NEC Corp. make their phones according to specifications supplied by service providers like NTT DoCoMo and Japan Telecom.

DEREGULATION AND PRICE EFFECTS OF INCREASED COMPETITION

The Japanese cabinet recently approved revisions to laws covering Nippon Telegraph & Telephone, but no agreement has been reached on controlling anti-competitive practices, according to a spokesman for the Ministry of Public Management, Home Affairs, Posts and Telecommunications.[27] The revisions will raise the limit on foreign ownership in NTT to up to one-third from a current ceiling of 20 percent and help two NTT domestic operators – NTT East and NTT West – expand their Internet businesses. In contrast, more work remains to be done on the proposed bill to outlaw anti-competitive practices by market-controlling mobile-communications companies, those with more than 25 percent of the market.

The Myline service, referred to earlier in connection with NTT's forecasted lower profit for the current year, also represents progress in deregulation. Introduced May 1, 2001, Myline allows Japan's 60 million phone customers to register for their preferred local and long-distance carriers. Until Myline went into effect, users of domestic phone services not operated by NTT group companies had had to dial additional prefixes.

Thereafter Japan Telecom promptly slashed rates to their lowest level by far for its local-call service. The company announced it would charge ¥8.5 (7 U.C. cents) for a local three-minute call, down from an originally planned ¥8.8. As a result of this step, the company

---

[25] Shannon, Victoria, "Tech Brief: Sony Phones Recalled," *International Herald Tribune*, July 5, 2001, p. 11.

[26] Bloomsberg News, "DoCoMo's Costly Error," *International Herald Tribune*, June 7, 2001, p. 17.

[27] Shannon, Victoria, "Tech Brief: Japan Revises Telecom Law," *International Herald Tribune*, April 11, 2001, p. 17.

expects revenue of ¥24 billion from local calling services according to Tsutomu Kotani, senior vice president of Japan Telecom's telephone business headquarters. But net profit will be flat in the financial year that began in April, he added.[28]

Rival firms matched Japan Telecom's move, signaling heightened competition in the world's second largest telecom market. Nippon Telegraph and Telephone Corp.'s two regional units, NTT East and NTT West, KDDI, and the Tokyo Telecommunications Network Co. decided to match Japan Telecom by cutting their rates to ¥8.5. All of them previously had charged either ¥8.8 or ¥8.7.

According to the Telecommunications Carrier Association, NTT nabbed 76 percent of pre-registration applications so far, while KDDI grabbed 16 percent. The low share in Myline subscriptions thus was a major factor behind Japan Telecom's rate-cutting move. Its share had been about 6 percent. Besides cutting rates, it spent ¥10 billion on Myline advertising and other expenses. Japan Telecom targets a 16 percent share of the local calling market.

For its part, a KDDI spokesman said his firm had matched Japan Telecom's move "so that our customers are not inconvenienced." KDDI also appointed Tadashi Onodera, 53, as president, replacing Yusai Okuyama, 69. Mr. Onodera vowed to introduce a new strategy to combat NTT DoCoMo.[29]

Meanwhile, Yahoo Japan Corp. announced plans for a high-speed Internet service to compete with Nippon Telegraph & Telephone and increase revenue as online advertising drops.[30] Yahoo Japan and Softbank Corp., which owns 51 percent of Yahoo Inc.'s Japan unit, started the service in Tokyo in June and expanded it nationwide in August 2001. Yahoo Japan, in which Yahoo Inc. owns 34 percent, expects to attract 1 million users by the end of the year. A recent decline in revenue from Internet advertising, which accounts for 90 percent of Yahoo Japan's sales, means the company must seek other revenue sources.

The new service, which will cost users ¥2,280 ($18.50) a month, will compete with NTT and Japan Telecom in the fast-growing market for Internet access based on asymmetric digital subscribers line technology. This technology enables data to move through copper phone lines at about 10 times the speed of conventional connections. The monthly rate is less than NTT and Japan Telecom charge for similar services. Japan Telecom has said the number of daily applications for its high-speed ADSL Internet access service slumped 30 percent since Yahoo Japan entered the market.[31]

NTT has 54 percent of the ADSL market in Japan, which totaled about 179,000 subscribers at the end of May, according to the Ministry of Public Management, Home Affairs, Post and Telecommunications. Japan's high-speed Internet services have lagged behind such services in other industrialized countries.

Analysts say the ADSL market is poised to surge in Japan. Merrill Lynch & Co. forecasts that subscribers will grow to 2.7 million by March 2002 and that the market for these services will be worth ¥575 billion by 2006. But competitors and analysts said Yahoo's effort probably would incur huge losses and wondered if it ever would be profitable. To cover the expected huge costs of ADSL, it therefore also likely will seek income from new businesses, such as charging for content viewing.

---

[28] Reuters, Bloomberg, "Rates Cut By Japan Telecom," *International Herald Tribune*, March 28, 2001, p. 19.

[29] Shannon, Victoria, "Tech Brief: Japan Telecom Rivalry," *International Herald Tribune*, April 11, 2001, p. 17.

[30] Bloomberg, Reuters, "Challenge to NTT's Net Service," *International Herald Tribune*, June 20, 2001, p. 17.

[31] Shannon, Victoria, "Tech Brief: Yahoo ADSL Hits Japan Telecom," *International Herald Tribune*, July 4, 2001, p. 11.

NTT DoCoMo Introduces I-Mode
in the United States and Europe

Years ago, Japanese firms scared American and European manufacturers first with their cutting-edge entertainment electronics, then with automobiles and computer chips, before finally making everyone happy with tamagotchis. Now they apparently intend to show the rest of the world how to sell mobile telephone services successfully.

NTT DoCoMo will begin offering wireless Internet services via i-mode in the United States through its American partner AT&T Wireless Group early in 2002.[32] The services probably will begin in the Seattle area and then expand nationwide a year or two later. Simultaneously, NTT DoCoMo also will make them available in Western Europe through its Dutch partner KPN NV. The partners hope to replicate i-mode's success in Japan. There the assortment of services accessible by handset already is gigantic: about 800 firms currently offer thousands of such i-mode services. Just in May and June of this year, they drew 200,000 new customers weekly into the Internet!

In Germany, which has the most Web-based commerce in Europe,[33] the country's third largest network operator, E-Plus, will market i-mode. It belongs to KPN's subsidiary mobile telephone company, in which NTT DoCoMo holds a minority interest. Despite i-mode's success in Japan, many Germans are skeptical about its prospects here due to both NTT DoCoMo's business strategy and KPN's seeming lack of one.

To begin with, i-mode is based on a Japanese standard, and makes use of handsets conceived especially for its use. Furthermore, the business model behind it is country-specific. In Japan, NTT has assumed the role of an integrator. That was possible only because the Japanese regulatory authorities – in contrast to their European counterparts – had no problem with the former monopolist's continuing to control much of the domestic telecommunications industry. For example, it alone still can dictate myriad technical details down to the question of which suppliers may sell their services from the Internet via i-mode. The company's ability to do so stems from the fact that it collects the sales revenue via telephone bill for all i-mode service suppliers, while charging a fee for each transaction.

The Japanese telephone giant thus dominates all aspects of this business. Such a situation is unthinkable in Europe, where the current technology, GSM embodies a common, open standard accepted by the entire industry. That standard constitutes the technological basis for competition not only among network operators, but also among handset producers and suppliers selling their services on the Internet.

Thus, while E-plus can attempt to implement NTT DoCoMo's business model on a smaller scale, it must reckon with countermeasures from the other five competitors (T-Mobile, D2 Vodafone, Viag Interkom, Mobilcom, and Group 3G) in Germany. Ron Sommer, the boss of Deutsche Telekom, which controls T-Mobile, is unimpressed by the NTT-KPN initiative. He believes no one can be successful with a closed standard on the European market because people want openness in the Internet.[34]

The group E-Plus/Hutchison will be among the first firms to use a UMTS-license in Germany beginning in 2003. From the outset, many observers regarded this Dutch-Asian

---

[32] Staszewski, Barbara, "Tech Brief: I-Mode in America," *International Herald Tribune*, March 15, 2001, p. 15.

[33] El-Bahay, Akram, "Deutschland ist beim Web-Handel führend," *Die Welt*, 4. August 2001, p. 14.

[34] Lütge, Gunhild, "Japan prescht vor," *Die Zeit*, 26. Juli 2001, p. 20.

alliance as the bidder with the best prospects at the German UMTS-license auctions. NTT DoCoMo participates in the group not only through its interest in E-Plus, but also through its minority participation in Hutchison. The group E-Plus/Hutchison paid DM16.42 billion for its license. E-Plus and Hutchison want to use it with separate offerings.[35]

Shortly after the group obtained its license, soccer fan Paul Smits scored a spectacular own goal.[36] The public invitation of the chairman of KPN's board of management to take over the Dutch telecoms conglomerate was not surprising because it underscored the concern's weakness relative to the international competition. Given the current conditions in Europe's telecommunications industry, other corporations also would be willing to flee to stronger arms. But neither has Mr. Smits been able to offer a strategic perspective, nor have close partners appeared to show much interest in a takeover of KPN. This disinterest applies to both the Italian TIM and NTT DoCoMo. Furthermore, U.S. Bell South, the other minority shareholder of KPN's German subsidiary E-Plus, availed itself of the option to swap these shares for the Dutch company's stock. As soon thereafter as it could, Bell South sold that stock for cash.

In light of the almost €22 billion in debts posted for the year just past against earnings before interest, taxes, depreciation, and amortization of €3.4 billion, a downgrading by the international rating agencies, which will make credit more expensive, and weak business prospects, KPN's lack of corporate suitors comes as no surprise either. To make KPN a more attractive takeover candidate, Mr. Smits wants to part with numerous stakes as fast as possible and use the proceeds to reduce its debt burden. But to date, little has happened.

JAPANESE COOPERATION AGREEMENTS IN CHINA

Besides Western Europe, Japanese telecoms also have been pursuing business opportunities in China actively. China had more than 100 million mobile-phone users at the end of March 2001, the Ministry of Information Industry claimed, thereby purportedly overtaking Japan as the world's Number 2 cell-phone market. The country supposedly soon will have more subscribers than the top market, the United States.[37] Consequently, the interest of Japanese firms in China has grown correspondingly.

For example, KDDI has signed an agreement with China United Telecommunications Corp. to cooperate in cellular and wireless Internet technologies.[38] China's Number 2 mobile phone company, known as Unicom, said that as part of the deal, the two companies would allow their mobile subscribers to use each other's networks in a roaming arrangement.

Unicom and KDDI are the only companies in their respective countries to have adopted Qualcomm's code division multiple access, or CDMA, wireless technology. A tie-up between the two could help popularize the standard, which 90 million cell-phone subscribers use worldwide.

Meanwhile, NTT DoCoMo has paid $30.4 million to increase its stake in Hutchison Telephone Co. of Hong Kong by 6.37 percentage points, to 25.37 percent. The holdings in the

---

[35] Zdf.msnbc.de, "Die UMTS-Gewinner im Porträt," 13. Februar 2001.

[36] Dunsch, Jürgen, "EuroCity Chat: A Dutch Own Goal," *Frankfurter Allgemeine Zeitung*, (English Edition), April 19, 2001, p. 5.

[37] Connell, James, "Tech Brief: Mobile China," *International Herald Tribune*, May 17, 2001, p. 20.

[38] Connell, James, "Tech Brief: China Telecoms Deal," *International Herald Tribune*, June 6, 2001, p. 17.

unit of Hutchison Whampoa Ltd. is part of the Japanese company's strategy to buy up stakes in key foreign partners.[39]

FOREIGN COMPETITORS IN JAPAN

While Japanese companies have been busy seeking opportunities to expand abroad, foreign firms, of course, have been active in Japan. Furthering its effort to reduce debt, AT&T Corp. has sold its stake in Japan Telecom.[40] Vodafone Group PLC, the British mobile phone company, agreed to buy AT&T's 10 percent stake in Japan Telecom for $1.35 billion, the companies said. AT&T also gave another reason for its decision to sell its stake in Japan Telecom: NTT DoCoMo had invested directly in Japan Telecom, despite the fact the two Japanese companies supposedly are direct competitors.

For its part, Vodafone's bet that a bigger footprint would be better has yet to generate the sizable returns investors have expected, prompting some to accuse the company of squandering its wealth by overpaying for assets.[41] Clearly, Vodafone's recent acquisitions and participations in China and Japan suggest the company still is betting a far-reaching network that will provide cost efficiency and retain customers will give it an edge over competitors.

For all the hoopla over the potential profitability of next generation services, though, Vodafone is sticking to cautious predictions. The firm estimates as much as 75 percent of its revenue will continue to come from voice traffic through 2004. In this regard, the comparison with NTT DoCoMo is not flattering for Vodafone, Europe's biggest mobile telephone service provider. Without new services, increasing revenue from existing customers will be that much harder.

Be that as it may, Vodafone Group also recently said that it planned eventually to list shares of its Japanese mobile telephone carrier J-Phone on the Tokyo stock market. "It would be a good idea at some stage to list J-Phone and have investors take a participating interest," the chief executive of Vodafone, Chris Gent said. Three J-Phone regional operators would have to be merged before a share sale could take place. The Vodafone Group controls about 60 percent of J-phone.[42]

CONCLUSIONS

The contribution of information technology and telecommunications to the Japanese economy has been subpar relative to other major industrialized countries. That situation, however, soon could change as UMTS-networks come into operation. Already, Japan appears to have learned important lessons from American and European mistakes in this regard. It has made large amounts of broadband spectrum available on a timely basis. Moreover, it has done so without financially overburdening either the telecoms or their customers.

---

[39] Connell, James, "Tech Brief: DoCoMo Bolsters Hutchison Stake," *International Herald Tribune*, May 17, 2001, p. 20.

[40] Kapner, Suzanne, "Vodafone to Take AT&T's Stake in Japan Telecom," *International Herald Tribune*, February 28, 2001, p. 17.

[41] Kapner, Suzanne, "A Big Spender Gets Put on Hold," *International Herald Tribune*, May 31, 2001, p. 18.

[42] Reuters, "Japan: J-Phone's Future," *New York Times*, July 31, 2001, p. W1.

Through its pioneering role in the development of e-commerce and 3G technology, NTT likely will play a major part in the change process. Both the parent company and its mobile telephone subsidiary are committed to implementing 3G for business and consumer purposes because their prospective growth otherwise will be flat. Their business model for FOMA seeks to replicate their success with i-mode. Although software glitches and manufacturing snafus have led to a scaled-down trial introduction of 3G service, the future nevertheless really seems to have begun – at least in Japan.

Whether NTT will prove successful in exporting its business model to Europe and the United States is unclear. Japanese regulatory authorities well may be reluctant to restrict NTT DoCoMo's anti-competitive practices. Their counterparts in Germany, the Netherlands, and the United Kingdom, though, unlikely will view limited access through billing procedures as well as exclusionary hard- and software favorably. Moreover, the long-run viability of NTT DoCoMo's Dutch partner, KPN, appears uncertain.

The efforts of Japan's telecoms to expand their business abroad also are evident in China, which currently is emerging as the world's largest mobile communications market. At the same time, the largest American telecom, AT&T, has exited the Japanese market, due in part to NTT DoCoMo's anti-competitive practices. That seems not to have troubled the American Internet provider, Yahoo, or Europe's Vodafone, each of which is using a different business model in trying to establish a presence in Japan. However neither American Internet providers nor European mobile telephone network operators so far have demonstrated that they can do things differently than NTT and still make money.

Chapter 4

STRATEGIES FOR CARBON TAXATION FOR REDUCING CO₂ EMISSIONS IN JAPAN AND KOREA

Toshihiko Nakata
Management of Science and Technology (MOST)
Graduate School of Engineering
Tohoku University
Aoba-Yama 01
Sendai 980-8579, JAPAN
Tel: +81 (22) 217-7004
FAX: +81 (22) 217-7004
E-mail: nakata@cc.mech.tohoku.ac.jp

ABSTRACT

This paper focuses on the impacts of using carbon and energy taxes to reduce carbon emissions from the energy systems of both Japan and Korea. Two countries have few domestic fossil fuels, resulting in shaky condition in current energy supply. Ensuring energy security is a national issue once again to stabilize economic development and to meet Kyoto protocol at a reasonable cost. Besides, the Japanese are increasingly keen to reduce the use of such 'dirty' fossil fuels as coal and oil in favor of gas. A partial equivalent model of the national energy sector has been developed to forecast changes in the energy system out to the year 2040. The model accounts for the changes in energy technology capacities, fuels, and consumption in response to policy initiatives, such as taxes. We find that carbon and energy taxes will decrease carbon dioxide emission to a proposed target. The total cost in terms of supplying energy will be similar for either approach. However, the model also indicates that carbon taxes cause a shift in resources used from coal to gas. Since energy security is a primary concern to Japan and Korea, maintaining a diverse base of resources is very important. Policies that would eliminate coal, and efficient coal based technologies, may not be desirable. The development of clean coal technologies and advanced transportation technologies suitable for national energy systems should be the next target to overcome the limit of carbon taxes. Another policy option for the reduction of CO₂ emissions is the Japan-Korea cooperation in energy technology. Coupling of utilities such as gas pipeline and electricity grid will have a great impact on ensuring energy security for Far East countries. Though the deregulation of energy markets is still on the way, cost effective and environmental sound strategies should be integrated to show up-to-date energy scenarios.

1. INTRODUCTION

The Kyoto conference calls for substantial reductions in the emissions of carbon from the world's energy systems. However, it is not clear how these reductions should be achieved. Each country has its own unique considerations of energy resources, economic demand patterns, and energy security concerns. Thus, the best strategy for each country will be different. In this paper we examine possible policy approaches for Japan and Korea. There are two questions that must be addressed for these countries: First, how can the energy system be configured so as to meet future CO_2 constraints, Second: what sorts of policies could be used to encourage the system into new configurations? The possible policies must be evaluated in light of their potential cost, emissions other that greenhouse gasses, and implications for national energy security.

Since almost all the energy resources are imported in Japan and Korea, energy security should have some priority over environmental constraints. Integrated analysis, which includes energy and environmental models, will make an important role to find out the most suitable scenario for national energy systems. Japan and Korea must assess different approaches to controlling CO_2 emissions. The impacts of controls on CO_2 emission from electricity in Canada and the USA have been studied (for example, Chung et al., 1997), however there are few papers concerning electric power reconfiguration in Japan and Korea.

The transportation sector has the characteristics of mostly using petroleum. Electric trains are powered indirectly from a variety of energy sources; however, their share of energy consumption in transportation was no more than 2.3 percent in Japan in the year 1997. Even when the cost of petroleum rises, conventional vehicles cannot switch right away to alternative energy sources. Hybrid vehicles, though still using gasoline as a fuel, could be one alternative technology in the transportation sector. Such vehicles have excellent fuel efficiency and a strong likelihood of drastically reducing CO_2 emissions.

Reaching the goals of emission reductions will require some action on the part of the government. There are a number of policy actions available to the government, ranging from regulatory incentives to taxes. Moreover, there are many energy alternatives in combination with technologies for energy conversion and with market forces. For example, the electric sector has more choices of energy resources than the transportation sector, in which only petroleum can meet most of the demand today. Electricity can be powered by fossil fuels, nuclear energy, and renewables such as hydro, wind and solar energy.

Nuclear energy has been an important energy source since the first oil embargo occurred in the early 1970s. Energy security has been a first concern for policy makers in Japan. Japan has increased its reliance on nuclear power because it has limited domestic energy resources. At present, 51 commercial nuclear power plants are in operation, and the government had wanted to build 10-13 more by the year 2010 (JPET, 1998; Kiso, 1998 and Matthews, 1998). Recently, the Ministry of Economy, Trade and Industry in Japan (METI) announced that nuclear power stations could be technically in use for sixty years under strict maintenance condition. Nuclear power has an advantage over fossil power stations in terms of CO_2 emissions. The government maintains that nuclear power helps to prevent global warming because nuclear power plants do not emit CO_2. In fact, as the nuclear power reactors operate past the period of paying off their capital costs, they produce electricity cheaper than any other energy source, because their operations and maintenance costs are the lowest. The capacity factors and safety records of power reactors have improves dramatically worldwide in recent years. In addition, the construction time and costs of power reactors have been improved, e.g., the Tokyo Electric/GE advanced 1,300 MWe BWR was built in just four years and within budget. By the year 2040 it becomes possible that the fast breeder reactors and high temperature helium gas cooled reactors will be built for a number of reasons. This will increase the efficiencies of electricity generation and lower the CO_2 emissions significantly, particularly in process of heat applications as well as in electricity generation.

However, current changes in ESI toward deregulation and privatization make electric power utilities conservative about future investment in nuclear power stations in Japan (OECD, 2001). The Japan's long-term recession forces investors to assume the risk of their investments. Independent Power Producers (IPP), which are recently allowed to come into the electricity market under competition, prefer combined-cycle power stations which use liquefied natural gas as a fuel. Combined-cycle plants have priority over nuclear power: Initial and capital costs are much lower, and gas turbines allows flexibility to meet the demand changes. Total heat efficiency of advanced combined-cycle exceeds 50 %, which saves fuel cost clearly.

Depletion and environmental effects of burning fossil fuels such as oil, gas and coal is also serious (Campbell and Laherrere, 1998; Banks, 2000 and Gan, 1998). External costs of atmospheric pollution are not included in the price of fossil fuels correctly. The irrationality of burning oil and gas rather than preserving them for the production of petrochemicals, etc, is not well discussed. The governments are compelled to find a solution to the problem.

The issue of nuclear safety has top priority at all time and economic aspects have an important role in developing nuclear energy policy. The question of what would be the best way to control the emission of CO_2 remains unsettled (US Department of Energy, Energy Information Administration, 1998a; Sato et al., 1998; Zongxin and Siddiqi, 1995; Romerio, 1998 and Bodde, 1998). The problem, which we have to consider next, is an integrated concept of national security to meet the environmental constraints. Nuclear power needs to be examined in detail now from the standpoint of what we call environmental security (Allenby, 2000; Kagramanian et al., 2000 and Kaya, 1997). Whereas we recognize the importance of nuclear power, it seems that its role from economic and environmental aspects in the future is not well organized in Japan. The point of Kyoto and greenhouse emissions is not to give nuclear power a free ride to bright future (Doucet, 1999).

This paper uses a multi-period market equilibrium model to explore the cost and energy security implications of carbon taxes as policies for reconfiguring the national energy system, for all sectors including electric power. Moreover, we explore the impact of hybrid vehicles on CO_2 emissions in the Japanese energy system. A BTU tax is hypothetically imposed to evaluate the effect of fuel cost on energy consumption in the transportation sector and on CO_2 emissions. Financial parameters such as capital costs and operating costs are included to estimate the profits for taxation purposes. The effect of factors such as capital investments, resource depletion, and the market penetration of advanced technologies were included, in addition to a multi-period modeling of the price-quantity equilibrium in various markets. The impact of regulatory policies involving devices such as taxes on emissions or constraints on quantities and prices has been modeled.

The role of nuclear power to reduce CO_2 emissions is also examined. To make it clear, nuclear power phase-out (Nordhaus, 1997; Andersson and Haden, 1997; Welsch, 1998; Hoster, 1998; Welsch and Ochsen, 2001 and Haas and Auer, 2001) is hypothesized in the model to evaluate the difference in CO_2 emissions. The carbon tax is tentatively introduced to stress the increases in fossil fuel consumption. An economic aspect of two cases, with or without nuclear power, is also examined.

Another policy option for the reduction of CO_2 emissions is the Japan-Korea cooperation in energy technology. We focus on the energy systems in Korea to see the possible options for reconfiguring energy networks between two countries in East Asia.

2. IMPACTS OF CARBON AND BTU TAXES ON ENERGY SYSTEMS IN JAPAN

2.1 Policy Approaches to Reduce CO_2 Emissions

Reducing carbon emissions will require some action on the part of the government. In recent years many studies on the cost of CO_2 emission abatement have been published (Richels and Sturm, 1996; Schultz and Kasting, 1997). There are a number of policy actions available to the government ranging from regulatory incentives to taxes. Here we outline a few of these possibilities.

The Government can encourage the construction of certain types of technologies through the permitting processes and financial encouragement. It has requested that Japan's electric power utilities construct twenty nuclear power stations between now and 2010 which means approximately a fifty percent increase in nuclear power generation capacity. It would be unrealistic for electric power utilities to build more nuclear power stations at this time without government encouragement because of its higher capital cost and the difficulty of obtaining public acceptance at local sites.

Another alternative is implementation of a carbon tax. A carbon tax will raise the price of high carbon fuels, such as coal, and lead to a greater reliance on low carbon fuels. Since this tax directly discourages carbon use, it is expected that will lead to the most efficient reconfiguration of the energy system to meet emissions limits (Environment Agency of Japan, 1998). However, coal appears to be one of the most abundant fossil fuels. From the viewpoint of energy security, it is expected that coal, especially when used with clean coal technologies, should have an important role in Japan's energy mix. In this sense a carbon tax may not be the best way to meet Japan's objectives. An energy tax applied to all fossil fuels could be another approach for meeting both the CO_2 emission constraint and providing a good mix of energy resources.

Because there are many alternative technologies and fuels available to meet emission targets, particularly in the electric sector, it is important for policy makers and engineers to understand the implications of different policies intended to meet the targets. The model that we discuss here includes effects such as the market penetration of advanced technologies, capital investments, capacity retirements, and resource depletion. The impact of regulatory policies can be modeled through devices such as taxes on emissions or constraints on quantities and prices.

2.2 National Energy Model for Japan

Modeling has been a tool for national energy planning since the mid-1970s. At that time models were used to understand the implications and means of coping with the first oil embargo. More recently global warming has become one of the most significant topics for decision-makers. Just as physical models can predict the impact of increased CO_2 on climate, energy-economic models can show the economic and technical impacts of alternative economic strategies to minimize emissions.

There are previous analyses of the Japanese energy system. An outlook for Japan's energy supply and demand is published (for example, Kibune and Kudo, 1996). By using the CRIEPI model, cost effectiveness of CO_2 emission controls were studied (Yamaji et. al., 1993). In this study a macro input-output model was used to predict the impact of subsidies on CO_2 emissions in Japan. However, the model included little in the way of market functions in each sector and energy prices were derived explicitly.

Impacts of carbon taxation on Japan's economy as a whole were examined by using general equilibrium model (Goto, 1995). Macro economic costs of CO_2 emission control were also studied (Goto and Sawa, 1993). In their model the industrial sector was divided into twelve sub-sectors. However, the electricity sector was treated as roughly one single sub-sector, making it difficult to estimate the effects of such policies on the structure of the electric sector. There are few analyses of Japan's energy system that disaggregate the electric generating sector so that the impacts of such policies on technologies and fuel use can be examined.

An Energy-Economic Model

An energy economic model for evaluating CO_2 emissions policies should incorporate energy technologies, economics, and environmental impacts. Technology innovation and its efficiency improvement are factors that should be included for this model as well.

There are several modeling approaches available in energy economics based on either optimization or equilibrium approaches shown in Table 1. We have used the META•Net economic modeling system developed at Lawrence Livermore National Laboratory (Lamont, 1990). META•Net is a partial equilibrium modeling system that allows for explicit price competition between technologies, and can constrain or tax emissions. It allows a user to build and solve complex economic models. It will construct an energy model as a network of processes such as end-uses (price sensitive demands), markets (which allocate market shares based on relative prices), conversion processes (which compute inputs required to meet output requirements based on efficiencies, and compute prices based on capital and operating costs), and resources (which can be exhaustible, or can follow a set price track).

Table 1: Comparison of META•Net to Existing Modeling Approaches

Modeling technologies	Tools	Developer	Feature
Fixed coefficient model	LEAP[a]	Tellus Institute	All impacts and inputs are set in a fixed ration to the out put required
Technology based market model	MARKAL[b]	BNL	Rigid structure of linear programming
Technology based market model	META•Net[c]	LLNL	Solves the economic equilibrium problem directly
General equilibrium model	Second generation model[d]	PNL	World scale modeling
General equilibrium model	GREEN[e]	OECD	World scale modeling

[a]Lazarus, M. Heaps, C. and Raskin, P. (1997). LEAP Long-range energy alternatives planning system. Stockholm Environmental Institute, Boston, Massachusetts.

[b]Lydick, J. Morris, S. C. Lee, J. and Goldstein, G. (1990). Demo MARKAL Abbreviated Version of the US MARKAL Energy Systems Model, Created for Demonstration: Abilities, Limitations, and Demonstration, BNL-47782, Brookhaven National Laboratory, Upton, New York

[c]Lamont, A. (1994). User's Guide to the META•Net Economic Modeling System Version 1.2. UCRL-ID-122511, Lawrence Livermore National Laboratory, Livermore, California.

[d]Edmonds, J. A. Pitcher, H. M. Barns, D. Baron, R. and Wise, M. A. (1995). Modeling future greenhouse gas emissions: The second generation model description. In Modeling global change, ed. Klein L. R. and Lo, F., pp. 295-362. United Nations University Press

[e]Lee, H. Oliveira-Martins, J. and Mensbrugghe, D. (1994). The OECD Green Model: An Updated Overviews. Technical paper No. 97, OECD, Paris.

Commodities flow through this network from resources, through conversion processes and market, to the end-users. META•Net finds the multi-period equilibrium prices and quantities. The solution includes the prices and quantities demanded for each commodity along with the capacity additions (and retirements) for each conversion process, and the trajectories of resource extraction.

Although the changes in the economy are largely driven by consumers' behavior and the costs of technologies and resources, they are also affected by various governmental policies. These can include constraints on prices and quantities, and various taxes and constraints on environmental emissions. META•Net can incorporate many of these mechanisms and evaluate their potential impact on the development of the economic system.

The Japan model which we have designed is shown in Figure 1. It has sixty-four processes including eight demand nodes in the industrial, commercial, residential and transportation sectors, eight resource nodes modeling purchases of coal, natural gas, petroleum and nuclear fuel on the world markets, along with domestic hydropower and other renewables. Additional processes model the conversion of fuels to heat, electrical services, and transportation services. Necessary operating parameters such as capital cost and operating cost are used based on the current references (The Federation of Electric Power Companies, 1998: US Department of Energy, Energy Information Administration, 1998b: MITI, Agency of Natural Resources and Energy, 1998). Table 2 shows capital and operating cost used for this study in the electricity sector.

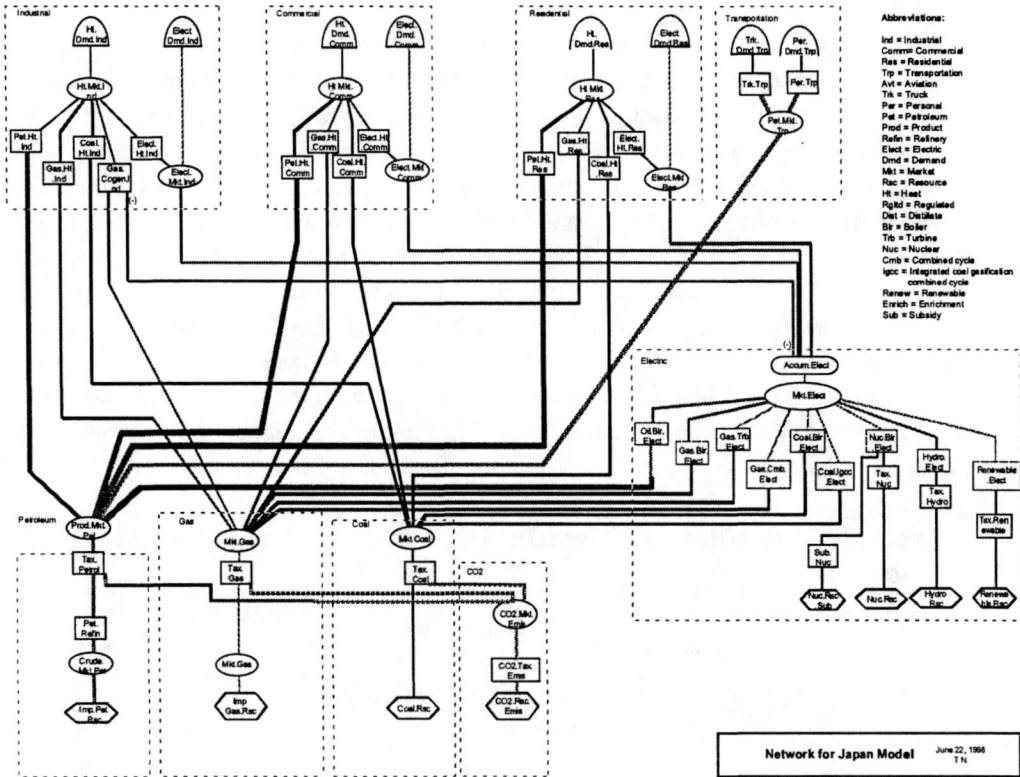

Figure 1: Network for Japan model

Table 2: Capital and Operating Cost in Electricity Sector

Electric power generation	Capital cost $/(mmBTU/Yr)	Operating cost $/mmBTU
Oil Boiler	49	9
Gas Boiler	51	10
Gas Turbine	30	10
Gas Combined Cycle	47	11
Pulverized Coal	68	14
Coal IGCC	110	13
Nuclear Boiler	80	16
Hydro	154	1
Renewable	50	4

Sources:

- The Federation of Electric Power Companies. (1998). *Handbook of Electric Power Industry*, Tokyo.
- US Department of Energy, Energy Information Administration. (1998). *Assumptions to the Annual Energy Outlook*, Washington DC.

Key Parameters and Assumptions

There are several key assumptions that drive any analysis of this type. These include growth rates, government policies to encourage particular technologies, and demand response to changes in price. We have assumed a moderate rate of growth over the model horizon. Table 3 presents assumptions about the growth rates and demand elasticities in each sector.

Due to government policies to maintain a nuclear generation capacity, it is assumed that the share of Nuclear Boiler power generation will remain constant at its 1995 level (about 35% of power generation output) until 2040. Hydropower is also set at constant generation quantity because of physical constraint on siting additional capacity. The Oil Boiler has maximum quantity constraint in accordance with the IEA agreement made just after the first oil embargo. New technologies such as coal integrated combined cycle and renewable power will be available in 2005. Their capacities are allowed to increase ten percent every year commencing 2005. Aviation transportation demand has not been included in this model since it is quite small in Japan.

Table 3: Growth Rate and Elasticity Assumptions for End-Use Sector

Process	Abbreviated name	Annual demand in starting period[a]	Annual rate of demand growth (at a constant price)[a]	Demand elasticity[b]
Industrial heat demand (mmBTU/yr)	Ht.Dmd.Ind	5.10E+09	0.002	-0.34
Industrial electricity demand (mmBTU/yr)	Elect.Dmd.Ind	1.24E+09	0.008	-0.34
Commercial heat demand (mmBTU/yr)	Ht.Dmd.Comm	9.00E+08	0.013	-0.24
Commercial electricity demand (mmBTU/yr)	Elect.Dmd.Comm	6.64E+08	0.020	-0.24
Residential heat demand (mmBTU/yr)	Ht.Dmd.Res	1.10E+09	0.006	-0.30
Residential electricity demand (mmBTU/yr)	Elect.Dmd.Res	7.37E+08	0.020	-0.30
Truck transportation demand (Ton-km/yr)	Trk.Dmd.Trp	2.14E+08	0.003	-0.17
Personal transportation demand (passenger-km/yr)	Per.Dmd.Trp	6.43E+08	0.010	-0.23

[a]The Energy Data and Modeling Center. (1998). *EDMC Handbook of Energy & Economic Statistics in Japan*, Tokyo.
[b]Based on the data by Nagata, Y. (2000, June 21). Personal communication.

2.3 Policy Scenarios Analyzed

The study focuses on a target rate of emissions of around 400 million tons of carbon (mmTC) by the year 2040. This is higher than the target of 280 mmTC in year 2010 that was specified by the Kyoto protocol (MITI, Agency of Natural Resources and Energy, 1998). Within this analysis, reaching the level of 280 mmTC appears to be difficult and might not be realistic for Japan. The discussion below outlines some of the issues raised by large carbon reductions. For most of the analyses, we have used a less stringent target.

The study evaluates the effects of carbon and energy taxes. In these cases we assume that government regulatory encouragement will keep the level of nuclear capacity at around 35 percent of the electric demand. Our investigation first developed a Reference Case analysis that showed the investments in energy technologies, resource use and emissions in the absence of policy actions. We then determined the level of tax needed to reach the required level of carbon emissions in the year 2040. We evaluated the cost of that approach and the configuration of the energy systems that results from it.

Reference Case Scenario

Under this scenario it is assumed that there is no intervention in the energy system.

Carbon Tax Scenario

A carbon tax is expected to be the most efficient approach to reducing carbon emissions. It has been already implemented in Sweden, Finland, Norway, Denmark and Holland in range of \$200/tonC (Sawa, 1997). In our study we evaluated several different tax rates to determine the rate that achieved the target reduction in the year 2040.

The taxes were introduced gradually over time, increasing the tax rate in uniform steps each period until the maximum rate in 2040 was reached. This avoids the dislocation caused by a sudden, drastic shift in the tax rate.

Energy Tax (BTU Tax) Scenario

An energy tax is another way to reduce emissions. In our study only fossil fuels such as petroleum, gas and coal are charged. Again, the tax rate was gradually increased over time.

2.4 Discussion for Taxation Scenarios

The discussion in this section highlights the changes in the energy system that result from reducing carbon emissions through carbon and energy taxes, and the costs of implementing these changes. Some figures in this section summarize the results from the year 2040, the last year of the analysis.

As the results show in Figure 2, the carbon tax suppresses the increase of CO_2 emissions. Without any taxation CO_2 emission will increase until reaching 491 mmTC in 2040. When the carbon tax is introduced, the increase of CO_2 emissions is strongly suppressed. At \$160/tonC, CO_2 emission will reach 391 million tons of carbon in 2040, which corresponds to a reduction of 100 mmTC.

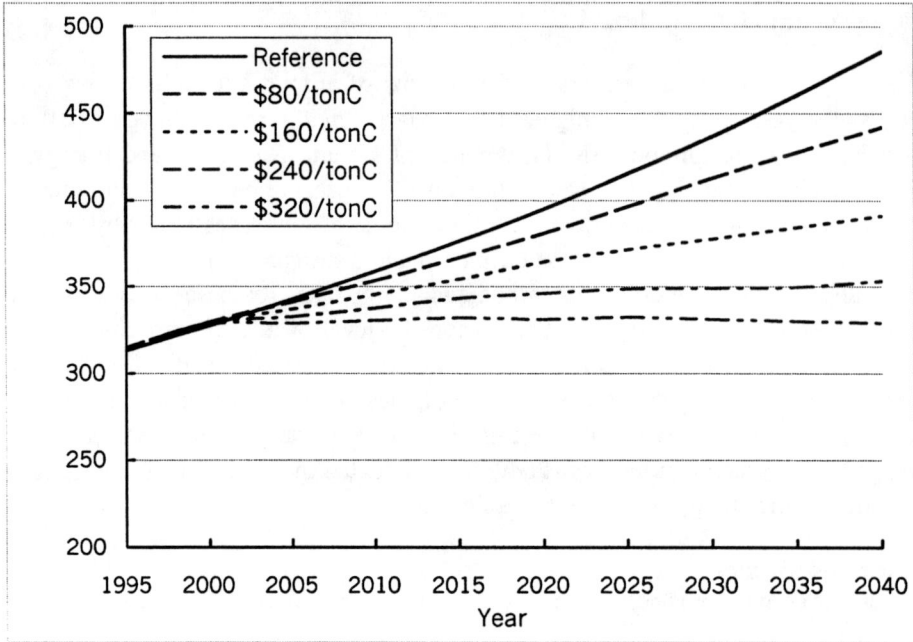

Figure 2: Impact of carbon taxes on CO_2 emissions

Using a similar analysis, we found that an energy tax of $4.5/mmBTU reduced carbon emissions to 400 million tons of carbon in 2040.

Changes in the System Leading to Reduction in Carbon Emissions

The taxes cause a reduction in carbon emissions through adjustments to the system. The costs of these adjustments are important for policy making. However, the *nature* of the structural changes may be equally important for Japan. In this section we discuss the structural changes and the costs resulting from the two taxes.

Figure 3 illustrates the development of the electric power sector to the year 2040 under the reference case. The quantities of coal boiler and gas power show steady increases corresponding to annual demand growth. Clean coal technologies such as Integrated Coal Gasification Combined Cycles (IGCC) are introduced to some extent. The quantities of nuclear power and hydroelectric power are set at a constant level based on the assumptions which we have made for this analysis.

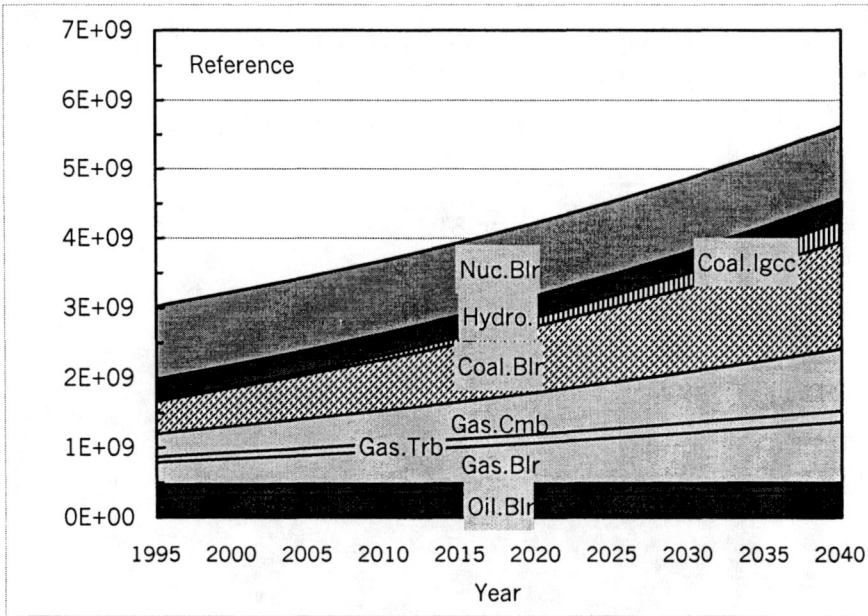

Figure 3: Changes in electric power generation for the reference case

Figure 4 shows the changes in electric power generation under carbon tax of $160/tonC. Under this tax, the coal boiler output decreases by about two-thirds (in 2040) while the output of the gas boiler and gas-combined cycle increases by about a quarter. IGCC does not penetrate the market in this tax case. Renewable energy does penetrate the market after about 2020.

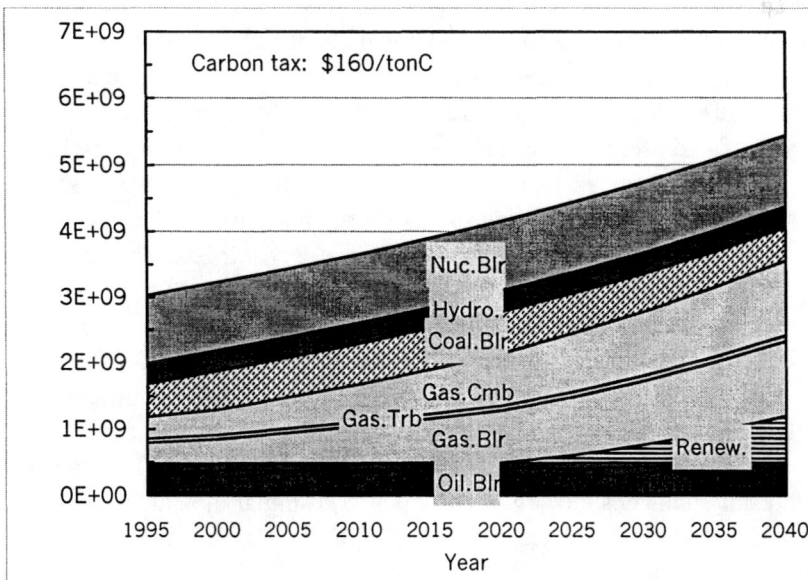

Figure 4: Changes in electric power generation for the carbon tax case

Figure 5 shows the changes in electric power generation under energy tax of $4.5/mmBTU. Under this tax, the coal boiler output as well as the gas boiler and gas-combined cycle decreases by about one-third (in 2040).

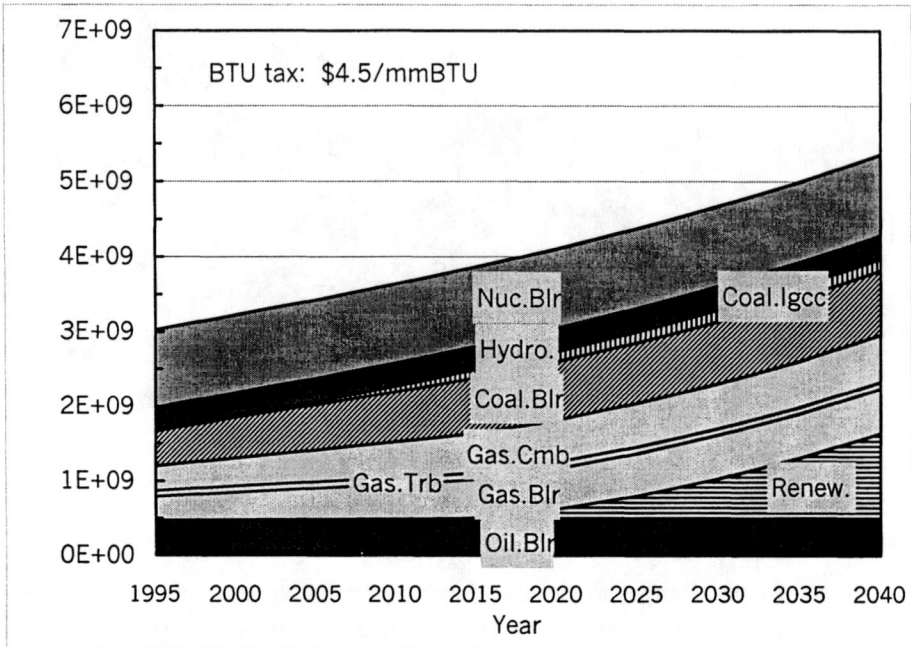

Figure 5: Changes in electric power generation for the energy tax case

Carbon emissions are also reduced through changes in the total energy services required. Figure 6 illustrates the changes in end-use energy under the two tax scenarios compared to the base case scenario. It shows that the industrial heat and residential heat end-use sectors have the largest percentage reductions (6 to 12 percent reduction). Industrial heat is the largest single category of end use, so the change in that sector accounts for a substantial amount of the carbon reduction. Such a reduction in energy use in these sectors could be achieved through improved efficiency, or shifting to less energy intensive products. On the other hand, personal transportation and truck transportation end-use sector have the smallest percentage reductions (1 to 2 percent).

Primary energy consumption for the three scenarios is shown in Figure 7. Under both scenarios coal consumption decreases, and natural gas increases under the carbon tax and decreases under the energy tax. The carbon tax greatly reduces coal consumption — coal is nearly replaced by natural gas under the carbon tax. Thus under the carbon tax, one major energy resource is nearly eliminated from Japan's energy mix. Petroleum decreases somewhat, but still maintains the largest share which is similar in both the tax cases.

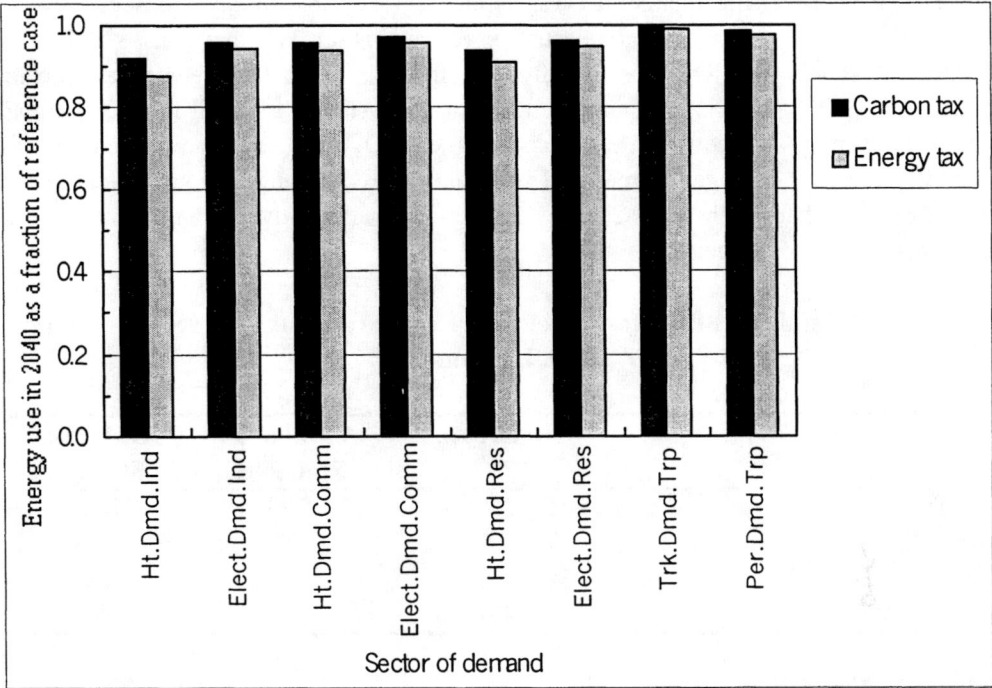

Figure 6: Energy used in each end-use sector under two scenarios in year 2040

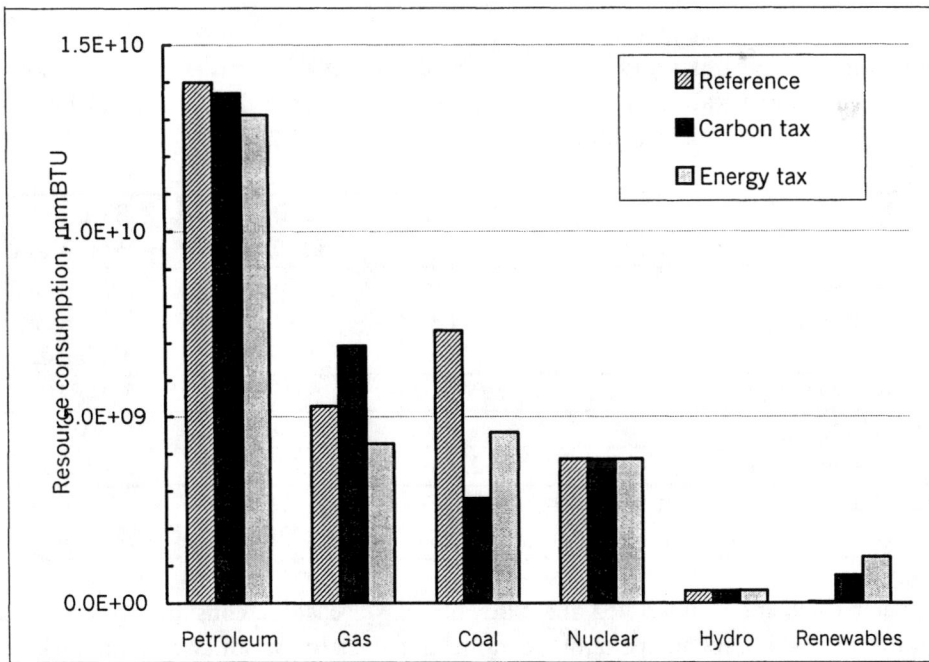

Figure 7: Primary energy used for two the scenarios in year 2040

Under the tax scenarios neither tax was applied to renewable energy. Consequently, both taxes encourage use of renewables in electric power generation.

Table 4 shows the CO_2 emissions from fossil fuels for both reference and taxation scenarios in year 2040. The emission characteristics are similar to fossil fuels consumption shown in Figure 7. As the tax rate becomes higher, CO_2 from coal combustion decreases drastically and CO_2 from gas increases. The amount of CO_2 changes in gas is less than the amount of CO_2 changes in coal. Changes for petroleum is relatively small compared with those of two other fossil fuels.

Table 4: CO_2 emissions from fossil fuels for reference and taxation scenarios in year 2040. Unit: mmTC

	Reference	Carbon tax $160/tonC	BTU tax $4.5/mmBTU
Petroleum	230	223	213
Gas	74	98	61
Coal	187	70	114
Total	491	391	388

Financial Impacts of the Taxes

A summary of the consumer costs and tax revenues is shown in Table 5. Total energy consumption for each case is also shown there. There is a reduction of total energy use in both tax cases. This is caused by the increase in prices due to the taxes, which results in less demand in each end-use sector.

Table 5: Summary of Costs and Tax Revenues for the Five Scenarios. The Costs are the Discounted Present Values of the Total Stream of Costs over the Time Horizon. The Discount Rate was 5%. Unit: US$ Billion

	Reference	Carbon tax $160/tonC	BTU tax $4.5/mmBTU
Capital cost	2.12E+03	2.10E+03	2.14E+03
Operating costs	5.27E+02	5.12E+02	5.14E+02
Fuel costs	3.70E+02	4.31E+02	3.57E+02
Total direct energy costs	3.02E+03	3.04E+03	3.01E+03
Tax revenue	0	6.30E+01	0
Total cost to consumers	3.02E+03	3.11E+03	3.10E+03
Total energy consumption in 2040 (Quads)	30.8	28.4	27.4

The cost calculations in Table 5 show that both taxes cost the consumer about the same amount for the cost of capital, operations, and fuel in the energy sector. We do not include the tax itself as a cost since it would offset other taxes. In these figures the total cost with the energy tax is slightly less than the cost with the carbon tax. This might appear to be anomalous since the carbon tax is assumed to be more efficient. However, under the energy tax, part of the reduction in carbon is achieved through the reduction of energy services, presumably through greater efficiencies in end uses or by foregoing services. The costs of those measures are not accounted for here. In addition, we note that the total tax revenues under the carbon tax are about one third less than under the energy tax scenario. Thus a dollar's worth of carbon tax is far more effective in reducing carbon emissions than a dollar's worth of energy tax.

3. IMPACTS OF HYBRID VEHICLES ON ENERGY SYSTEMS IN JAPAN

3.1 Policy Scenarios Analyzed

In this section we see the transportation sector which still shows demand increases for decades in Japan. In order to understand technology innovation and its impacts on CO_2 emissions, hybrid vehicles are taken into account for our energy-economic model. It is assumed that hybrid vehicles will be available for passenger transportation in 2005 in a particular maximum quantity, which will increase ten percent every year commencing in 2005. Based on the reference (Energy Data and Modeling Center, 1998) the performance factors of both conventional and hybrid vehicles are shown in Table 6.

In this investigation a reference case analysis was first developed to model the expected emissions, resource use, and investments in energy technologies in the absence of policy actions. The next step was to model the effects of imposing a BTU tax with the goal of a reduction of 100 mmTC by the year 2040.

Table 6: Performance of vehicles

Type of passenger vehicles	Hybrid[a]	Conventional[b]	*Hybrid/Conventional*
Specific capital cost $/(mmBTU/Yr)	824	687	*1.2*
Ancillary operating cost $/mmBTU	27.46	34.33	*0.8*
I-O coefficient (mmBTU/K passenger mile)	1.431	3.578	*0.4*

[a]Based on Hybrid Car PRIUS, (1999) TH0015-9903, Toyota Motor Corporation, Nagoya.
[b]Based on Energy Data and Modeling Center. (1998). *EDMC Handbook of Energy & Economic Statistics in Japan*, Tokyo.

In the reference case scenario it is assumed that there is no intervention in the energy system, except that nuclear power is subsidized as needed to maintain a 35 percent share of the electric market (the share in 1995). Under this scenario, CO_2 emissions rise to 491 mmTC by the year 2040.

Next, the impact of hybrid vehicles on the transportation sector is examined. A BTU tax is expected to be one of the most efficient approaches to reduce carbon emissions (Sawa, 1997). This study evaluated several different tax rates to determine the rate that would achieve the target reduction in the year 2040. Both cases – with and without BTU tax – were extrapolated to explore the difference in fuel prices. The cost of each approach and the configuration of energy systems that results from it are evaluated.

In the taxation case, the BTU tax was assumed to be imposed in increments, starting at zero in the first period and then rising by a fixed amount in each subsequent period until reaching the target amount of the tax. This approach avoids the sudden shock to the system and the stranded assets that can result from rapid market changes.

It was found that a tax rate of $4.5/mmBTU produced an emission rate of 388 mmTC in 2040, achieving a reduction of 100 mmTC in the emission rate. The tax was introduced gradually over time, increasing the tax rate in uniform steps in each period until the maximum rate was reached in 2040.

In the scenarios involving hybrid vehicles, both cases – with or without BTU taxes – were again studied. In the reference case without BTU taxes, CO_2 emissions rise to 472 mmTC by the year 2040. With a BTU tax at the rate of $4.5/mmBTU, CO_2 emissions rise to 350 mmTC by the year 2040. Again, the tax rate was gradually increased over time.

3.2 Discussion for the Passenger Transportation Sector

The discussion in this section highlights the changes in the energy system that result from reducing CO_2 emissions through the use of hybrid vehicles and a BTU tax, and the costs of implementing these changes.

First, the changes in the passenger transportation sector from introducing hybrid vehicles in 2005 are illustrated in Figure 8. We can see a way in which the system has adjusted to the introduction of hybrid vehicles in 2005. There is an increase in the use of hybrid vehicles from the year 2005 until 2040. The share of hybrid vehicles eventually reaches 50 percent in 2040.

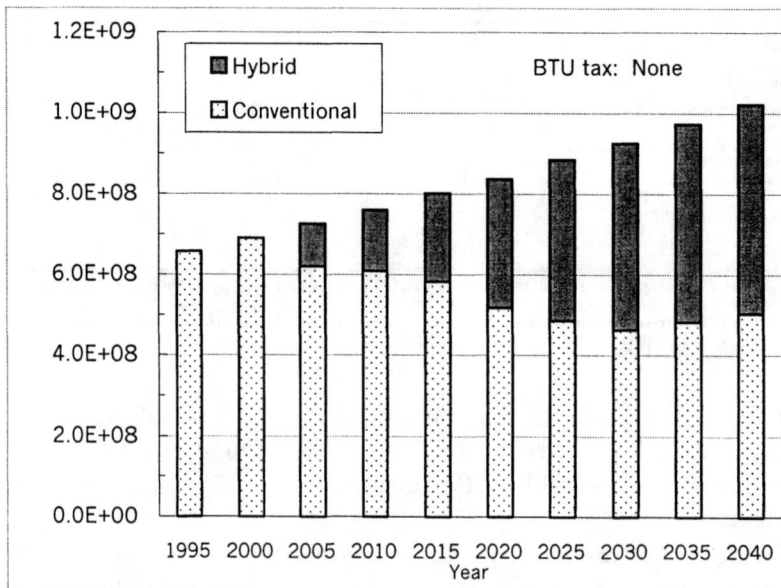

Figure 8: Passenger transportation using hybrid vehicles

Second, the changes in the passenger transportation sector resulting from introducing BTU taxes as well as hybrid vehicles are shown in Figure 9. A BTU tax of $4.5/mmBTU is charged on fossil fuels such as gas, petroleum, and coal. This results in an increase in the share of hybrid vehicles, which reaches 75 percent in 2040.

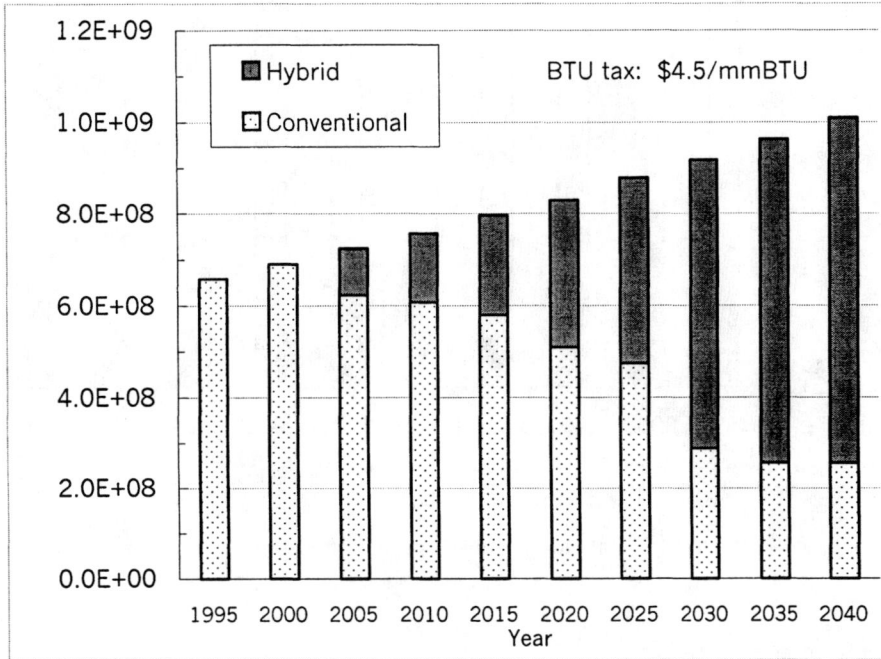

Figure 9: Passenger transportation using hybrid vehicles under the BTU taxes scenario

Third, the changes in energy consumption in the transportation sector under the BTU tax scenario are shown in Figure 10. There are four ways that the system has adjusted to lead to a reduction in carbon emissions:

1. There is a reduction in the use of conventional vehicles.
2. There is an increase in the use of hybrid vehicles. However, the use of these is relatively low because of higher fuel efficiency, which result in a lower I-O coefficient in the study.
3. There is an increase in the use of trucks.
4. There is a reduction of total energy use for transportation. This is mainly caused by the increase of hybrid vehicles.

Total energy use in each resource sector in 2040 under the four scenarios is illustrated in Figure 11. We can see that the BTU tax reduces coal use the most. Under BTU taxation the cost of fossil fuels becomes higher, which orients the energy user toward more energy efficient choices. The BTU tax encourages the use of renewables, which enter the electricity market at competitive prices.

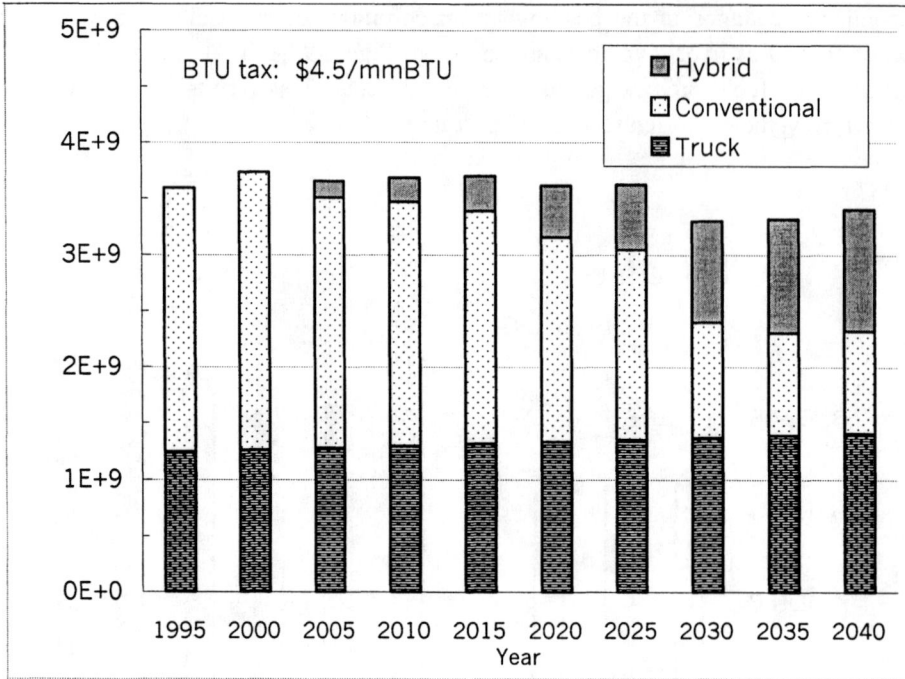

Figure 10: Total energy consumption in transportation sector

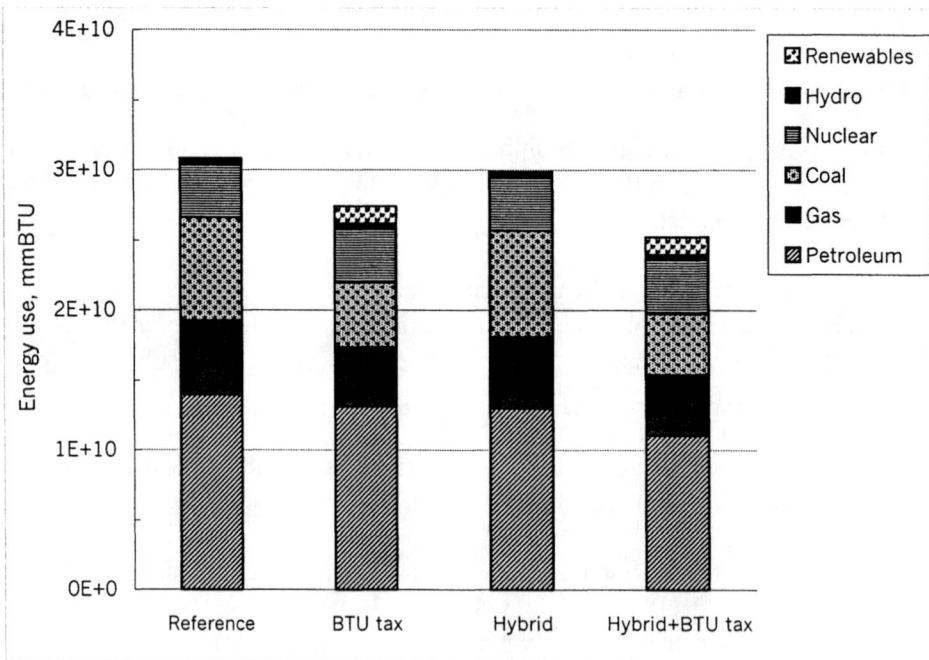

Figure 11: Total energy use in resource under the four scenarios in 2040

A summary of CO_2 emissions for the four scenarios is shown in Table 7. We can observe the following impacts of hybrid vehicles:

- Hybrid vehicles are effective to reduce carbon emissions from petroleum consumption for transportation use.
- With hybrid vehicles, CO_2 emissions rise to 350 mmTC by the year 2040 under the BTU tax scenario, producing a 122 mmTC reduction compared with the tax-free case.
- A BTU tax is effective to decrease carbon emissions from petroleum consumption for non-transportation use. In other words, carbon emissions from petroleum consumption for transportation use cannot be reduced even when BTU taxes are imposed.

Table 7: Summary of CO_2 emissions for the four scenarios in 2040

	Without hybrid vehicles		With hybrid vehicles	
	Reference	BTU tax $4.5/mmBTU	Reference	BTU tax $4.5/mmBTU
Petroleum	230	213	211	180
(Transportation)	(97)	(95)	(76)	(65)
(Non-transportation)	(133)	(118)	(135)	(115)
Gas	74	61	73	62
Coal	187	114	188	108
Total	491	388	472	350

Changes in the costs to consumers are seen in Table 8, which shows a summary of the costs and tax revenues for the four scenarios. The costs are the discounted present values of the total stream costs over the time horizon. In the hybrid vehicle cases, the capital costs are relatively higher than in the conventional vehicle cases because of the high capital costs of producing hybrid vehicles. In terms of fuel costs, we can see slightly less expensive costs using hybrid vehicles. Considering the total direct energy costs and the BTU tax revenue, the total cost to consumers is increased under the hybrid vehicles with BTU tax scenario. However, these differences in the cost to consumers are small, remaining within a ten-percent difference.

Another consideration is the differences in total energy consumption for the four scenarios. The case involving hybrid vehicles and BTU taxes results in less energy consumption. In this case, 25.2 Quads represents an 18 percent saving in energy consumption compared with the reference case scenario.

Table 8: Summary of Costs and Tax Revenues for the Four Scenarios. The Costs are the Discounted Present Values of the Total Stream of Costs over the Time Horizon. The Discount Rate was 5%. Unit: US$ Billion.

	Without hybrid vehicles		With hybrid vehicles	
	Reference	BTU tax $4.5/mmBTU	Reference	BTU tax $4.5/mmBTU
Capital costs	2.12E+12	2.14E+12	2.31E+12	2.42E+12
Operating costs	5.27E+11	5.14E+11	5.18E+11	5.24E+11
Fuel costs	3.70E+11	3.57E+11	3.63E+11	3.42E+11
Total direct energy costs	3.02E+12	3.01E+12	3.19E+12	3.29E+12
BTU tax revenue	0	9.06E+10	0	8.47E+10
Total cost to consumers	3.02E+12	3.10E+12	3.19E+12	3.37E+12
Total energy consumption in 2040 (Quads)	30.8	27.4	29.9	25.2

4. IMPACTS OF NUCLEAR PHASE-OUT ON ENERGY SYSTEMS IN JAPAN

4.1 Policy Scenarios Analyzed

Phasing-out of nuclear power is hypothesized to understand the role of nuclear energy for both strengthening energy security and reducing CO_2 emissions in Japan. In this investigation, a reference case analysis was first developed to model the expected emissions, resource use, and investments in energy technologies in the absence of policy actions. The reference case scenario means a business as usual condition. Under this scenario, it is assumed that there is no intervention in the energy system. In other words, reference case scenario is a base condition which result is already analyzed, evaluated and confirmed. The next was to model the effect of nuclear power phase-out and a carbon tax with a goal of a reduction of CO_2 by the year around 2040. A variety of approaches to reduce energy-related emissions of CO_2 and other greenhouse gases are possible. Under the term of The Kyoto Protocol, Japan would agree to reduce their carbon emissions by 6 % below 1990 levels, corresponding to a 22 - 25 % reduction from projections for 2010 (Environment Agency of Japan, 1998). This study focuses on a target rate of reductions of around 20 % of CO_2 by the year around 2040 since reaching the target in 2010 appears to be difficult and might not be realistic for Japan. We then determined the level of tax needed to reach the required level of CO_2 by the year around 2040. We evaluated the cost of that approach and the configuration of energy systems that results from it.

In the taxation case, the carbon tax was assumed to be imposed in increments, starting at zero in the first period and then rising by a fixed amount in each subsequent period until reaching the target amount of the tax. This approach avoids the sudden shock to the system and the stranded assets that can result from rapid market changes.

Reference Case Scenario

Nuclear boiler is assumed to be having constant generation quantity as it has in 1995 until 2040 considering government concern. Under this scenario, it is assumed that there is no intervention in the energy system, except that nuclear is subsidized as needed to maintain a 35% share of the electric market, the share in 1995. The trend of electric power generation under the reference case scenario is shown in Figure 3. Under this scenario, CO_2 emissions rise to 490 mmTC by the year 2040. The nuclear subsidy is our original term to remain the share of nuclear power boilers in the electricity sector at current output level. Without this subsidy, the price of nuclear power rises, resulting in nuclear's dying out in the electric market. The value of the subsidy is set at \$9/mmBTU at most.

Nuclear Phase-Out Scenarios

In this case, we assume that the level of nuclear capacity will begin to phase-out in 2015 and will be reached at zero in 2035. Under this scenario, it is assumed that there is no intervention in the energy system. The CO_2 emissions rise to 530 mmTC by the year 2040.

Carbon Tax Scenarios

A carbon tax is expected to be the most efficient approach to reduce CO_2 emissions. It has been already implemented in Sweden, Finland, Norway, Denmark and Holland in range of \$200/tonC (Sawa, 1997). This study evaluated several different tax rates to determine the rate that would achieve the target reduction by the year 2040. Both cases –with and without a carbon tax- were extrapolated to explore the difference in fuel prices. We found that a tax rate of \$160/tonC produced an emission rate of 390 mmTC by the year 2040, achieving a reduction of 20 % in the emission rate.

Nuclear Phase-Out with Carbon Tax Scenarios

In the case of nuclear phase-out, at \$205/tonC of carbon tax, CO_2 emissions rise to 390 mmTC by the year 2040. Again, the tax rate was gradually increased over time.

4.2 Discussion for Nuclear Energy

The discussion in this section highlights the changes in the energy system that result from reducing CO_2 emissions through carbon taxes, and the costs of implementing these changes.

Changes in the electricity sector in nuclear phase-out

Figure 12 illustrates the changes in the electric power generation under the nuclear phase-out case. The total energy consumption and the CO_2 emissions for four scenarios in the year 2040 are shown in Table 9. We can see three ways in which the system has adjusted to make up the nuclear boiler after its phasing out:

- The use of coal boiler and coal IGCC rise, and the total coal consumption rises by four times.
- The use of gas combined-cycles and gas boiler rise gradually, and the total gas consumption grows by three times.
- The renewables is not seen in the electricity market.

- There is a reduction of total energy use. This is mainly caused by the increase in efficiency in power generation shifting from nuclear boiler to gas boiler and gas combined-cycle.

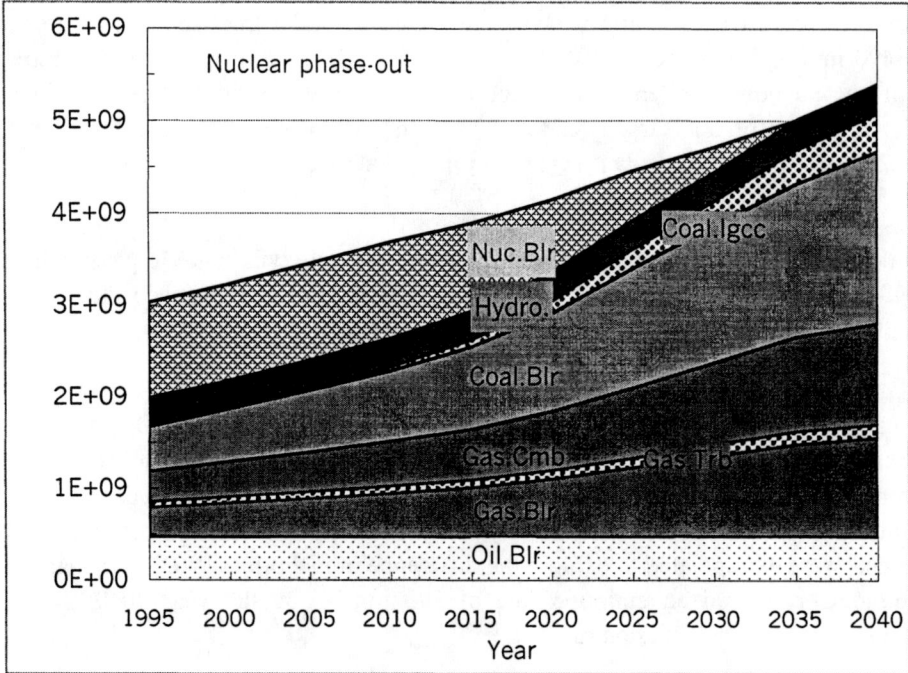

Figure 12: Electric power generation under the nuclear phase-out

Table 9: Summary of Costs and Tax Revenues for the Four Scenarios. The Costs are the Discounted Present Values of the Total Stream of Costs over The Time Horizon. The Discount Rate was 5%. Unit: US$ Billion.

	Reference	Nuclear phase-out	Carbon tax	Nuclear phase-out & carbon tax
			$160/tonC	$205/tonC
Capital costs	2.12E+12	2.10E+12	2.10E+12	2.09E+12
Operating costs	5.27E+11	5.15E+11	5.12E+11	5.03E+11
Fuel costs	3.70E+11	3.73E+11	4.31E+11	4.44E+11
Total direct energy costs	3.02E+12	2.99E+12	3.04E+12	3.04E+12
Carbon tax revenue	0	0	6.30E+10	7.97E+10
Total cost to consumers	3.02E+12	2.99E+12	3.11E+12	3.12E+12
CO_2 emission in 2040 (mmTC)	490	530	390	390
Total energy consumption in 2040 (Quads)	30.8	29.0	28.4	25.2

Figure 13 shows the changes in the electric power sector under nuclear phase-out with the carbon tax condition. The carbon tax is set at \$205/tonC to reach the emission rate of 390 mmTC by the year 2040. We can see three ways in which the system has adjusted to lead the reduction of CO_2 emissions:

- The use of coal boiler falls, and IGCC's dying out in the electricity market.
- The use of gas combined-cycles and gas boiler rise, and the total gas consumption grows by four times.
- The use of renewables grows commencing the year 2015.
- There is a reduction of total energy use. This is mainly caused by the increase in price due to the taxes.

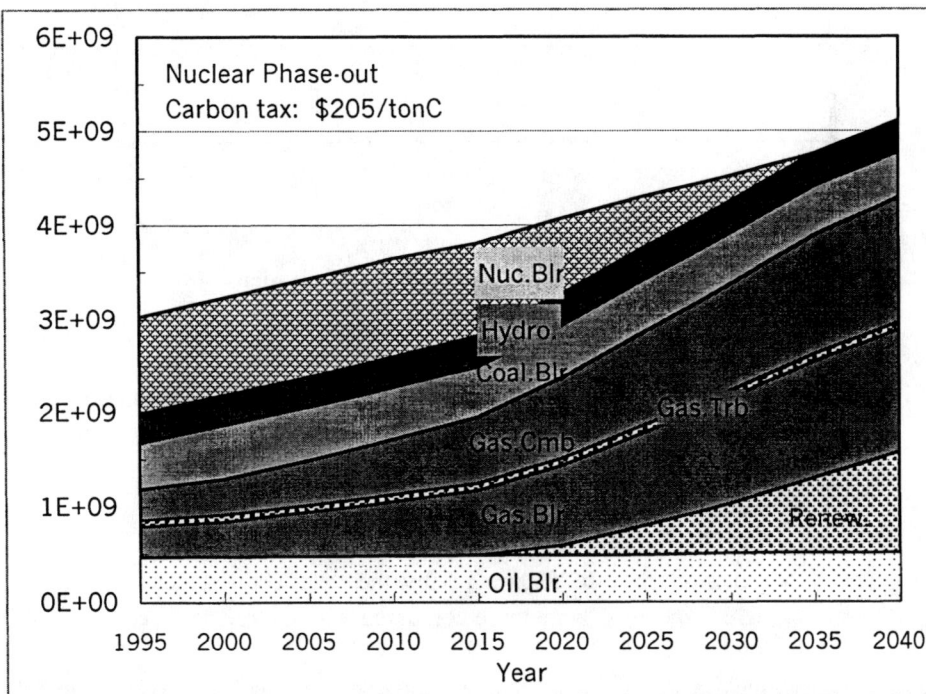

Figure 13: Electric power generation under the nuclear phase-out with carbon tax

By comparing Figure 3, Figure 12 and Figure 13, we can get a sense of the difference in electricity supply. Nuclear power will be replaced by fossil fuels combustion such as coal boiler, gas boiler and gas combined-cycle. Because the price of electricity produced by coal is still cheaper than the price of gas fueled electricity, coal shows priority over gas fuel in case carbon tax is not charged. On the contrast, the price of coal rises more than the price of gas under the taxation case, resulting in the growth of gas power in the electricity supply (see Figure 14). The renewables are allowed to come into the market, when the price of renewable power becomes somewhat competitive under carbon taxes.

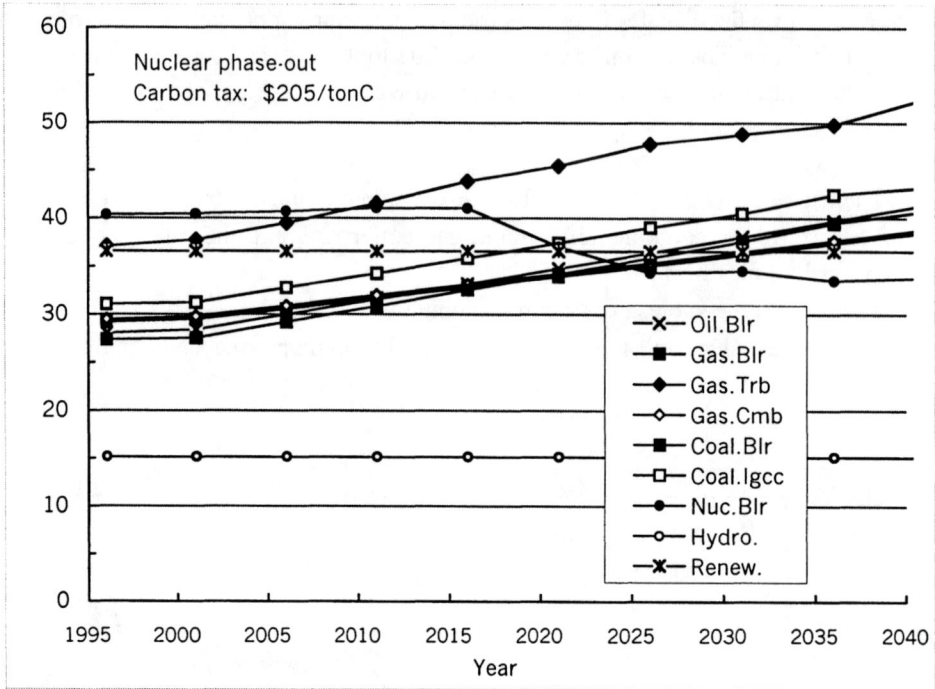

Figure 14: Changes in the price of electricity

Impacts of the Taxes with or without Nuclear Phase-Out

Figure 15 shows energy use in each resource sector under the four scenarios in the year 2040. We can observe the following impacts of a carbon tax:

- The carbon tax reduces the coal use the most.
- The carbon tax encourages the use of renewables.
- The CO_2 emissions rise to 530mmTC by the year 2040 under nuclear phase-out condition, which means 8 % increase compared with the reference case (see Table 9).

From the changes in the share of each resource, we can see the alternative scenarios without nuclear power. It looks possible to replace nuclear by fossil fuels as shown in Figure 6, however, the problem of local emissions and the fuel depletion are not considered adequately. Moreover, except for the slight reduction under the taxation case, the petroleum consumption remains stably at a constant level. Unlike the electricity sector, the transportation sector and some parts of the industrial sector have no alternatives to switch petroleum fuel easily. Renewables are another alternative which we can expect to produce electricity without emitting any environmental pollution. Besides its low intensity in energy conversion, renewable power requires optimum range of climate conditions to operate it. In the management of transmission grid, renewables cannot secure stable distribution to end-use customers.

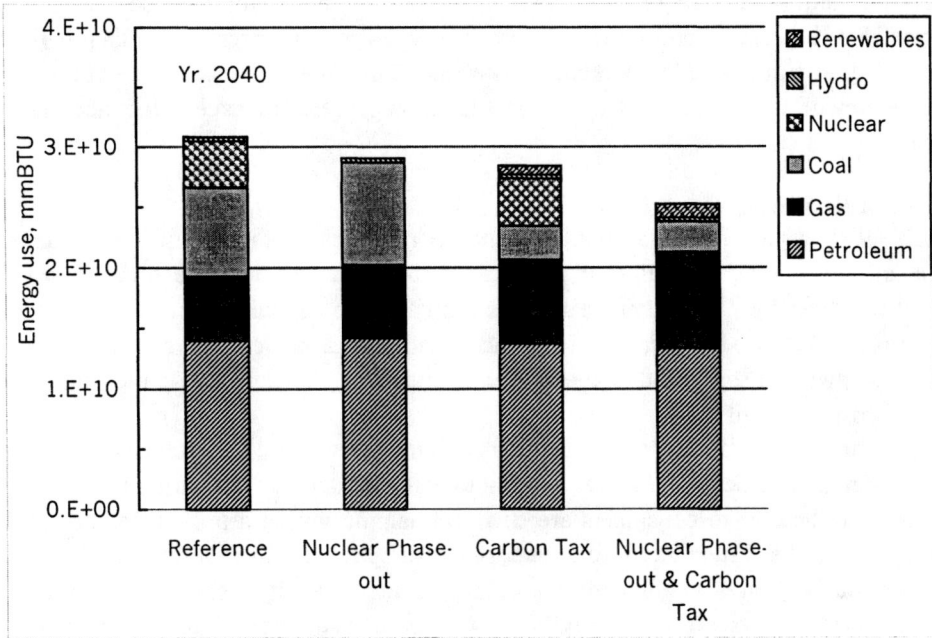

Figure 15: Total energy use in resource under the four scenarios in 2040

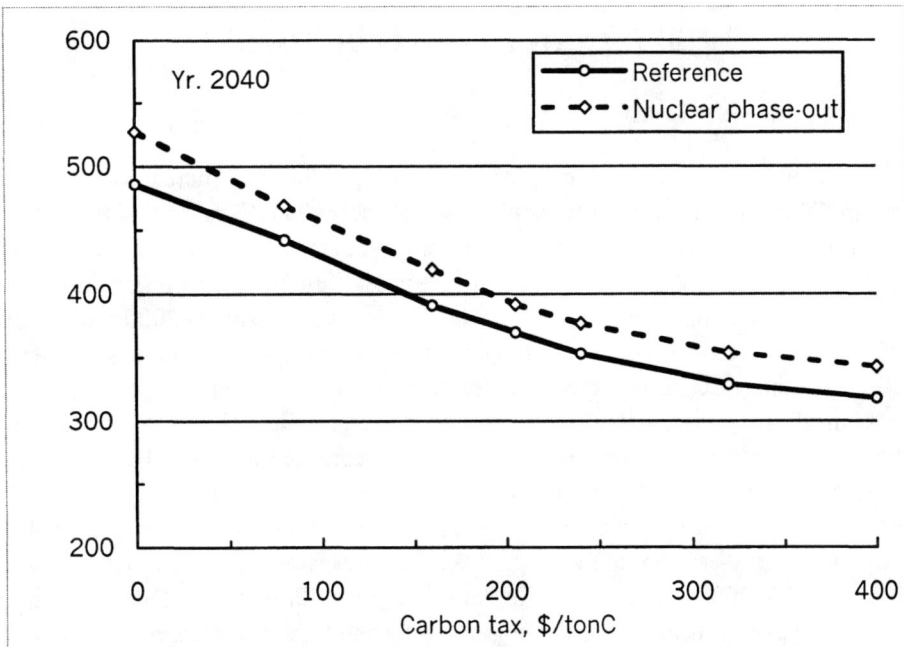

Figure 16: Impact of carbon taxes on CO_2 emissions

Figure 16 shows the impacts of carbon taxes on CO_2 emissions. It is reasonable to suppose that a higher rate of carbon tax will be necessary when in nuclear phase-out to reach the same emission levels by the year 2040. This characteristic is mainly affected by the demand elasticities in each sector shown in Table 3. We carefully chose this value and confirmed its reliance in our previous study many times. However, there should be some changes in elasticities when carbon tax takes effect in the future. We believe that the trend in the reduction of CO_2 emissions by carbon taxation is reliable except the uncertainty of demand changes.

Changes in the Cost to Consumers
Table 9 shows a summary of the costs and tax revenues for the four scenarios. The costs are the discounted present value of the total stream of costs over the time horizon. The discount rate was 5 %. In the nuclear phase-out case, the capital costs are relatively lower than the reference case because of the absence of additional nuclear power stations. In terms of fuel costs, we can see slightly expensive cost under the nuclear phase-out case because of increased costs of fossil fuels.

Considering the total direct costs and the carbon tax revenues, the total cost to consumers will be increased under the nuclear phase-out with carbon tax scenario. However, these differences in the cost to consumers are small, remaining within a 5 % difference. Another consideration is the difference in total energy consumption for the four scenarios. The case involving nuclear phase-out and carbon taxes results in less energy consumption. In this case, 25.2 Quads represents an 18 % saving in energy consumption with the reference case scenario. The discussion of GDP, which could be analyzed by using macro economy model, is not included in this study.

5. ENERGY SYSTEMS IN KOREA

5.1 Policy Scenarios Analyzed

In the Republic of Korea, as the gross domestic product has increased rapidly, energy consumption also has increased at an annual rate of more than 10 percent since 1985 till the IMF crisis in 1997 (Table 10). Among the energy sources while the shares of coal and hydropower have decreased, the share of petroleum and liquefied natural gas have increased (Asia Development Bank, 1998, Korea Energy Economics Institute, 2000). Most of fossil energy is imported from abroad except small amount of domestic coal sources. The emissions of GHGs including CO_2 have increased in proportion to the energy consumption. The consumption of energy is closely related to economic growth and environmental problems. Therefore it is necessary to establish and implement energy policies for the balanced pursuit of economic development and environmental conservation.

Both two cases, carbon taxation case and the BTU taxation case, are analyzed by designing an energy-economic model for Korea. Necessary data are given by current references (OECD, 2000) and by some Korean colleagues (Shin, 2001). The results are shown in Figure 17 for carbon taxation, and in Figure 18 for the BTU taxation, respectively. We can expect reductions of CO_2 emissions in the future by introducing carbon or BTU taxation into Korean economy. The carbon tax tends to suppress the consumption of carbon-heavy fuels such as coal, whereas the BTU tax appears to reduce the overall fossil fuels. In this sense, the BTU tax would be favorable for Korean energy security to reduce CO_2 emissions we well as keeping stable shares among energy sources.

Table 10: Energy Statistics for Two Countries

Yr.	Country	GDP, billion US$	Population, million	Primary energy consumption, Mtoe	CO_2, mmTC
1973	Japan	2,561	108	324	245
1973	Korea	89	34	21	18
1998	Japan	5,319	126	510	312
1998	Korea	516	46	163	100

Sources:
- OECD, International Energy Agency. (2000). *Energy prices and taxes*. Paris.
- OECD, International Energy Agency. (2000). *Energy balances of OECD* countries. Paris.
- OECD, International Energy Agency. (2000). *Energy statistics of OECD* countries. Paris.

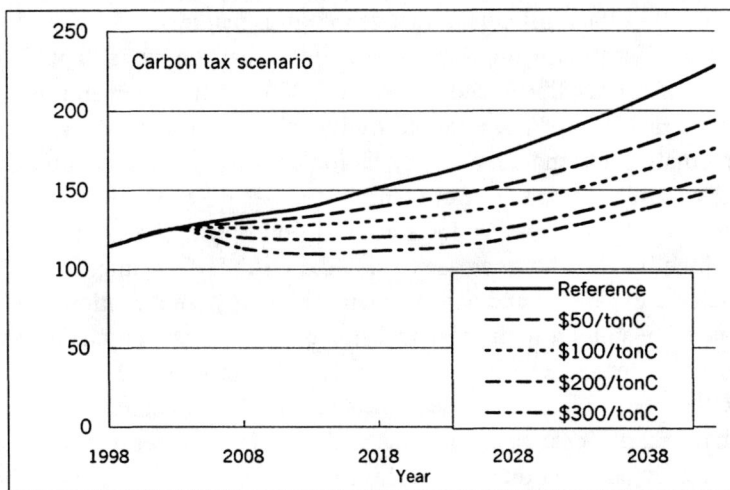

Figure 17: Carbon tax scenarios in Korea

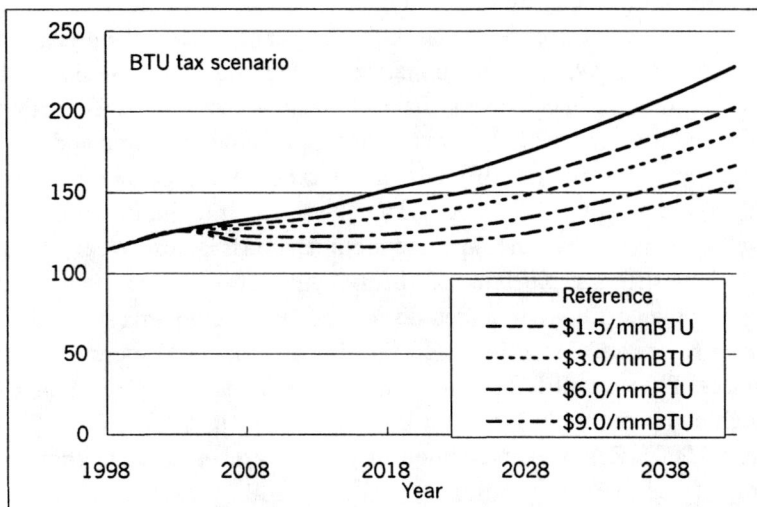

Figure 18: Btu tax scenarios in Korea

5.2 Discussion for Energy Cooperation between Japan and Korea

There are some differences between Japan and Korea for current energy industries.

In order for competition to develop in electricity markets, monopolistic activities such as the operation of the transmission network need to be effectively separated from the potentially competitive activities such as power generation (OECD, International Energy Agency, 2001). The main objective of unbundling is to avoid discrimination in the competitive segments of the ESI (Electricity Supply Industry). On April 2, 2001, the Government of Korea unbundled former utility KEPCO (Korean Electric Power Cooperation) into new six power generation subsidiaries, and a power exchange. As the Korean electric power monopoly is ending, competition is being introduced in the process of restructuring. Customers will create a new order in the competitive electric power marketplace. Most of the functions and roles of the government will be replaced by market forces and behavior of customers which will be the most crucial factors in power markets.

On the contrast, Japan still looks to be studying what measures should be taken. The retail electrical market was liberalized in March 2000 for high-demand customers, which represented approximately 30 % of total electricity sales. This was the first attempt to catch up with the international standard of deregulation in fifty years' monopolistic history of Japanese ESI. As a result, companies from other industries have entered the power generation business and the practice of bidding for electrical power has expanded. Growth in power consumption, which has steadily increased since the utility's founding, is distinctly slowing amid weak economic expansion and advancements in energy conservation. However, the rest of 70 % customers are still put in the classical situation where neither choice nor competition is allowed for both customers and utilities. The price of electricity per kWh for residential use is 28 JPY (23 US cents), which shows the highest fare in OECD countries.

Along with the market changes toward deregulation and competition, we can see possible approaches for energy cooperation between Japan and Korea. First, there can be competitive pools or power exchanges such as NordPool between two countries. NordPool is a voluntary electricity exchange open to traders from Norway, Sweden, Finland and parts of Denmark. As of 1997, over 40 % of electricity trade in that area was handled by the pool. The geographical location between Japan and Korea is similar to that of Scandinavian countries, and the electric utilities of both countries have point of similarity in generation, transmission and distribution systems. The new pool market can give a chance to operate the ESI in efficient way as well as empowering the end user, and meeting security of supply, environmental and social goals.

Second, Japanese government officials and Exxon Mobil Corporation executives are talking up a 2,100 km pipeline that would carry natural gas from the Russian far East to either Tokyo or Niigata, halfway down the Japanese archipelago (Business Week, 2001). In Korean peninsula, the domestic gas pipeline has been built between Seoul and Pusan, and its extension from China to Seoul is under discussion by foreign investors. Provided that a pipeline between Korea and Japan is designed, this network could secure natural gas supply for both countries. The current LNG price for industry in Japan is $96.45 in 2000 which is unnaturally high compared with $41.95 in UK and $26.50 in the US (OECD, International Energy Agency, 2000). Regional integration of gas market and the electricity network will make an important role for two countries.

CONCLUSIONS

Both the carbon tax and the energy tax can be effective in reducing nation's carbon emissions. The total cost to the consumer will be approximately the same under either scenario — although the energy tax will result in larger tax revenues. However the carbon tax tends to eliminate coal as an energy resource for Japan. Since Japan must import nearly all of it fossil fuels, narrowing its mix would leave Japan more vulnerable to price variations in the international petroleum and natural gas markets and would reduce their bargaining power in negotiations. Thus, the energy tax would be a more stable approach for Japan.

The transportation sector uses one-fourth of total primary energy. Because there are no alternative fuels for transportation except petroleum, the effects of carbon or energy taxes are relatively small. Hybrid vehicles, which have excellent fuel efficiency, could be one of the breakthrough technologies to meet the environmental constraints. Either carbon or energy taxes would encourage the penetration of hybrids.

In the long run, renewable resources may contribute more to carbon reductions than envisioned here. In our study renewables are only included in the electric sector, as renewable technologies in other sectors are not widely available. If renewable technologies could be used in the transportation sector (e.g. through electric or hydrogen vehicles fueled by renewable generation), petroleum consumption and CO$_2$ emissions would be drastically reduced.

Moreover, there are uncertainties about the future capacity of nuclear power. MITI recently announced that nuclear power stations could be technically operable for sixty years under strict maintenance conditions. This suggests that the Government may change its nuclear policy from building new stations to extending the life of existing stations. Over the long term this could result in a decrease in the share of nuclear capacity. Since our study is based on the assumptions that nuclear will supply 35 percent of electricity to the year 2040, a decrease in nuclear power will affect the capacities in electric power generation. Nuclear's role in abating carbon emission should be re-evaluated as the government's policy becomes clearer.

Based on these analyses, we can draw the following conclusions:

- Achieving carbon reductions *with the set of technologies considered here* will mean reduction in energy use as well as shifts to lower carbon fuels. Introducing other technologies, such as a greater reliance on renewables or hybrid vehicles, might ameliorate the projected reduction in energy use.
- The total cost in terms of supplying energy will be similar for all three cases. However, the carbon reduction cases imply reduction in energy use. This will probably be achieved through more efficient end use process or other shifts which may require additional capital investment (though it is not clear that higher capital investment is inevitable)
- The carbon taxes have their advantages and disadvantages. The carbon tax is efficient in that smaller tax revenues are raised and the energy use reduction is smaller. However, the energy tax maintains a diversity of energy resources which is an important consideration for Japan's energy security.

Second, the main impact of hybrid vehicles is a decrease in petroleum consumption in the transportation sector (Nakata, 2000). As hybrid vehicles are introduced into the passenger transportation market, the share of conventional vehicles decreases proportionally, leading to a decrease in CO_2 emissions.

BTU taxation has a positive impact on reducing the consumption of fossil fuels such as coal, gas and petroleum for non-transportation purposes. As there are no alternative choices in the transportation sector, BTU taxation has no effect on petroleum consumption for transportation. However, when hybrid vehicles become available, higher fuel prices promote a shift by consumers from conventional vehicles to hybrid vehicles, which results in reducing carbon emissions drastically.

From the viewpoint of financial parameters, higher dependence on hybrid vehicles involves relatively high capital costs. The total cost in terms of supplying energy will be similar for all four cases. However, the carbon reduction cases imply a reduction in energy use. This would probably be achieved through more efficient end-use processes or other shifts which would likely require additional capital investment.

Third, the main impact of nuclear phase-out is an increase in fossil fuels consumption in the electricity sector (Nakata, 2002). As nuclear power begins phasing out, the output of coal and gas fired power generation grows proportionally, leading to an increase in CO_2 emissions.

A carbon tax has a positive impact on reducing the consumption of fossil fuels such as coal and gas. The carbon tax will raise the price of high-carbon fuels, such as coal, and lead to greater reliance on low-carbon fuels. Even for clean coal technologies such as coal IGCC does not penetrate the electricity market. The carbon tax tends to eliminate coal as an energy source for Japan.

From the viewpoint of financial parameters, higher carbon tax will be necessary under nuclear phase-out scenario to achieve the same target of CO_2 emissions. However, carbon tax scenario tends to be relying on gas resource increasingly. Taking into consideration of energy security issues, BTU tax scenario (Nakata, 2001) would be more stable solution for Japan where all the fossil resources are imported.

Another consideration is the use of renewable resources and the technologies for their conversion into energy. In our study, renewables are only seen in the electricity sector, as renewable technology in other sectors is not yet on the horizon. If future technology were to enable the use of renewable resources in the transportation sector, decreased petroleum consumption could contribute lead to drastic reductions in CO_2 emissions.

Based on these analyses, we can draw the following conclusions:

- Nuclear power phase-out will mean shifts from nuclear to fossil fuels such as coal and gas, resulting in increase in CO_2 emissions in the electricity sector.
- There is a dramatic difference in the carbon tax between reference case and nuclear phase-out case. To achieve the same level of CO_2 emissions without nuclear power in the future, it will be necessary to charge a 30 % higher carbon tax than in a similar scenario with nuclear power. However, the presented results are derived from a fixed set of initial condition such as price elasticity in energy demand. It is therefore necessary to note some changes in real energy supply in the future caused by unexpected matters.

Finally, the regional pool market of electricity in Japan and Korea are discussed. The extension of gas pipelines is also suggested to secure energy supply and to meet environmental and social goals in efficient way. The concept of energy grid between two countries will make an important role both in strengthening energy security with economical way and in building a more market-oriented economy, resulting in stabilized political situation in East Asia.

REFERENCE

Asia Development Bank, 1998. *Asia least-cost Greenhouse gas abatement strategy, Republic of Korea.* Manila, Philippines.

Allenby, BR., 2000. Environmental security: Concept and implementation. *International Political Science Review*, **21**(1), 5-21.

Andersson, B. and Haden, E., 1997. Power production and the price of electricity: An analysis of a phase-out of Swedish nuclear power. *Energy Policy*, **25**(13), 1051-1064.

Banks, F., 2000. Oil, electricity deregulation, and nuclear energy. *Petromin*, March 24-27.

Bodde, D., 1998. Strategic thinking about nuclear energy: Implications of the emerging market structure in electric generation. *Energy Policy* **26**(12), 957-962.

Does Japan really need a $16 billion gas pipeline? 2001. *Business Week*, October 22, 37.

Campbell, C. and Laherrere, J., 1998. The end of cheap oil. *Scientific American*, March 78-83.

Chung, W., Wu Y. J. and Fuller, J. D., 1997. Dynamic energy and environmental equilibrium model for the assessment of CO_2 emission control in Canada and the USA, *Energy Economics* **19**, 123-124.

Doucet, G., 1999. The inevitability of nuclear power generation. *Proceedings of the Uranium Institute 24th Annual Symposium*, 1-6.

Edmonds, J.A., Pitcher, H.M., Barns, D., Baron, R. and Wise, M.A, 1995. *Modeling future greenhouse gas emissions: The second generation model description. In modeling global change*, ed. Klein L. R. and Lo, F., pp. 295-362. United Nations University Press Tokyo.

The Energy Data and Modeling Center, 1998. *EDMC Handbook of Energy & Economic Statistics in Japan*, Tokyo.

Environment Agency of Japan, 1998. *White Paper on Environment*, Tokyo.

The Federation of Electric Power Companies, 1998. *Handbook of Electric Power Industry*, Tokyo.

Gan L., 1998. Energy development and environmental constraints in China. *Energy Policy* **26**(2) 119-128.

Goto, N., 1995. Macroeconomic and sectoral impacts of carbon taxation. *Energy Economics* **17**(4), 277-292.

Goto, N. and Sawa, T., 1993. An analysis of the macroeconomics costs of various CO_2 emission control policies in Japan. *The Energy Journal* **14**(1), 83-110.

Haas, R. and Auer, H., 2001. How to ensure effective competition in western European electricity markets. *International Association for Energy Economics Newsletter*, Third quarter, 16-20.

Hoster, F., 1998. Impact of a nuclear phase-out in Germany: Results from a simulation model of the European Power Systems. *Energy Policy*, **26**(6), 507-518.

MITI's new ten-year plan calls for development of 11.3million kW nuclear power to raise its generating capacity to 56.1 million kW by end of FY 2007, 1998. *JPET*, May; 2-9.

Kagramanian, V., Kononov, S. and Rogner, H., 2000. Climate change driving forces, Nuclear energy & the latest IPCC emission scenarios. *IAEA Bulletin*, 42(2), 31-35.

Kaya, Y., 1997. Japanese strategy for mitigating global warming. *Energy Conversion and Management*, 38, 19-23.

Kibune, H. and Kudo, H., 1996. Structural changes in Japan's economy and society and outlook for long-term energy supply and demand. *Energy Policy* 24 (12), 1119-1125.

Kiso, A., 1998. Trends of nuclear power development in Asia. *Energy Policy* 26(7), 577-582.

Korea Energy Economics Institute, 2000. *Yearbook of energy statistics*, Seoul.

Lamont, A., 1994. *User's Guide to the META•Net Economic Modeling System Version 1.2.* UCRL-ID-122511, Lawrence Livermore National Laboratory, Livermore, California.

Lazarus, M., Heaps, C. and Raskin, P., 1997. *LEAP Long-range energy alternatives planning system*. Stockholm Environmental Institute, Boston, Massachusetts.

Lee, H., Oliveira-Martins, J. and Mensbrugghe, D., 1994. The OECD green model: An updated overviews. *Technical paper No. 97*, OECD, Paris.

Lydick, J., Morris, S.C., Lee, J. and Goldstein, G., 1990. *Demo MARKAL abbreviated version of the US MARKAL energy systems model, created for demonstration: abilities, limitations, and demonstration*, BNL-47782. Brookhaven National Laboratory, Upton, New York.

Matthews, J., 1998. Challenges for nuclear power in Japan, Korea and Greater China at the turn of the century. *Nuclear Energy* 37 (4), 233-239.

MITI, Agency of Natural Resources and Energy, 1998. *Interim Report on General Energy Supply and Demand*, Tokyo.

Nagata Y. *Personal communication*. June 21, 2000.

Nakata, T., 2000. Analysis of the impact of hybrid vehicles on energy systems in Japan. *Transportation Research*, Part D 5, 373-383.

Nakata, T. and Lamont, A., 2001. Analysis of the impacts of carbon taxes on energy systems in Japan. *Energy Policy*, 29(2), 159-166.

Nakata, T., 2002. Analysis of the impacts of nuclear phase-out on energy systems in Japan. *Energy*, printing.

Nordhaus, W., 1997. *The Swedish nuclear dilemma: Energy and the environment. Resources for the Future*, Washington, D.C.

OECD, 2000. *OECD economic surveys, Korea*. Paris.

OECD, International Energy Agency, 2000. *Energy prices and taxes*. Paris.

OECD, International Energy Agency, 2000. *Energy balances of OECD* countries. Paris.

OECD, International Energy Agency, 2000. *Energy statistics of OECD* countries. Paris.

OECD, International Energy Agency, 2001. *Competition in electricity markets*. Paris.

Richels, R. and Sturm, P., 1996. The costs of CO_2 emission reductions. *Energy Policy* 24 (10/11), 875-887.

Romerio, F., 1998. The risks of the nuclear policies. *Energy Policy* 26(3), 239-246.

Sato, O, Tatematsu, K. and Hasegawa, T., 1998. Reducing future CO_2 emissions – The role of nuclear energy. *Progress in Nuclear Energy* 32(3/4), 323-330.

Sawa, T., 1997. *Chikyuu Ondanka Wo Fusegu*. Iwanami Shoten Publishers, Tokyo.

Shin, E., 2001. Personal communication. August 21, 2001.

Schultz, P. A. and Kasting, J. F., 1997. Optimal reductions in CO$_2$ emissions, *Energy Policy* **25** (5), 491-500.

US Department of Energy, Energy Information Administration, (1998a). *Impacts of the Kyoto Protocol on U.S. energy markets and economic activity*. Washington D.C.

US Department of Energy, Energy Information Administration, (1998b). *Assumptions to the Annual Energy Outlook*, Washington D.C.

Welsch, H., 1998. Coal subsidization and nuclear phase-out in a general equilibrium model for Germany. *Energy Economics*, **20**, 203-222.

Welsch, H. and Ochsen, C., 2001. Dismantling of nuclear power in Germany: sectoral and macroeconomic effects. *Energy Policy*, **29**, 279-289.

Yamaji, K. Matsuhashi, R. Nagata, Y. and Kaya, Y., 1993. A study on economic measures for CO$_2$ reduction in Japan. *Energy Policy* **21** (2), 123-132.

Zongxin, W. and Siddiqi, T., 1995. The role of nuclear energy in reducing the environmental impacts of China's energy use. *Energy* **20**(8), 777-783.

Chapter 5

INTERVENTION IN EAST TIMOR AND ELSEWHERE

I. QUASI-GENOCIDAL VIOLENCE DEMANDS A RESPONSE

Stanley Hoffmann
Harvard

In Kosovo, the United States and its allies had to choose between two important norms of international relations: respecting a state's sovereignty and protecting human rights. When they chose to stand for the latter principle, and to use force on its behalf, it seemed that a new standard was being established at last – that no state was allowed to commit gross human rights violations even on its own territory, and that those who were guilty of having ordered them and carried them out could be indicted as criminals.

Now we seem to be backpedaling from that principle, and in a country where the sovereignty issue shouldn't hold us back at all. In East Timor, where rampaging militias supported by elements of the Indonesian Army are terrorizing the population, there's no conflict between the fundamental principles of human rights and a nation's self-determination. Indonesia is an illegal occupier of East Timor, not a legal sovereign.

Its annexation of the island more than 20 years ago has never been recognized by the international community. Behaving as if we need Indonesia's consent to protect the East Timorese discredits the United Nations and its leading member nations, whose commitment to human rights now looks scandalously selective.

Whatever the strategic importance of East Timor, the symbolic significance of allowing militias to murder civilians and to nullify the results of a United Nations-sponsored referendum on independence cannot be overestimated. The withdrawal of most United Nations personnel from East Timor evokes disturbing echoes of Srebrenica, the Bosnian town where United Nations peacekeepers stood by while thousands of civilians were massacred.

Such violations cry out for a response. Chapter VII of the United Nations Charter, which deals with international peace and security, permits the Security Council to make decisions, not just recommendations. And the Security Council is not likely to be paralyzed by a Russian or Chinese veto as it could have been in Kosovo; neither country has much sympathy for a military regime that 34 years ago massacred hundreds of thousands of ethnic Chinese.

Indonesia is not, as Russia is in its war against Dagestani rebels in the Caucasus or as China is in oppressing Tibet, a major power capable of turning any military intervention into anything beyond a regional war. It's a bankrupt state with a weak President, shaky and incomplete democratic institutions and a repressive military. And the West has supported Indonesia for far too long for reasons of economic interest and obsolete cold war balancing.

The Clinton Administration, which once defined its mission in foreign affairs as the spread of democracy, has responded in a weak, dilatory manner by doing no more than suggesting a Security Council resolution asking Indonesia to accept an international force. Instead, it should take the initiative not by sending ground forces, but by rallying the Security Council and getting together a collective force to keep the peace and enforce the results of the referendum-with or without Indonesia's consent.

What the crisis points to once again is the need for regional organizations-like the Asian Pacific Economic Cooperation forum-to take over in emergencies like this one and put together a common force before its too late. At the same time, the United Nations must call on its members to provide men women and material for the kind of volunteer army-in-readiness that Sir Brian Irquhart wisely called for several years ago.

The 21st century will be full of ethnic conflicts and disintegrating states. It will not be possible to prevent, stop or resolve all of them, but cases of extraordinary quasi-genocidal violence like Kosovo and East Timor need to be considered as inherently dangerous for international peace and security, and intolerable on both ethical and prudential grounds.

II. THERE IS NO SCIENCE TO INTERVENTION

Ronald Steel
University of Southern California

"Because we bombed in Kosovo doesn't mean we should bomb Dili," said Samuel Berger, the national security advisor, about the atrocities in East Timor, which seem to have been committed by militias supported by elements of the Indonesian military. Well, why not?

The case for intervention in Dili is stronger than it was in Kosovo. Kosovo, after all, was a province of Serbia and had been for centuries. East Timor was never a part of Indonesia until it was seized by the Jakarta Government in 1975. Its people overwhelmingly voted for independence in a recent United Nations-monitored election that the Indonesian Government promised to honor. Yet, after days of violence and hundreds of deaths, the West has only asked, albeit forcefully, that Indonesia allow international peacekeeping troops into East Timor.

If the United States intervened for humanitarian reasons to support the Kosovars, even to the point of bombing Serbia, why shouldn't it do the same against Indonesia?

One reason is that-all the rhetoric aside-we did not intervene in Kosovo primarily for humanitarian purposes. The plight of the Kosovar refugees is what tugged at the public's heartstrings. But, if American foreign policy were driven mainly by such concerns, we would have sent a few thousand troops to Rwanda to stop the genocide of the Tutsis by the Hutus.

What tipped the balance in the case of Kosovo, as in the case of Bosnia, were two concerns: that the conflict would spread to other areas of the Balkans and beyond, and that

American leadership of NATO-and even the alliance itself-would be thrown in to question. The Kosovo operation was in part meant to prove that NATO was still relevant in a post-Soviet Europe.

None of this applies to conflicts outside Europe. Witness, for example, the West's non-response to, and even lack of interest in, the Russian repression in Chechnya. Unless Indonesia changes its mind and allows in troops, the East Timorese will most likely be left to fend largely for themselves. This will happen not only because East Timor is far from the North Atlantic world, but also because of the size and importance of Indonesia.

It is the world's fourth most populous nation, rich in natural resources and a prime trading partner for American corporations. It is a logical counter to any potential Chinese expansion. Furthermore, unlike puny Serbia, it is a serious military power.

Moreover, we have good reason to avoid weakening the Indonesian Government. This is because the civilian officials do not appear to be in control of the military units carrying out repression in East Timor. Punishing the fledgling democratic Government by military action could defeat our own purposes.

So where does that leave the noble principle of humanitarian intervention, so triumphantly affirmed in Kosovo? About where it began: as the exception rather than the rule.

Intervention will occur where it can be done relatively cheaply, against a weak nation, in an area both accessible and strategic, where the public's emotions are aroused, and where it does not get in the way of other political, economic or military needs.

However realistic this may be, it is deeply regrettable on moral grounds. The special tragedy of this case is that the "international community" monitored an election whose predictable results-an overwhelming vote for independence-it had no intention of guaranteeing.

But in the end, the quest for self-determination-which it what led to the current murderous repression-is relative, not absolute. People have the right to seek their own independent state. But others will come to their defense only where they believe that their own self-interest is involved. That is where the line is being drawn today in East Timor.

III. The UN Instead of the US (Table 9-1)

Stuart Nagel
PSO-DSI-MKM Center and University of Illinois

The key conservative goal in this context, relating to the role of the US in helping the UN to bring peace to East Timor or elsewhere is to save US dollars and save lives. The conservatives weren't always so oriented toward isolation. They were very interventionist back in the days of the cold war, especially with regards to curtailing the expansion of the Soviet Union. But at the present time, they do espouse more of an isolationist, less of in intervention policy than liberals do. The conservative alternative for saving US dollars and lives is to keep US troops at home. The feel it's more important to develop the policemen of the world traveling around with the goal of promoting world peace. More idealistic or maybe more naive, they believe what is sometimes referred to as a social worker ideology. That necessitates intervention.

Table 9-1: U.S. and the U.N.

ALTERNATIVES / GOALS	CONS Save U.S. Dollars and Lives	LIB World Peace
CONS Isolationism	+	-
LIB Intervention	-	+
NEUTRAL Sometimes and Moderately	0	0
SOS or WIN-WIN Volunteer U.N. Force	++	++

A. A Standing UN Force

The win-win solution saves US dollars, US lives, and promotes world peace simultaneously. An approach recommended by some who specialize in international relations is the idea of a volunteer UN force. What this would mean is that American troops would not be sent to East Timor or anywhere else. The UN would have its own volunteer force, a force similar to the French Foreign Legion. It would consist of people from all over the world who would join partly out of idealism, partly because it pays some money. They would not be allowed to join unless they've had some military experience of some aptitude for military training. It would provide an opportunity for Vietnam War veterans, Russian soldiers who had fought in Afghanistan, and others to participate in a force which would be devoted to a righteous cause. The officers would be officers who had served in the militaries of their various countries.

As a result there would be no American soldiers in this UN force. There may be Americans in the UN force, but they would be Americans acting on their own. They would be volunteering to serve. They would not be drafted, or as in the case of the current Americans serving in East Timor, ordered to go because their unit was called. They are not completely volunteers. These would be pure volunteers, pure 'in the sense they would be joining the UN force with the agreement to go wherever they are sent. If they won't go, for ideological or other reasons, then an option can be provided where they can quit. In such a case it might be fair to have them pay back something in return for their training. Such an arrangement has many possibilities.

Such a plan has been opposed in the past by the US because it was feared that the UN could not be trusted to have its own volunteer force. Strictly by the numbers, the UN in the past has been too much under the control of developing nations or nations under the control of the Soviet Union. But now, with the breakup of the Soviet Union, the US dominates the UN as the only super power in the world. The volunteer force could not be a threat to the US. Though a bit behind in its payments, the US is the leading source of funds to the UN, which further adds to its influence. If the US doesn't like what the volunteer force is doing, it could just cut off the funding, use its veto power in the Security Council, or use its influence among countries of the world. This kind of volunteer force would mean that no American lives or American dollars would be used, yet it could still be very effective In promoting world peace.

It's possible that the volunteer force might call upon member countries to supply additional troops at some time, but this would be handled as the need arose. This represents another kind of win-win solution.

The feasibility problem for this issue is psychological. It would be conceived that such a force might represent the muscle behind some type of world government which could partly deprive the US or its sovereignty. Some might fear the volunteer is going to march in and take over. As with all the other obstacles, it's necessary for this one to be overcome if this win-win solution is going to be adopted. People have to realize that a UN volunteer might not be a threat to them. In no way would the people with blue helmets serving in East Timor invade the US.

B. An Ad Hoc UN Force

The above material on "The UN instead of the US" was written at the time of Bosnia, but it applicable to East Timor and elsewhere. However, there may be no need for a standing UN volunteer force. It could be an ad hoc LIN force, as is currently operating in East Timor in November 1999. An ad hoc force has the disadvantage of having to be mustered quickly to meet emergency needs, although most trouble spots brew for awhile before they need intervention.

An ad hoc force has the advantage of making use of existing seasoned troops of countries that are neighboring to the trouble spot. Such an arrangement provides coordination within each group of national soldiers, as contrasted to having groups that are multi-national down to the lowest units. It is easier to have coordination at the top as was the case with the Allies in World War I, the Persian Gulf, Kosovo, and elsewhere. There was, however, no UN intervention in those three instances because the UN either did not exist or Security Council veto would have occurred. The veto is less likely to occur now that the Cold War is over.

If it is impossible to muster an ad hoc set of countries, then the US can consider going it virtually alone as was done in Korea and Vietnam. The ad hoc UN force is a good first resort, and it may sometimes be widely endorsed as in East Timor. Bosnia and the East Timor situation illustrate the ad hoc volunteer force of contributed troops under the UN (rather than the US or NATO) and rather than just UN observers. Such a force could maybe be mustered to intervene in (1) Afghanistan, Sudan, Angola, the Congo, and elsewhere if the UN, the US, and other major countries were willing to support symbolically, financially, or otherwise the peacemaking of intervention of neighboring countries. This type of ad hoc UN intervention could satisfy the conservative goal of keeping US combat troops out and the liberal goal of more effective peacemaking and peacekeeping.

Chapter 6

CAMBODIA AS BAD FOREIGN POLICY

Stuart Nagel
University of Illinois

I. LACK OF PEACE, PROSPERITY, OR DEMOCRACY

American foreign policy as of the year 2000 seems oriented toward producing world-wide peace, prosperity, and democracy. The motification may not be altruism, although that may be partly involved. The motivation is mainly to (1) create more customers for U.S. goods, (2) create more supplies to U.S. buyers, (3) create better outlets for U.S. investment, and (4) obtain investment money from overseas.

Cambodia may be the worst off country in the world on a combined index of lack of peace, prosperity, and democracy. Internal peace requires an effective legal system to deal with violence. In contemporary Cambodia, the main source of violence is the legal system. The main function of the police these days seems to be to encourage the people to form a circle around criminal suspects so the police can beat the suspects to death.

On the matter of prosperity, the UN defines poverty as earning less than $1 a day. The overwhelming majority of Cambodians qualify by that extremely low standard of poverty. Worse than that, government officials earn about $20 a month which is substantially below the poverty line. The $20 may also have to feed, clothe, and shelter children in the breadwinner's family.

This leads to the pits of corruption, contrary to meaningful democracy. Under meaningful democracy, the people control the government. Under such an underpaid system, the government constantly extorts and intimidates the people for protection money (although sometimes called tips) in order to supplement their impoverished incomes.

II. U.S. SANCTIONS

Cambodia would be a lot better off if it were not under a government boycott by the U.S. government. Private U.S. business firms can deal with businesses in Cambodia. The sanctions, however, prohibit the U.S. government from dealing with the government of

Cambodia. This is justified because in about 1995, the closest thing to a democratic change in government that Cambodia has known in a generation was declared to be rigged in favor of the current president who did assume power under questionable circumstances.

One could argue that American presidents regularly assume power under questionable circumstances when they are only elected by a fraction of the adult population. Fifty percent of the adult U.S. population is discouraged from voting partly by not providing for on-site registration. Fifty percent of those registered are discouraged from actually voting by not providing an election-day holiday. That leaves 25% of the adults who vote. A 14% victory is then considered a landslide.

A key reason the sanctions continue is because Cambodia is so poor and hurt by the sanctions that there is not much incentive for American business to seek the removal of the sanctions in order to open up economic opportunities. This is unlike China, Vietnam, North Korea, and Cuba. Cambodia also does not have the oil of Iran, Iraq, and Libya. All those places on your list of sanctioned countries are way better off and much more likely to have sanctions removed than Cambodia is. In fact, the sanctions probably remain on Cambodia because almost nobody in the U.S. much cares or is interested.

III. FROM VICIOUS CIRCLE TO UPWARD SPIRAL

This is a vicious circle because the sanctions make Cambodia poorer, more lawless, and less democratic. That causes American business to want to have less to do with Cambodia. That in turn causes Cambodia to become poorer, more lawless, and less democratic and so on until maybe things get so miserable that somebody gets a New York Times story out of it. The story might be called something like "The Killing Fields Become the Slow-Dying Fields in Cambodia?"

I just returned from Cambodia where in a few days, I encountered examples of how bad things can be. None of the events were reported in the New York Times. One example is that Cambodia relies heavily on tourism to the Ankhor Wat ruins, which are up river from Phnom Penh. While I was there, a tourist boat was hijacked by well-armed men with AK47 weapons. They were subsequently identified as members of the army and the police, supplementing their incomes. That kind of semi-government action temporarily destroyed a substantial chunk of the income of Cambodia. It would not be so likely to happen elsewhere.

To move out of this vicious circle into an upward spiral, Cambodia public policy with the aid of the U.S. could and/or should:

> Seek to introduce new technologies in agriculture, commerce, manufacturing, transportation, communications, and other activities. The private sector can be encouraged to invest by a payroll tax that is 100% refundable if the money that would be used to pay the tax is instead used for new technologies.
>
> Seek to introduce more adult training to use the new and the old technologies. Encouragement can be provided through whatever training vouchers Cambodia public policy can afford.
>
> Encourage competition in the sale of electricity, telephoning, and other highly essential or useful services by offering to multiple providers blocks of numerous potential customers in return for competitive discounts.

Encourage free trade regarding both exporting and importing so as to enable Cambodians to sell overseas for increased income, to buy from overseas for increased quality of life, and to buy from overseas raw materials and merchandise for commercial resale.

Cambodia is in bad shape. It was once a relatively thriving country until more bombs were dropped on Cambodia than in much of World War II. The bombs fell in order to bomb out the alleged Vietnamese headquarters that was never found. The U.S. should help Cambodia not out of Cold War guilt, but because Cambodia (like Vietnam and the other Southeast Asia Tigers) can be a good customer, supplier, and investment outlet for the U.S. and other industrial countries. For that matter, so can the potential Tigers of Africa, Latin America, and other parts of Asia besides Southeast Asia.

Chapter 7

SCIENCE IN THE FUTURE OF INDIA AND ELSEWHERE

C. N. Rao
Third World Academy of Sciences

As a developing nation, India faces a situation that may be unique among democratic countries in recent human history. On the one hand, it is committed to taking care of the minimum needs of a huge and rapidly growing population. On the other, it must compete with the most advanced countries in a global economy. Unfortunately, it is becoming increasingly difficult for Indian researchers who work at the cutting edge science and technology to do their jobs well because of the poor infrastructure and facilities at most institutions, in particular the universities. As a result, the gap in the level of science technology between the advanced countries and India is increasing.

Why is that the case? There are several reasons. A disquieting tendency in India and in many of the developing countries is the increasing disinterest in science among the younger generation. Many colleges are closing down science departments because students prefer to take courses in management, commerce, and related areas. And there are fewer bright students studying for careers in science and engineering research or higher education. This situation has to be remedied by promoting talent and by offering incentives. It is likely that the vast population of India and other developing countries harbors more than a few geniuses, possibly future Faradays and Newtons. But we have to find them and encourage them to pursue science.

The situation facing universities is quite depressing because of deteriorating facilities, poor administration, vested interests, and overemphasis on examinations rather than education. Although institutions that provide a proper environment and facilities continue to attract young scientists in spite of modest salaries, they are negligible in number. There has also been a downward trend in basic research in the past few years. India will face a no-win situation unless there is a radical structural transformation of the system. Oppressive administrative practices, political interference, and person animosities tend to impede creativity and innovation, as in most other developing countries. The bureaucratic procedures that run the country have hardly changed from the days of British rule. They are the same cumbersome institutions for science, revenue service, and municipal administration. The labyrinths in the government buildings, and the mountains of files piled high within them, make one shoulder. It takes 2 years or more to obtain a grant, and government departments are generally not responsive to scientists, especially those of the younger generation.

In spite of major gains and accomplishments, India remains poor and backward, with innumerable problems and challenges fueled by its burgeoning population. Science has much to contribute toward creating a nation that is economically sound and where social justice prevails. Because science has become a key component of communication in the world at large, a nation unable to speak the language of science cannot adequately deal with other nations in matters of vital interest. It has therefore become incumbent on even the smallest or the poorest of nations to have an optimal science base and the associated institutional structure. A majority of the population in India has yet to become literate and develop the scientific awareness needed to face new and difficult situations. Scientific literacy is equally needed among the educated citizens, including politicians and administrators.

To achieve these goals, pragmatic efforts are essential on several different fronts. First and foremost is the need to carry out programs in science and technology that focus on the minimum basic needs of the common person and on the promotion of sustainable development, which will provide meaningful employment, particularly in rural areas. The country also must develop an adequate infrastructure for energy, transportation, and communications. A large country such as India faces an additional challenge. It has to develop its own expertise at the highest level, at least in a few chosen areas of science and technology, so as to be able to compete and excel in the international arena. India has to invest much more in education [6% of gross domestic product (GDP) rather than the current level of around 3%] and in science (about 2% of GDP rather than 0.9%). It is only by making use of a strong knowledge base that India can ever hope to become a great nation.

Chapter 8

STRATEGIC DIMENSIONS OF THE CRISIS IN ASIA

Bob Catley
University of Otago
New Zealand

INTRODUCTION

In a realist analysis, the states of East Asia have emerged from the period of colonialism and Cold War to form a classic regional inter-state system in which each pursues its own interests within the confines established by the advantages of membership of the system itself. The partial exceptions to this are North Korea (Buzo 1999), which has recently shown quite strong indications of wanting to emerge from its isolationism, and Myanmar, which has tried to do the same thing. There are also residues of the Cold War in the form of several remaining communist regimes in North Korea, the PRC, Vietnam and Laos, and other governments with personnel whose careers were first forged during that contest, including the USA, South Korea and, arguably, Australia and New Zealand. What marks out the Asian regional international system from other regional systems in the contemporary world is that there is little by way of a generalised regional institutional architecture in the security, political or even economic sphere. The partial exceptions to this generalisation are limited in either geographic or functional scope.

The geographically based institutions include most notably the Association of South East Asian Nations (ASEAN). ASEAN was formed in 1967 and was until recently depicted as one of the world's most successful regional political associations. It ranked only perhaps behind the European Union in its historical record of producing cooperation and integration among its member states when previously there had been conflict and discord. During the last four years that record has come to look less impressive as the old long-term leadership personnel and regime structures of the member countries have changed, often as a result of the regional financial crisis and its knock on effects. The 'ASEAN way' of mutual admiration has given way to more determined pursuit of individual interest and, in some instances, ready criticism. In many respects this new openness may be no bad thing. But ASEAN is geographically limited.

Nonetheless, ASEAN did spawn in the 1990s the ASEAN Regional Forum (ARF), which expanded out of the dialogue partners' meetings to produce regular, annual contacts between the major powers of the region and then ASEAN plus three (PRC, Japan, South Korea). Coupled with other bilateral relationships, this has produced a growth in commitments to confidence building measures, such as publishing annual defence white papers to reassure other states about military intentions, dialogues about difficult issues like the South China Sea, cultural, educational and diplomatic exchanges, and even regular summit meetings to provide some person-to-person contacts. In the world of international power politics such developments of an international civil society can surely do no harm.

In contrast, the Asia Pacific Economic Cooperation (APEC) has proven to be almost entirely an instrument for economic liberalisation – and costume manufacture and distribution – but one that could not act in the face of a real economic/financial crisis for several of its members in 1997-98. Its inability to act even in its designated sphere – economics – left little confidence in its capacity to intervene in strategic issues. It was merely an accident of timing that enabled the New Zealand APEC summit of 1999 to be the site of important negotiations which produced the INTERFET intervention in East Timor.

This scant regional security architecture compares unfavourably with what has emerged in Europe since the end of the Cold War. There, the expansion of NATO and the European Union, both of which are still proceeding, promises to produce parallel, overlapping but differentiated mechanisms for economic, social, political and strategic integration and problem resolution. Neither ASEAN nor APEC have gone this far, nor seem likely to.

In the Asia Pacific region there are also a number of more limited multilateral organisations. These include: the US security agreements with South Korea and Japan; the emerging relationships between China and Russia and between China and Myanmar; the South Pacific Forum; and the ANZUS and ANZAC treaties. In the main, however, these are not so much systems of regional security as treaty relationships designed to pursue joint national interests. They are, in other words, with the partial exception of the South Pacific Forum, which is somewhat more than just an organisation for administering Australian regional hegemony, classical tools of power politics. The region of East Asia/western Pacific has an international system which has more in common with the world of nineteenth-century European power politics than it does with the twenty-first century Atlantic world of states being integrated into a larger political community.

In Asia, while it is the case that for most states of the region the problems of adjustment to the age of globalisation have replaced strategic issues as the dominant priority, national security always lurks near the surface of much state decision making.

In simple realist terms the major attributes of the region are:

1. a dominant great power, the US (which is also systemically hegemonic);
2. a declining great power, the Russian Federation;
3. two potentially rising great powers, in China and Japan;
4. a number of lesser powers with different interests to pursue like Thailand, Malaysia and Vietnam (some of which are quite large and potentially powerful, but temporarily disabled, like Indonesia, and a unified Korea);
5. many lesser states unlikely to be strategically important for the foreseeable future, like Laos, Cambodia, Brunei and East Timor;

6. and the mostly even smaller states of the western Pacific including Australia, Papua New Guinea, and New Zealand.

THE USA: THE HEGEMONIC POWER

Since its victory over the Soviet Union the United States has emerged as the hegemonic power in the international system. It is the dominant military, economic and political power in the global system and this applies regionally to East Asia and the entire Pacific (Mosler and Catley 2000).

The Presidency of Bill Clinton marked the transformation of an uncertain but victorious US finding it difficult to define its strategic goals as a hegemon, to an ascendant and confidant 'Global America' pursuing globalisation with considerable success. While much of this objective can be defined in terms of economics and then, to a lesser extent, culture, it has had to be buttressed by the application of state power. This has been most evident in the use of force against what were then and are now again, called 'rogue states' by the US. Military power was used directly against Iraq and Serbia, vicariously against Syria, Afghanistan and Sudan, and threatened against North Korea and even the PRC (Catley 1999).

The instruments of US power in East Asia are the global power projection capabilities which have been able to transform almost the entire US military structure into a medium time (about a month) deployment force; a naval and air power based military command which extends from California to the Persian Gulf; and pre-positioned forces and installations in states as diverse as Japan, South Korea and Australia. These forces have stood behind US political activities in the region for the last decade and are the foundations for its capacity to constrain China, deter North Korea and restructure East Timor (Weeks and Meconis 1999).

Does US policy look likely to continue in this vein under the new administration?

There are four main indicators for the direction of US policy under the new administration of President George W. Bush: the stated policy intentions of its personnel; the existing DOD document, recently published in 2000 and not disowned; the inaugural Presidential address of 16 January; and the continuing interests of the US.

*   The personnel of the new Bush administration are represented by its critics as being dominated by the staff of his father's team of the last stanza of the Cold War. There is of course much substance to this claim. As a result, it may be expected that some of the strains in relations with both Russia and China of a decade ago will re-emerge. This is particularly so over the issues of an anti-ballistic missile (ABM) defence system and Taiwan, although, in the latter case, a clearer US doctrine than 'strategic ambiguity' may well be an improvement.

Colin Powell, the Secretary of State, made his name during the application of US military power to the protection of access to that most important of tradeable commodities, oil, against the attempts of the Iraqi militarist regime to control half the world's known reserves. In this his career does not differ markedly from that of his predecessor who waged war against another militarist regime, that of Serbia, to establish US domination across the European continent via NATO. Kosovo was Madeleine's war.

According to the semi-official pen portrait in the *New York Times* (2000), Donald H. Rumsfeld began his first tour of duty as Secretary of Defense when the Vietnam War had just been lost. His supporters say Rumsfeld, 68, will not be stuck in the Cold War. His one-time protégé Dick Cheney, a former Defense Secretary under George Bush, is now the Vice-President. The Bush administration will seek to increase defence spending and win Congressional approval for a national missile defence program.

During his first stint at the Pentagon, Rumsfeld also tried to increase the defence budget, and re-emerged as a leading force in Republican circles on national security issues. He led an independent commission which in 1998 found that the ballistic missile threat from countries like North Korea and Iran was growing, and appeared more serious than the intelligence community had previously concluded.

Rumsfeld, Cheney and General Powell are all advocates of a strong US military force and substantial defence spending.

Condoleezza Rice, the new National Security Adviser, is less well known than many of her predecessors but has revealed some of her strategic thinking, particularly about Russia, her speciality. In 'Promoting the National Interest', in *Foreign Affairs* (Rice 2000), she wrote:

> Power matters, both the exercise of power by the United States and the ability of others to exercise it. Yet many in the United States are (and have always been) uncomfortable with the notions of power politics, great powers, and power balances. In an extreme form, this discomfort leads to a reflexive appeal instead to notions of international law and norms, and the belief that the support of many states – or even better, of institutions like the United Nations – is essential to the legitimate exercise of power. The 'national interest' is replaced with 'humanitarian interests' or the interests of 'the international community'.

She added:

> The Kosovo war was conducted incompetently, in part because the administration's goals kept shifting and in part because it was not, at the start, committed to the decisive use of military force....If it is worth fighting for, you had better be prepared to win. Also, there must be a political game plan that will permit the withdrawal of our forces – something that is still completely absent in Kosovo....The president must remember that the military is a special instrument. It is lethal, and it is meant to be. It is not a civilian police force. It is not a political referee. And it is most certainly not designed to build a civilian society....
>
> Foreign policy in a Republican administration will most certainly be internationalist....But it will also proceed from the firm ground of the national interest, not from the interests of an illusory international community. America can exercise power without arrogance and pursue its interests without hectoring and bluster.

•   The Department of Defense annual report document of 2000 shows that under the Democrats the US was continuing its policy of essentially maintaining military superiority from California to the Gulf to the extent of the 'two and a half wars' doctrine. The Republicans only criticised this as being too little and under-resourced. We may expect US military capabilities in the Asia Pacific region, as elsewhere, to be augmented. To judge by other statements, however, notably those of Colin Powell, US forces would be used more specifically for US national interest purposes. Issues of humanitarian intervention would be downgraded and regional security issues hand-balled to allies wherever possible. The DOD Report already said:

East Asia and the Pacific Rim

U.S. Defense Objectives. The United States seeks a stable and economically prosperous East Asia that embraces democratic reform and market economics. Central to achieving this goal are the United States' strong alliance relationships within the region, especially with Japan, Australia, and the Republic of Korea (ROK). In addition, it is critical to continue to engage China so that it contributes to regional stability and acts as a responsible member of the international community. The United States desires a peaceful resolution of the Korean conflict resulting in a non-nuclear, democratic, reconciled, and ultimately reunified Peninsula, as well as the peaceful resolution of the region's other disputes, including that between Taiwan and the People's Republic of China. Successful counters to terrorism, illegal drug trafficking, and nuclear proliferation are also major U.S. goals for the region.

U.S. Regional Defense Posture and Activities. The United States is committed to maintaining its current level of military capability in East Asia and the Pacific Rim. This capability allows the United States to play a key role as security guarantor and regional balancer. The United States will continue a forward presence policy, in cooperation with its allies, that reflects its interests in the region and allows for adjustments in the U.S. force posture over time to meet the changing demands of the security environment. Today, the United States stations or deploys approximately 100,000 military personnel in the region. Of these personnel, over half are stationed in Japan and close to 40 per cent are in the ROK. The United States will seek to continue and build upon bilateral and multilateral exercises with key states in the region, including the ROK, Japan, Thailand, the Philippines, and Australia.

The most significant near-term danger in the region is the continuing military threat posed by the Democratic People's Republic of Korea. The United States remains fully committed to its treaty obligations to assist the ROK in defending against North Korean aggression. The United States also seeks a Korean Peninsula free of NBC weapons – a goal shared with the ROK and other allies and friends in the region. The U.S.-North Korean Agreed Framework froze North Korea's nuclear facilities at Yongbyon and Taechon under International Atomic Energy Agency inspection. The Agreed Framework still provides the best means to secure North Korean compliance with its non-proliferation commitment under the Nuclear Non-Proliferation Treaty. The Department is also working with its Pacific allies to enhance their collective capabilities to deter and defeat use of chemical or biological weapons.

The U.S. security alliance with Japan is the linchpin of its security policy in Asia and is key to many U.S. global objectives. Both nations have moved actively in recent years to strengthen this bilateral relationship and update the framework and structure of joint cooperation to reflect the security environment. U.S. efforts to build on strong alliances with other nations in the region, especially Australia, buttress the U.S. goal of ensuring stability in Southeast Asia, an area of growing economic and political importance. The continued strengthening of U.S. security dialogues and confidence-building measures with the members of the Association of Southeast Asian Nations (ASEAN) through the ASEAN Regional Forum is one of many ways in which the United States is working to enhance political, military, and economic ties with friends and allies in Southeast Asia. The Asia-Pacific Center for Security Studies is a key U.S. initiative that promotes mutual understanding and cooperation by providing an academic forum for military and civilian decision makers from the United States and Asia to exchange ideas and explore regional security challenges.

The Asian financial crisis has shaken the region's assumptions about uninterrupted economic development. Indonesia's economic and political difficulties in particular will pose challenges to the established order both internally and in the region. Continued U.S. engagement in Indonesia will help promote the stability necessary to manage this difficult period of change.

Because of China's critical importance in the Asia-Pacific region, the United States is working to integrate China more deeply into the international community. Specifically, the United States engages China in order to promote regional stability and economic prosperity while securing China's adherence to international standards on weapons non-proliferation, international trade, and human rights. The United States also seeks greater transparency in China's defense program, including its planning and procurement processes, and will continue to engage China in dialogue aimed at fostering cooperation and confidence-building. Military exchange programs, port visits, and professional seminars contribute to this dialogue and are aimed at building lasting relationships that will foster cooperation and build confidence among U.S. and Chinese leaders. (US Department of Defense 2000a)

• During the 2000 US Presidential elections, less emphasis was placed on foreign policy than had been the case during the last five decades. In part, this was due to agreement on the major issue, globalisation. In his inauguration address President George W. Bush also placed little emphasis on foreign policy issues, although he stated:

We will build our defenses beyond challenge, lest weakness invite challenge. We will confront weapons of mass destruction, so that a new century is spared new horrors.
The enemies of liberty and our country should make no mistake, America remains engaged in the world, by history and by choice, shaping a balance of power that favors freedom. We will defend our allies and our interests. We will show purpose without arrogance. We will meet aggression and bad faith with resolve and strength. And to all nations, we will speak for the values that gave our nation birth. (*New York Times* 2001a)

• Finally, of course, US interests in the regional have not substantially changed because of a change in administration. In the past these have been described as including: over US$500 billion in trade (1998); the maintenance of open trade routes and Sea Lanes of Communication (SLOCs); extensive investments; the maintenance and expansion of open, growing, capitalist economies; and the prevention of a single power, or allied group of powers, establishing their control over the region. To that end, the US has maintained an extensive military presence in a command which stretches from California to the Gulf:

US overseas presence in the Asia-Pacific region, including the continued maintenance of approximately 100,000 military personnel for the foreseeable future, will continue to promote regional strategic interests, and provide evidence of undiminished US commitment and engagement. Our force structure will continue to reflect our conception of regional strategic requirements and the capabilities necessary to support them, and remain the subject of continued consultation with our allies. In coming years, the United States will also examine new modes of sustaining and supporting this presence within the region. The continued development of support – outside the traditional basing structure – in such nations as Australia, Indonesia, Thailand, Malaysia, Brunei, Singapore and the Philippines will enhance US strategic interests in maintaining regional stability and a credible power projection capability in the region and beyond, including to the Arabian Gulf when necessary. (US Department of Defense 2000a)

In the substantial policy area of globalisation there seems little reason to believe that the Bush administration will differ much from that of Clinton. Indeed, it may be anticipated that with organised labour and protected industry supporting the Democrats – and in some instances Ralph Nader – Bush's pursuit of a free trading global economy may be even more determined than Clinton's. His personnel are otherwise even more oriented towards the national interest. The Democrats developed into a liberal, institution building and power projecting team under Clinton, and especially under Madeleine Albright in his second administration. As far as may be determined, Colin Powell, the Gulf War notwithstanding, is less keen on the use of force than Albright.

The thrust of the late Clinton administration was economic globalisation, although the threat or use of US military power was periodically deployed to achieve that outcome – as against North Korea, the PRC, Serbia, and Iraq. The Bush administration is more likely to be more geo-politically realist. Rumsfeld will probably be more committed to building greater US military power and expenditure than Cohen, Dick Cheney more oriented to geo-political power than the Internet and ecology than Al Gore, and Dr. Rice is more classical in her realist posture than Sandy Berger.

This provides a picture of a US which is likely to be more committed to: free trade and a liberal economy; the use of military power to pursue US national interests; a reduced inclination to act multilaterally; and a lesser inclination to use US power for systemic purposes depicted in Albright's phrase, 'the indispensable nation'. The new personnel are less ideological, less liberal, a trifle more isolationist and rhetorically more realist. But, of course, it is early days.

On specific issues, the Republicans seem less committed than the Clinton administration to the liberal belief that economic growth will produce political development, liberalisation and a greater harmony of interests with the old adversaries of the US in East Asia like China, North Korea and even Russia. They are more likely, therefore, to take out military insurance policies, like the regional anti-missile defence system. They are also likely to be more precise about their intention to use force in protection of their allies in Taiwan and South Korea, if this should become necessary. This may involve the abandoning of the doctrine of 'strategic ambiguity'. There will probably be less rhetoric and policy based on the idea that the more the PRC and North Korea can be brought into the community of nations, the better will regional security be served, and more emphasis placed on the need for the US to maintain its military superiority, in order, they may well believe, to avoid the need to use it.

This is not to say the Bush administration will not pursue a global economy; it is to suggest that this will be seen as a distinct agenda from that of regional stability, that will be regarded as more dependent on its strategic policies than on modernisation theory. In short, the basis for US hegemony in the system as a whole, and in East Asia in particular, will not be eroded by the new Republican administration. But it will be less likely to resort to the use of force in support of it.

Finally, the so-called unipolar moment of US power is now coupled with a less clearly dominant US electoral support for a coherent global role. The US Congress is now evenly divided, and thus is likely to be more resistant to (and the people are more sceptical about) Clinton's idea of a US global responsibility – or Albright's concept of the 'indispensable nation'. The US, it seems, is more interested on those inside its tent than outside. In this mood it may well expect friends and allies to do more as it has already made clear to both Australia, which seems likely to respond, and to New Zealand, which is unlikely to respond.

STATE CHALLENGERS TO THE US: THE RUSSIAN FEDERATION

There are three states which might have the capacity to pose a substantial challenge to US regional hegemony: the Russian Federation, the PRC and Japan.

The collapse of the Soviet Union in December 1991 marked the end of the Cold War. The decisiveness of this defeat was masked by the decision of the US not to celebrate its victory in order to support more readily the new Russian administration in Moscow headed by its ally/client, Boris Yeltsin. But the impact on the former client states of the Soviet Union in East Asia should not be underestimated. North Korea was most severely effected because its subsidised, cheap oil supply from the Soviet Union was cut off with considerable impact on its economic performance. Much of the North Korean economic collapse can be attributed to that cause (together with the inability of its rigid economy to adjust to it). Some of the Vietnamese problems of economic development also derive from its difficulty in adjusting a COMECON (Council for Mutual Economic Assistance; Communist Economic Conference) oriented economy to one located in a globalised world economy.

Russia no longer represents the failed ideal of communism and is merely the successor state of the Soviet Union. Its power is now based on a diminished economy still finding any growth difficult to achieve, a population halved and now shrinking, a military under-funded, poorly serviced and damaged by a succession of defeats, and an inability to project power even into its own near abroad (Mosler and Catley 2000, ch.6). During the Clinton administration this was somewhat offset by the determination of Washington to treat the Yeltsin and then Putin regimes as a co-superpower because of the Russian nuclear arsenal. This diplomacy got Moscow into the G-8 and other serious high level negotiations where it had otherwise little right to be.

The Republicans seem determined to treat Russia more as a rival than an ally. Dr. Rice has already suggested that the US has little interest in building the power of Russia in order that it may better rival US strategy. The commitment to continue with the ABM deployment is likely to produce greater Russian hostility amid claims that this breaks treaties which go back as far as 1972 and 1974. But in the end Russia can do little about it. Yeltsin was committed to containing Russian military expenditure to 3 per cent of GDP – a similar percentage to the US, pre-Bush. This will not produce a military machine to rival that of the US, nor indeed provide a significant power projection capability except where the Russian land forces can engage even weaker forces. This probably means only Central Asia. As a player in the wider diplomacy of East Asia, Russia is of extremely limited importance. As in the European theatre, Russia has demonstrated a model descent, achieved rapidly, and now shows no significant power projection capacity.

Under Boris Yeltsin, Moscow was committed to winding down its military forces to an expenditure level of under 4 per cent of GDP. Since the economy was in apparently permanent decline, this amounted to a rapid demobilisation of the kind that occurred throughout the 1990s. President Putin is unlikely to change this policy dramatically, although he is more dependent than his predecessor on military force for his legitimacy, having eased himself into power at the same time as finally achieving some sort of victory in Chechnya. Nonetheless, unlike its Soviet predecessor, the Russian Federation regime is not dependent on revolutionary ideology, global expansion or military might for its survival. As such, it is as likely as that of Yeltsin to continue to give highest priority to the economic reforms in the surviving hope that these will generate substantial growth. There is now some literature describing the failure of the rapid economic liberalisation of the early 1990s in Russia. There is also some by participants apologising for their rather over-enthusiastic application of the World Bank/IMF canon. Whatever their validity, it now seems that the creation of a successful, liberal democratic political and economic structure requires more than state deregulation. It may involve a broader range of sociological, cultural and legal artifices than have yet been obtainable in Russia.

Under Vladimir Putin, the dictatorial aspects of the Russian political system are commonly believed to be already more in evidence. The recreation of the capacity to project serious power is still far from the official Russian agenda, notwithstanding the recent despatch of a Russian naval flotilla into East Asian waters for probably the first time since the Cold War. While Russia may complain at US behaviour – over, for example, a missile defence system – it is difficult to envisage it putting these developments before US assistance for its economic plans, assistance which will be more difficult to win from a Bush administration if Dr. Rice's views are a guide. Even if it were to do so (and in 2001 there are signs of such action involving, particularly, weapons and technology transfers to the PRC and Iran), its power base is presently insufficient to mount a general or even regional strategic opposition to the US.

STATE CHALLENGERS TO THE US: THE PRC AND JAPAN

The PRC

In 1989 the People's Republic of China (PRC) turned from being a US ally in the global contest against Soviet-backed communism, to a more carefully scrutinised, old-style communist political dictatorship. The Tiananmen Square repression marked a key event in this transition. The regime itself, almost paradoxically, also changed its orientation, but away from Marxist Leninist ideology for regime legitimation towards a more market-oriented economy and nationalistic political vocabulary. The regime became more determined in its pursuit of lost territories, the People's Liberation Army seemed to achieve greater influence in resource allocation politics, and economic growth was given even greater attention and indeed accelerated.

The PRC is clearly, so far, a frustrated aspirant for the status of a regional dominant power (Ji 1999). The evidence for this is not to be found in its Cold War behaviour under the previous communist leadership, nor in its statements about its peaceful intentions, nor in the signs of the modernisation of its political and economic system. Rather, it has been modernising its military forces in such a way as to give it the capacity to project power into the regional order. In the realist methodology there is nothing anti-PRC in this conclusion. All states behave like this, including the US as just described. Under Clinton, the US described its pursuit of national interest in terms of liberal ideology. In the case of the PRC, whereas previously it used the rhetoric of socialist and even revolutionary ideology, it now utilises Chinese nationalist terminology and sometimes irredentism, particularly with respect to Taiwan and the South China Sea.

Chinese military forces are being improved with the objective of giving them the capacity to project power. During the 1970s and 1980s PRC military forces were moved away from a pro-Soviet posture to one designed to defend the country against Soviet attack. In the last ten years they have been re-jigged to provide the PRC with an augmented power projection capacity. Alongside this the PLA is trying to develop a rudimentary capacity to fight the US in the event of military conflict and to deter the US from using its vastly superior nuclear arsenal. Important in this respect are the stated purposes of achieving a naval blue water projection capacity; an air strike capability based on the 300 plus SU 27 Flankers acquired from Russia; modernising its nuclear arsenal with a view to being able to strike more distant targets (including the US mainland); a presence in space which might deliver some capacity to disable US space stations for detection, surveillance and targeting; and participation in the so-called Revolution in Military Affairs which could enable a rapid catch-up on US technology by leaping a technological generation. Few of these objectives are likely to be achieved in the near future, particularly while the military embargoes by the US and allied powers stay in place. This explains severe US reactions to transfers of military technology to the PRC by Israel or espionage activities.

The PRC has a long way to go to match the US in military, economic or political terms. Its military capacity does not enable it to project power against the Republic of China (ROC) merely 100 miles across the Taiwan Strait. Its economy is between 10 and 20 per cent of the size of the US economy. Its political system and nationalist/military ideology has the attraction of that of the Burmese dictatorship to anyone who is not ethnic Chinese and for many who are.

Periodically, the PRC attempts to make up for these weaknesses by seeking to establish allies against the dominance of the US. So far it has been unable to form a coalition by the traditional Balance of Power behaviour which realist theory would anticipate. It has purchased military equipment from the Russian Federation and has on several occasions achieved joint declarations that have, among other things, taken a sideswipe at American power. But no lasting and durable anti-American partnership has been possible with either Yeltsin or Putin. It has had more success in forging an anti-US posture with Myanmar, a pariah for other reasons, but this adds little to PRC power. It has won a few friends in the Middle East by weapons and other diplomacy, but these are assets of questionable utility. Similarly, the provision of arms to Pakistan has been of limited diplomatic value, particularly when it has continued to alienate India. The qualified support of Serbia during the Kosovo War yielded limited gains, almost all of which were lost with the fall of Milosevic.

Part of the problem for the PRC involves its inability to offer rewards as great as the US can in the form of access to the processes and institutions of globalisation. Part of the problem is that the PRC claims are nationalist and attract little support from other states which have no interest in whether the PRC controls Taiwan and the South China Sea – or more often are against it. Of course, being both Chinese and (ostensibly, anyway) Marxist, the PRC regime may just be taking a longer term perspective on the matter in looking for outcomes closer to, say, 2050 than this paper intends to allow for. After all, after nearly 50 years the PRC got Hong Kong and Macao back; it may take another mere 30 to do the same for the ROC and the South China Sea. By then the US will have worked its way through at least another four administrations of quite unpredictable complexion.

Japan

The Japanese state was touted as recently as in the 1980s as a potential rival to the power of the US as the Soviet Union declined. Japan has, in the last 50 years, achieved the most rapid rise to over-maturity (Mulgan 2000; and compare with the more optimistic Helweg 2000). The model of political management of a capitalist economy which appeared for 30 years to be more effective than the *laissez faire* practices of the Anglo-Saxons or the welfare statist behaviour of the western Europeans, now looks too ossified to accommodate new technological requirements or commercial organisations. The Japanese economy has been effectively stagnant now for a decade, during which time it has progressively expanded its state sector by continuing but ineffective fiscal stimulations and contracted its foreign trade surpluses. The combination of a sclerotic domestic economy and hollowed out manufacturing sector, exacerbated by sociological trends in demography, immigration and cultural aspirations, has retarded its economy.

This economic stagnation has only worsened the geo-political ambivalence of the political elite. It was already undertaking strategic objectives only at the behest of the Americans. By the late 1980s, however, some politicians were urging an expansion of its strategic responsibility under the US alliance. Some statements had been made to this effect and Japan contributed modestly to some UN peacekeeping operations. In the later 1990s this expanding role was progressively abandoned as a series of administrations came and went, losing further authority with each change of political leadership and the corresponding capacity to lead an expansion of Japan's power projection. By the time of the revision of the responsibilities under the US-Japan Security Treaty in 1998, the Japanese armed forces' role – and indeed that of its territory – had been reduced almost entirely to one subordinate to that of regional US forces.

By 2001 Japan had a lame duck Prime Minister in Mr. Mori, whose authority was further eroded by a renewed deceleration of economic growth and maladroit handling of the collision between a US navy submarine and a Japanese vessel. This account of recent Japanese developments demonstrates the triumph of political will over economic competence. Japan has a limited but real capacity for military power projection; it lacks almost entirely the will to use it.

SITES OF GREAT POWER CONTESTATION

The US, then, is the most powerful nation in the world. For the most part it seeks its objectives in the East Asia region with only limited opposition from the other major powers, which for reasons just described are hamstrung in their capacities.

This is not to say that there are not substantial regional problems involving conflicting claims between important states. Indeed there are several, and every so often they break out into crises, which often have both regional and wider dimensions. The three that are of greatest significance are, in part, remaining legacies of the Cold War. They are, in declining order of short-term importance, the Koreas, Taiwan and the South China Sea.

The Koreas

The total power of a united Korean state of 70 million and a large economy with advanced technological capabilities and strong military forces would be considerable. It is unlikely, however, that it would have the aspiration to project such power substantially, since the focus of both Korean states has been on the peninsula. Since one very costly war and half a century of strategic competition between these two states has involved all major regional powers and the deployment of forces from another 50, there is considerable interest in a peaceful resolution of this issue.

The developments of the last year have been among the most promising of the last 50 years. The lurch towards unification has been occasioned by the economic crisis in North Korea; the regime modification there; the democratisation in the South under a President deeply committed to national unification; and the interests of all great powers involved in a peaceful resolution to the dispute. The end of the Cold War has, albeit belatedly, brought a relaxation of the tensions attendant on the problems of the division of the Korean nation into two hostile states.

The end of the Cold War itself has stimulated these positive developments by weakening the capacity of the North Korean state to sustain its revolutionary character, and by liberalising the South Korean regime and unleashing thereby nationalist sentiments which were previously subsumed by Cold War ideology.

Taiwan

Taiwan remains the most important single site of direct conflict between US and PRC interests. In 1996 it was the occasion for the most public display of force by the US against the PRC since the end of the Cold War. Since then the issue has been hosed down substantially by an apparently unlikely series of events, including the election of a non-KMT ROC President on the island state with an apparent commitment to developing an independent state. Nonetheless, President Chen Shui-bian did not bring with him an eight decade long history of hostility with ideological, personal, family and financial dimensions.

The democratisation of the ROC has provided the impetus for an acceleration of the process of cross-strait dialogue. This contains the possibility of a negotiation of terms for the long-term settlement of the sovereignty dispute which has prolonged a Cold War conflict for more than a decade beyond its use-by date. As in Korea, the possibility of a resolution or more stable accommodation of this seemingly intractable issue arose only a decade after the Cold War itself was resolved. Again, the diminution of Cold War ideological imperatives on both sides of the Taiwan Strait has enabled a more realistic posture of accommodation to emerge in both of the previously competing political regimes.

The South China (and East China) Sea

The South China Sea is claimed in its entirety by the PRC (Catley and Keliat 1997). This is not, however, strictly a Cold War issue and arguably worsened after that strategic conflict ended with the increasingly nationalist direction of the PRC regime. If this claim were successful and complemented by its claims in the East China Sea, it would add a territory of about 50 per cent of the existing PRC state territory. It would also add some territory which is presently claimed by Malaysia, Indonesia, Brunei, the Philippines, Taiwan, Japan and the Koreas.

This claim is a continuing but, at present, fairly low order irritant to PRC relations with many neighbouring states. If it were to be prosecuted successfully and lead to the PRC control of the strategic Sea Lanes of Communication contained within the claimed waters, further complications would arise within PRC relations with users of these SLOCs including the US, Japan, Korea and Russia, not to mention other more distant powers with similar interests in the EU, Australia and the oil exporting countries of the Middle East.

These PRC claims are a continuing and distressing indication of what PRC regional hegemony might bring for other neighbouring states. Nonetheless, since the Taiwan Strait crisis of 1996, the PRC claim has been pursued with less vigour. Some of this declining enthusiasm may be attributed to that demonstration of superior US power, but some also to the continuing dialogues about the South China Sea held under Indonesian auspices throughout the 1990s. These processes made the PRC aware of both its military deficiencies and the diplomatic costs of pursuing this ambitious territorial claim.

LESSER POWERS: ASEAN

ASEAN

The history of ASEAN has gone through three main phases: accelerating success 1967-97; regional financial crisis, during which it was largely impotent, 1997-99; and a modest recovery 1999-2001. The ASEAN states each now have their own individual concerns which are related to the maintenance of regime stability and the remaining consequences of the financial meltdown. In the foreign policy arena they also have some collective problems involving the ambitions of the PRC, US pressures for the acceleration of globalisation and, in several countries, regional disputes with neighbours. The problems for twenty-first century ASEAN are multi-layered, multi-fissured and multi-dimensional. They are no longer able to be defined in simple Cold War terms, nor indeed within the competing agendas of the regional Great Powers. They deserve careful and individual consideration and regional mechanisms to address them.

Within that context each of the ASEAN states has had mixed fortunes.

Indonesia, the largest of the ASEAN states, is presently going through a process of deep restructuring, the precise dimensions and consequences of which are impossible to predict. It now has an unstable political structure, a resentful armed forces, several actually or potentially rebellious provinces, and a mass population deeply divided along a number of fissures. While its economy has shown some sign of recovery, it is far from recovering the Tiger status that it almost acquired in the mid-1990s. These multi-dimensional pressures could, of course, lead to the disintegration of Indonesia as a post-colonial state, although most observers discount this possibility (Emmerson 2000).[1] By March 2001 the Indonesian Armed Forces were appealing to the US for more assistance to fulfil their task of maintaining national unity. This responsibility would be more appropriately addressed by regional states – if necessary with the support of the US.

The Vietnamese state has clearly long since abandoned its external aspirations for the projection of revolutionary impulses. But its leadership has been unable to agree on an appropriate strategy for dealing with the opportunities and dangers of the processes of globalisation (Nathan 1999). It seems to be almost permanently "twixt reform and retreat". It has, however, abandoned the militaristic impulses that the success of its war against the US generated a quarter century ago. The synonym for strategic theories of the mid-twentieth century, Vietnam in the twenty-first is unlikely to conjure much more than notions of stagnation, irresolution and isolationism. Again, effective regional economic organisations might assist the Vietnamese leadership in its search for an appropriate resolution to these problems. In this effort, US resources would be an invaluable combination with regional states' enabling activities.

Myanmar/Burma, under the continuous although changing rule of its military forces for the last four decades, was unable to access the East Asian Miracle. During the last decade its military has enforced harsher repression assisted by PRC military equipment. While this has brought a higher degree of national unification with the defeat or accommodation of most of the secessionist and revolutionary movements within its territory, it has not brought substantial economic growth. Burma/Myanmar remains one of the region's least developed countries but with a powerful state apparatus nonetheless. The legitimacy of the ruling elite's hold on power has been continually questioned by the National League for Democracy (NLD) led by Aung San Suu Kyi, of course. The only opportunity to assess this occurred in the elections of 1990 when four fifths of the population voted against the government, which ignored the verdict. Recent negotiations with the NLD have raised some optimism for a negotiated settlement. It is too early to tell whether these may succeed, or indeed whether they are genuine. Despite the efforts of the PRC to recruit the military regime to its anti-US cause in the early 1990s, however, Myanmar still stands aside from the regional strategic balance.

Thailand enjoyed its economic hyper-growth for three decades when administrations changed frequently. But the power of the military was a continuing political factor, only exacerbated by the Cold War and continuing competition with Vietnam. In 1997 it was the first country to be hit by the Asian financial meltdown. Thailand has revived somewhat from the 1997 financial crisis. It had a change in government in November 1997 and the new administration subsequently undertook notable but, as elsewhere in the region, limited reforms. Although the results of the 2001 election are still being disputed at the time of writing, it can be said that the influence of the military has been reduced.

On 6 January 2001 Thailand voted in an election that was expected to produce not only a new parliament but also several months of political and constitutional uncertainty. Dozens of winners in the five hundred seat parliament might be disqualified by an aggressive new election commission for vote buying and other irregularities. The apparent victor is Prime Minister, Thaksin Shinawatra, of the Thai Rak (Loves) Thai, who is under indictment and could be removed from office if he fails in an appeal.

The focus now is on Thailand's renewed campaign, under a new constitution, against corruption. Again, this may involve an attack by the regime on itself. This has led to fears of political instability and economic stagnation after the economic crisis of 1997. The former Prime Minister, Chuan Leekpai, came to office during that crisis, in November 1997 when the economy was contracting by 10 per cent a year and the International Monetary Fund (IMF) was administering a $17 billion rescue package. Chuan stabilised the economy and restored growth to 5 per cent a year, but the IMF package caused widespread pain.

Thaksin, a telecommunications tycoon who became one of Thailand's richest men during the decade-long boom that preceded the crash, formed his own party two years ago. Thaksin's own image as a new-style politician was badly damaged when the National Counter Corruption Commission, a centre-piece of the reformist constitution passed three years ago, found he had hidden assets. The military, so powerful in Thai politics since the 1930s, is now apparently on the sidelines. It remains politically influential, although it has said there would be no coup. Since 1997 Thailand has wound back its previously quite ambitious arms procurement policy as it has tried to re-ignite economic growth.

Malaysia has been one of the success stories of East Asia in the last several decades. Its regime has been successful in securing a surprising level of stability among geographically and ethnically distinct political elites. It has used the resulting New Economic Policy to sustain a rapid rate of economic development and to spread widely (if nepotistically) the growing resources thereby generated. It has been among the leading advocates of a regional grouping which excludes external powers, including the US and Australia. Mahathir was a stand out from taking IMF advice in 1997-98, and following the recent admissions from the IMF about mistakes it made in the 1997 crisis, Mahathir's standing is further enhanced. Malaysia has done well, and its government won an election victory on that basis in 1999. It is of course a small if noisy player in the strategic environment. In addition its recent record has exhibited a slowdown in its success. The economy is slowing and the several high prestige one-off projects – including the twin high rise towers, new airport and high technology corridor – are looking less successful.

Malaysia's pursuit of an exclusivist regional grouping, while understandable, is not conducive to regional stability. There is and can be no regional counterweight to the PRC. Without a US presence in East Asia, presently aligned with Australia, South Korea and Japan, PRC dominance will be assured. Given PRC claims and historic aspirations, which includes claims against Malaysian administered territory in the South China Sea, this would not provide a healthy long term strategic balance.

Singapore has been showing more alarm as ripples from the financial crisis of 1997 has spread more widely geographically and into the political sphere. Singapore's assured and rapid ascent to the ranks of High Income Economies and developed countries has depended on regional stability, growing trade and an inflow of capital. All these factors have been at risk since 1997. The Indonesian regime was an early casualty, but the stability of Thailand and the Philippines has not been spared entirely.

Since the dictatorship of Marcos the Philippines has had trouble in joining the East Asian economic miracle. It had a weak economy during the dictatorship and did not become a new Tiger economy after Marcos, especially with a continuing potential political legitimacy crisis. During the period of President Aquino nationalist sentiment and resentment against the perceived US relationship with Marcos led to the eviction of the US military bases but no corresponding buildup of domestic military strength. The result was some panic when the extent of PRC ambitions on adjacent islands became clearer in the mid-1990s. While President Ramos was able to generate economic growth, it was always fragile and seemed vulnerable to his departure. Estrada's populist base in Philippines mass commercial culture at the cost of substantial policy confirmed these fears.

The removal of the populist Estrada and his replacement by the more cerebral new Philippine President Gloria Macapagal Arroyo in January may be a good development. But the country still has not developed a major economy either in bulk or growth rate. It is a small power, with very limited military force projection capacity and may remain politically unstable for a while.

The larger states of ASEAN have become generally more problematic, less self-confident and more self-centred since the onset of the 1997 crisis. Arguably, their regimes are more responsive but also more fragile. The stability of the region is more unpredictable than during the Cold War, and this may be politically healthier. But it also makes the need for a more coherent regional security architecture more pressing, in order that a now more likely domestic disturbance does not readily become a regional crisis.

SOUTHEAST ASIA: THE LESSER STATES

Southeast Asia also contains some smaller states with lesser power.

Cambodia and Laos

Cambodia and Laos were previously peculiar communist powers. The Cambodian regime was viciously introverted and much of its personnel survive in the present authoritarian and incompetent administration. Laos has been little more than a Vietnamese protectorate for a generation. It is unlikely to change much in the foreseeable future. Both these countries weigh lightly in the strategic balance and are more likely to be sites of contestation than sources of power projection.

Brunei

Brunei is an oil rich Muslim dictatorship, aka a Sultanate, important only for its dominant resource. Its independent existence is a result of the policies of the British colonial administration and oil diplomacy in the 1960s. It is unlikely to survive independently forever but the precise nature of its demise is impossible to predict.

East Timor

East Timor is the newest of the states of the region and will only assume its full sovereignty in late 2001. It must be questioned whether that sovereign status will ever be any more than imaginary. East Timor was birthed by the unusual combination of a temporarily determined Australian government and a vacillating regime in Jakarta. Neither may have wanted an independent East Timor state had they been directly polled. They have nonetheless got one. It is unlikely it can survive with any degree of sovereignty without Australian tutelage and, probably, Indonesian benevolence. How long these two strategic characteristics will survive is problematic.

It is often observed that Southeast Asia is in transition from a region of relative success to relative failure. There has been a cyclical recovery in ASEAN countries, but the bulk of structural economic reform still lies ahead. Corporations are weak; and banks have not restored their balance sheets. As a result, ASEAN's share of investment into Asia has fallen dramatically. The World Bank and International Monetary Fund have warned of its vulnerability to a further external shock. ASEAN as a regional group has been drifting since 1997.

THE SOUTHWEST PACIFIC

Australia

The only country of the Southwest Pacific with any substantial power projection capability and strategic importance is Australia. Australia is a global middle power and a dominant regional power in the Southwest Pacific (just). Its capacity is levered up by its alliance with its major US ally. But it is, on its own, not a substantial power to its north, where it is unable to wield power alone in contested circumstances. Its power projection capacity is limited to 'the arc of instability' (or, more accurately, weakness).

Australia is in danger of being excluded by East Asia. Australia's new opponents in Southeast Asia are Malaysia and Indonesia. For 50 years Australia has been a close security partner of the US through the ANZUS treaty. The Howard Government is prepared to become a close economic partner of the US for the first time. This has been widely criticised in Australia as reversing the Asian direction of the last decades. Nonetheless it has substantial economic, financial, cultural and strategic advantages.

The Australia-Indonesian security agreement is finished and the Canberra-Jakarta shared vision (Catley and Dugis 1998) for the region has evaporated. Canberra and Jakarta now struggle to retain a civil relationship, whereas previously they cooperated to shape the strategic architecture of the region. Indonesia has undergone a hugely destabilising transformation. The move to democracy has been coupled with Islamic assertion, virulent nationalism, religious tension and the risk of fragmentation. A democratic Indonesia will be a challenge for Australia and harder than arranging things with Suharto. Indonesia is increasingly a regional opponent of Australia. The dispute over Irian Jaya involves Australia's churches, non-government organisations, media and trade unions supporting self-determination. Australia may be treated in Jakarta as an enemy seeking the dismemberment of the Indonesian nation, as it may yet do.

New Zealand

Australia's other major ally is New Zealand under the 1944 Canberra Pact and a plethora of subsequent agreements. New Zealand is economically in steep decline and has been, for a decade or so, the worst performing of the developed or OECD economies. This has substantially reduced its capacity to contribute to either the global or regional strategic configuration because it lacks the finances to upgrade continually the technology of its armed forces. It also now lacks the will. The Labour/Alliance coalition government is filled with politically good intentions, but it has shown no economic calculations. Partly as a result, the economic decline continues. It is not punching above its weight except where the US permits, for example in the UN. This is paradoxical since the governing Labour Party has taken an anti-US position since the nuclear ships controversy of the 1980s, when the Lange Government refused to support the US in its final and decisive confrontation with the Soviets.

The Nationals Government led by Jenny Shipley in 1998-99 had plans to revive the relationship with the US and took an option on maintaining some air power capacity by leasing/purchasing 28 F-16s. This deal was dropped by the present coalition/Labour government last year. It has also been accused of intending to drop its air strike capability altogether and has, indeed, publicly canvassed this option.

New Zealand will, however, maintain some existing but limited naval capacity to intervene in strategic problems in the South Pacific region. It has already done so in conjunction with Australia in Papua New Guinea (Bougainville), East Timor and the Solomon Islands. How determined it will be in pursuit of such activities in the longer term is questionable in view of the cost and political will which would be required (Catley 2001).

'Australia now finds itself surrounded by states that are either unviable (several states of the South Pacific and possibly East Timor), unstable (Papua New Guinea and Indonesia) or useless (New Zealand)', one participant in an Australian defence seminar was recently quoted as saying.

Arc of Instability

Elsewhere in the region of the South Pacific it is widely feared that an 'arc of instability' may be emerging. This is not entirely fanciful, but for the most part is limited to Melanesia.

In Fiji 2000 witnessed the third coup against the rise of ethnic Indian organised political power. Although both Australia and New Zealand applied sanctions against the new regime – Australia under the Liberals ironically to a greater extent than New Zealand under a more moralistic Leftist government – it is unlikely that Melanesians will permit Indian political rule on the islands and political instability will continue.

In Fiji, Papua New Guinea, and other Melanesian states it may be that recent political upheavals should be viewed as the victory of the pre-colonial over the post-colonial. As in a number of other countries, the Fijian political order is once more decisively in indigenous hands. In West Papua a series of demonstrations have been held against Indonesian rule, which have escalated the 1980s independence movement from a fringe organisation into something to be taken seriously in its secessionist aspirations – as it has already been by sections of the Australian political community.

In Papua New Guinea central government control over the entire country appears to have become progressively more tenuous as regional political aspirations combine with a general economic and administrative retreat to produce the possibility of a fracture in the state apparatus (Standish 1999). This is likely to be exacerbated by the possibility of a military revolt that re-emerged in March 2001.

Ethnic and linguistic tensions have been long endemic in Vanuatu – although they have been more recently contained. In the Solomon Islands a more extensive conflict has broken out over the last few years with quite substantial casualties and the need for an Australia-New

Zealand evacuation program. Most of these problems may be seen as the triumph of the pre-colonial over the post-colonial political structures.

In Polynesia, on the other hand, where the post-colonial states have more or less coincided with the pre-colonial authority and loyalty patterns, there is a greater degree of stability in evidence. In Samoa, Tuvalu and Tonga, pre-colonial political structures have largely re-emerged with some modification into the twenty-first century; in the Cook Island, Niue, Hawaii and New Zealand indigenous political societies have been absorbed into the politics of a larger nation state with resulting greater stability. Micronesia contains no state of sufficient size or geopolitical weight to count for much in this survey.

OPTIONS FOR THE BUSH ADMINISTRATION

The strategic architecture of the Asia Pacific region is still in transition from that of the Cold War. The chief faultline between the major powers still runs along the border between US and PRC power, that is to say, through the Koreas, the Taiwan Strait and between much of ASEAN and the PRC. Unlike during the Cold War, however, discernable progress is being made in the resolution of these disputes along that fissure, notably in the cases of Korean reunification, easing relations between the PRC and ROC, and the PRC's regaining lost territory in Hong Kong and Macao. The PRC pursuit of its claims to adjacent seas has been wound down in recent years.

As the ideological dimension of this great power confrontation eases, however, the regional system of international politics looks more classical and less ordered. For regimes, problems of development, democratisation, identity, and statehood are replacing those of ideology and geo-politics. The region may become less predictable as a result. What is required for the pursuit of regional stability is no longer the strategic architecture of the Cold War and the containment of PRC or Soviet power along the faultline of the rim of mainland East Asia, but a structure of institutions which enable interstate regional solidarity and provide a set of mechanisms to resolve the now more likely problems of regime stability, national cohesion and inter-state dispute.

Post-Cold War US interests coincide with these objectives. The main threat to US objectives is no longer communist aggression, but rather a series of inter-layered social, economic and political issues that break out from a variety of sources with unpredictable regularity. Cold War alliance patterns will not deal with them. Nor will direct US intervention in pursuit of clearly defined US interests always provide an appropriate policy, still less one that is acceptable to regional powers.

If there were one direction in which US policymakers might probe during the next few years to enhance the prospects for stability in the region, it might be a firmer foundation for a regional security architecture along the lines that have been constructed in Europe. The viability for such a project will lie largely with the policies of and relations between the PRC and the US. If President Bush had not been too determined in his unilateral pursuit of US national interests and Beijing more accommodating in its determination to restore China's regional power, this may have been a task within reach. In fact it moved in the other direction.

THE BUSH ADMINISTRATION'S TAIWAN POLICY 2001

Asia has become more of a focus for the foreign policy of USA during the Bush administration. This is largely because the other major area of geo-political power, Europe, presents fewer problems which require urgent attention at the onset of the twenty-first century. The third area of major geo-political contestation, the Middle East, has been designated for low key US diplomacy by a Republican administration less eager to pursue and support Israeli interests. In East Asia, the opportunities and risks are greater, largely because it is the location of the only serious potential rival to US power – the PRC. The Republicans have also long espoused a policy that shows stronger support for the integrity of the Taiwanese state. As the ROC has developed economically, democratised, and then, in the elections of 2000, thrown off the KMT, so support for a more overtly pro-ROC policy has spread. Since support for such a policy has long been strong in both the Congress and the Republican Party, it is hardly surprising that it has seen some expression in the foreign policy of George W. Bush.

During the 1990s, especially during the period of President Clinton's second term, the US administration clearly paid considerable attention to its relationship with the PRC. Broadly, it tried to establish a 'strategic partnership' after the rifts which emerged after the Taiwan Strait crisis of 1996 and, later, the US bombing of the PRC Embassy in Belgrade in 1999. This policy not only put the ROC in an unfavourable position, but also neglected the most important ally of the US in East Asia – Japan. Therefore, many conservative Congressmen, and particularly Republicans, frequently made strong criticisms of the Democratic administration's seemingly pro-PRC stance. It was matched by frequent and appropriate warnings about the considerable military buildup being undertaken by the PLA and the fact that this was most commonly directed at strengthening the PRC capacity to deal with the United States, should the need arise.

During the campaign for the year 2000 US Presidential election, the Republican camp, including its candidate George W. Bush and most of his aides, had clearly shown their own taste for a tougher stance toward the PRC. After their victory, US policy toward the Taiwan Strait certainly became a noteworthy issue for checking any policy movement. The previous pro-PRC policy was indeed adjusted, and this impacted on the US-ROC-PRC triangular relationship. Central to the Clinton policy had been the 'strategic ambiguity' posture, which did not unequivocally commit the US to defend Taiwan against the PRC, thereby limiting Taiwan's room for manoeuvre while – it hoped – leaving sufficient deterrence against a PRC attack on the island state.

In early 2001 the new administration seemed to abandon the doctrine of 'Strategic Ambiguity'. On 25 April 2001, President Bush released what was claimed by critics to be a statement of an 'ambiguous strategic ambiguity' policy[2] towards the Taiwan Strait. He expressed his resolve to defend the ROC against the PRC, while supporting the 'one China' policy at the same time. On the program 'Good Morning America' on the ABC, on the morning of 25 April, Bush replied to an interviewer that the US had an 'obligation' to defend the Taiwanese and 'the Chinese must understand that'. When asked whether that would be 'With the full force of American military?', Bush responded, 'What ever it took to help Taiwan' (*Washington Post* 2001a).

Bush's declaration on the ABC show immediately raised a new controversy over America's Taiwan policy. Many US China experts, such as Kenneth Leiberthal and David M. Lampton, said that Bush's initial comments on the ABC went beyond previous American commitments and would have serious implications for the US-PRC relationship (Babington and Milbank 2001). 'This clearly does go beyond what any previous administration has indicated either orally or in writing', said Leiberthal, previously Director of Asian Affairs at the Clinton administration's National Security Council. He said Bush even went beyond the US commitment under the 1955 US-ROC defence pact, which was abrogated as one of the preconditions to establishing the formal US-PRC relationship in 1979 (Mufson 2001).

At hearings before the House Subcommittee for Asian and Pacific Affairs, Professor David Shambaugh commented that President Bush might have been misunderstood and would probably correct himself later (*China Times* 2001b). Senator Joseph R. Biden Jr (Democratic, Delaware) also criticised Bush's comments, which he said infringed the 1979 Taiwan Relations Act, as the TRA had not promised Taiwan defence from the US against the PRC (Biden 2001).

Several hours later, in a CNN interview, Bush stressed that 'the Chinese must hear' that his administration 'is willing to uphold the spirit of the Taiwan relation law, the Taiwan Relations Act'. He also said, 'Nothing has really changed in policy, as far as I'm concerned. This is what other presidents have said, and I will continue to say so'. Nevertheless, he did not again say he would 'defend Taiwan'; instead, he repeatedly stressed his resolve to 'help Taiwan to defend herself'. Besides, he also said that 'at the same time, we support the one-China policy, and we expect the dispute to be resolved peacefully'. When asked by the interviewer, 'What if Taiwan declared independence first?', Bush replied, 'First, I have said that I will do what it takes to help Taiwan defend herself, and the Chinese must understand. Secondly, I certainly hope Taiwan adheres to the "one China" policy. And a declaration of independence is not the "one China" policy, and we will work with Taiwan to make sure that that doesn't happen. We need a peaceful resolution of this issue' (*Washington Post* 2001a).

Bush's remarks on CNN seemed a retreat from what he had said on the ABC. The main point, however, was whether the US under Bush would change or had changed its Taiwan policy. Although Bush himself and his National Security Advisor, Condoleezza Rice, have both said that they did not change the long-standing US Taiwan policy, they indeed had changed their policy. The Bush administration had abandoned the ambiguous policy concerning Taiwan's security, and most of its ranking officials, including Vice-President Cheney, Defense Secretary Rumsfeld, and Rice herself, stressed a few days later that Bush's remarks meant 'we are very serious about defending Taiwan' (*Agence France Presse* 2001; *China Times* 2001d). Cheney also stressed that the Bush administration is 'less ambiguous around the world', with a style that differs from that of former President Bill Clinton. 'What we have now is a straight-talking president from Texas who says exactly what he thinks, people around the world will get used to that', added Cheney (*Agence France Presse* 2001).

To some extent, this was actually merely an adjustment of US Taiwan Policy. At the very least, the Bush administration had clearly expressed its resolve of upholding the TRA and helping Taiwan defend herself, which the Clinton administration had never done. In fact, before the US 2000 Presidential election, George W. Bush had on many occasions shown his tough stance toward the PRC and his resolve to adjust Clinton's apparently pro-PRC policy. On 6 December 1999 and 2 March 2000, he remarked at Republican Presidential nominee debates that if the PRC got aggressive with the Taiwanese, he would help Taiwan defend itself (*Washington Post* 1999; 2000a). On 21 November, he also said that, 'to Taiwan, I think it's important for us to have a viable anti-ballistic missile system that'll help keep the peace' (*Washington Post* 2000b). In addition to these statements, he also said that he supported the Taiwan Security Enhancement Act, which was overwhelmingly passed by the House of Representatives in 2000.

During the campaign for the 2000 US Presidential election, under Paul Wolfowitz's guidance, the Republicans strongly criticised Clinton for his supposedly pro-PRC policy. With respect to the 'one China' policy, the Republicans just 'acknowledged' its existence without endorsing it. The Republican platform reads, 'America has acknowledged the view that there is one China. Our policy is based on the principle that there must be no use of force by China against Taiwan'. Bruce Jackson, Chairman of the Republican platform subcommittee on foreign policy, further rejected the 'one China' policy as the basis of their foreign policy toward Asia. Instead, he stressed that 'our policy in Asia is based on freedom, democracy and the peaceful resolution of disputes'. As for the policy of 'strategic ambiguity' toward Taiwan's security, the Republicans also eroded it by stating in the platform that if the PRC attacked the ROC, 'America will help Taiwan defend itself'. Jackson also said, 'What we said is that it should be resolved peacefully. We are correcting the imprecision that has been creeping in' (Mufson 2000).

These developments set the stage for changing the US Taiwan policy by the new administration. In fact, most of the Bush administration's ranking officials, including Vice-President Cheney, National Security Adviser, Condoleezza Rice, Secretary of Defense, Donald H. Rumsfeld, and Deputy Secretary of Defense, Paul D. Wolfowitz, have been regarded as hard-line, anti-PRC conservatives. Some of the other senior officials, such as Deputy Secretary of State, Richard L. Armitage, had also explicitly advocated the scrapping of 'strategic ambiguity' in the past (Mufson 2001). For example, a report was published by the US *Business Week* in May 2001, which said that during a visit to Beijing in 1999, the now Defense Secretary Rumsfeld found that Jiang Ze-min was dubbed the 'unifier' on the archway of a museum, and a mural inside the museum showing Chinese military attacking Taiwan with massive missiles, ships, submarines, and tanks. Rumsfeld was jolted and believed that the Clinton administration's pro-PRC position had made the PRC doubt US resolve to risk its soldiers and commercial interests to fight for Taiwan. Wolfowitz delivered a speech in Washington in November 1999, saying that previous US policies of ambiguity had elsewhere been misunderstood and led to the 1950 Korean War and the 1990-91 Persian Gulf War. He feared that the PRC would doubt that the use of force against the ROC would be met with strong American response in the future. He also emphasised, 'If we leave any ambiguity about that, all we are doing is encouraging Chinese actions that could get both of us in trouble' (*Business Week Online* 2001).

In addition to Bush's strong remarks about defending Taiwan against military threats from the PRC, there were other signs that demonstrated the Bush administration's Taiwan policy was different from that of the Clinton administration. These included an increase in US arms sales to Taiwan. Since the 1982 US-PRC Communiqué, US arms sales to the ROC have been a controversial issue between the US and the PRC and a larger indicator of the US-ROC relationship. In recent years, as the PRC modernised its military forces and it deployed about 300 short- and medium-range missiles in its southeastern coast opposite the ROC, the balance of military force across the Taiwan Strait gradually shifted, to the detriment of the ROC. On 26 February 1999, the Pentagon sent a report to the US Congress concluding that, by 2005, the PLA would 'possess the capability to attack Taiwan with air and missile strikes, which would degrade key military facilities and damage the island's economic infrastructure' (US Department of Defense 1999). This caused deep Congressional concern over Taiwan's security. The Clinton administration, however, refused to sell many advanced weapons which had been requested by the ROC. In 2000, in spite of the prompting of many pro-ROC Congressmen, the Clinton administration deferred selling to the ROC the sophisticated Aegis destroyer, which could effectively reduce the threat of a PRC missile attack and was strongly opposed by the PRC.

In 2001, before the annual US-ROC military meeting about the arms sales, due in April, the issue drew broad domestic and external attention, and was viewed as an indicator of the Bush administration's Taiwan Strait policy. Many pro-ROC congressmen urged the new administration to carry out the TRA and provide Taiwan with more sophisticated arms. In order to try to block the arms sale, the PRC announced it would dispatch its Vice-Premier, Qien Qi-chen, and some previous PRC Ambassadors to the US to visit President Bush, his father, Henry Kissinger, and some of former President Bush's influential aides in March, before the scheduled US-ROC arms sales meeting.

In response, on 8 March, Secretary of State, Colin Powell, answered a question from Senator Jesse Helms, Chairman of the US Senate's Foreign Relations Committee, by saying that the US would observe the 1982 'Six Assurances' and would not consult with anyone from the PRC regarding arms sales to the ROC (*Taiwan Headlines* 2001). During the hearing, it was also noteworthy that Powell twice used the term 'Republic of China', which was taboo during the Clinton administration.

On 23 April, just two days before Bush pledged to help the ROC to defend itself, the US approved the sale to Taiwan of a weaponry package estimated at more than $US4 billion, which included four Kidd-class destroyers, eight diesel-powered submarines, a dozen P-3 Orion surveillance aircraft, known as submarine-hunters, and some submarine-launched Harpoon anti-ship missiles. This was the largest US arms sale to the ROC since 1992, when under the previous Republican administration the US sold the ROC 150 F-16 fighters.

According to the US Defense Department, because Taiwan's military was not up to speed, it would take eight or ten years to build, develop, sell and deliver the Aegis missile systems. Therefore, the Bush administration decided against unnecessarily irritating the PRC by selling the Aegis system to Taiwan (CNN 2001). The Kidd-class destroyers, which are less sophisticated than the Aegis destroyers but could be delivered to the ROC within two years, provided the best and most effective substitute. In addition, Bush administration officials assured some influential conservative congressmen, who demanded a more muscular arms package to Taiwan, that the President was open to a later sale of the more high-tech weapons, if the PRC continued to deploy short and intermediate range missiles targeting the ROC (CNN 2001). The US had kept the 'one China' policy, even though it was gradually being eroded.

Although the ROC did not get the Aegis destroyers this year, most other items on its shopping list were approved. The most significant was the sale of submarines and anti-submarine forces, because 'Underwater defense is the most fragile front in Taiwan's efforts to modernize its forces', according to Yang Chih-heng, deputy director of the Taiwan-based Division of Strategic and International Studies (*China Times* 2001a). The Pentagon's 2000 *Annual Report on Military Power of the PRC* agreed, saying, 'Chinese numerical superiority in submarines constitute a threat to the Taiwan Navy...the Taiwan Navy probably would have an extremely difficult time opposing a naval blockade with its existing resources' (US Department of Defense 2000a). The ROC had tried to buy submarines for many years but had failed to acquire them even from US allies keen for sales, such as Australia. Fearing submarines would be considered as offensive weapons by the PRC, previous US Presidents had declined to sell submarines to the ROC. Nevertheless, Bush was convinced that the ROC needed a more up-to-date submarine capability to defend itself against PRC attack and/or economic blockade (*New York Times* 2001b). Furthermore, with the P-3's range of 2,500 km, the ROC could expand its anti-submarine capabilities from the Taiwan Strait to as far as the South China Sea or the Pacific (*Taipei Times* 2001a). The Bush administration decided on the arms sales to the ROC in spite of diplomatic warnings and strong opposition from the PRC. The deal won praise from the US Congress. Senate Chairman of Foreign Relations Committee, Jesse Helms, praised President Bush for his 'courageous' decision, and said that 'the US, at long last, has an administration that is taking the critical matter of Taiwan's defense seriously' (*Taipei Times* 2001a).

On 25 April, in an interview with the US-based *Time* magazine, Bush defended this decision saying that upholding the TRA was his obligation, although the US-PRC relationship would be more complicated in the future (*China Times* 2001c). Bush's decision seemed to signify that the ROC had come out of the shadow of the 1982 US-PRC Communiqué, which had seriously restrained US arms sales to the ROC.

Two other developments demonstrate the new US determination over Taiwan's security. On 27 April, the *Washington Post* reported there was a secret US plan for military operations toward the Taiwan Strait stored in the headquarters of the US military forces in the Pacific (*Washington Post* 2001b). And in early May, the ROC military confirmed that Admiral Blair, Commander of US forces in the Pacific, had made an extremely rare and secret visit to Taiwan on 1 April. He had then quickly returned to Hawaii to attend to the incident of a collision between a US surveillance plane and a harassing PRC fighter jet (*Taipei Times* 2001b). Of course, this incident exacerbated the other dimensions of increasing strain between Washington and Beijing. Admiral Blair's staff stayed in Taiwan to assess the ROC Army's defensive capabilities and to discuss with the ROC military plans for establishing a 'safe corridor' in the Taiwan Strait for US aircrafts and ships, should the US need to come to Taiwan's aid (*China Times* 2001e).

Clearly, the Bush administration was more strongly determined to help the ROC to defend itself against the PRC than was its Democratic predecessor. In fact, this more hard-line position had been expressed since 1999, when the US 2000 Presidential election was effectively launched. The Pentagon Report on Implementation of the TRA, released on 19 December 2000, would merely have strengthened Bush's determination. It says, 'The US takes its obligation to assist Taiwan in maintaining a self-defense capability very seriously...This is not only because it is mandated by US law in the TRA, but also because it is in our own national interest' (US Department of Defense 2000b).

In addition to Bush's remarks about assisting Taiwan to defend itself and the US-ROC arms sales, there were other messages showing that the long-standing US 'one China' policy was being gradually eroded. In late April 2001, the Bush administration approved a visa for the ROC President, Chen Shui-bian, for two stopovers during his visit to and from Latin America in the next May. Chen was, of course, elected to the Presidency in early 2000, was the first non-KMT leader of ROC/Taiwan, and had long been associated with popular and DPP agitation for Taiwan to become an independent state. This stopover was a breakthrough in US-ROC diplomatic history, as Chen became the first incumbent Taiwan President to visit New York since the ROC retreated from the Chinese mainland in 1949. Besides, the US accorded President Chen considerable freedom, including permitting his meeting with over 20 Congressmen in New York. It was a sharp contrast to his previous stopover in August 2000, when the Clinton administration set strict conditions for a brief layover that kept him in political quarantine. In 2001, the Bush administration explicitly announced that meetings between the US Congressmen and a foreign President would 'advance US interests'. The Department of State also assured Chen in advance that his stopovers should be 'convenient, comfortable, and safe'. The Bush administration's treatment of President Chen was widely regarded by many as being a 'visit' of almost official status.

Although the US Republican camp expressed a tougher stance toward the PRC during the 2000 Presidential campaign, some observers believed that Bush would, like previous US Presidents, including Reagan and Clinton, criticise the PRC at the beginning of their tenure and change afterwards. But the current international situation is different. In Reagan's era, the US was continuing to play the 'China card', which Kissinger and Carter had dealt, to contain the USSR; in Clinton's era, the US was eager to 'comprehensively engage' the PRC to deal with other international issues. Both these administrations had to cooperate with the PRC to pursue their other strategic goals.

The situation in 2001, however, is different. The PRC is regarded by the Bush administration as the only existing serious competitor to US hegemony and its probable rival in the future for regional dominance and systemic superiority. In such circumstances, geo-political competition may well replace strategic partnership. The more determined US policy towards the protection of the ROC state may well be the early signs of this evolution and harbinger of a new relationship.

CONCLUSION

Unlike in the European/Atlantic sphere, no regional security or economic architecture has been constructed in post-Cold War Asia to enable multilateral resolution to major issues and disputes. In the late stages of the Clinton administration the opportunity for creating such an environment appeared to exist. The ASEAN initiative, the AFR had extensive contacts with 'dialogue partners' and APEC had survived the Asian financial meltdown, even with its reputation degraded. The reduced regime confidence in many of the regional states reduced economic growth, and renewed apprehension about PRC aspirations, combined to present the opportunity for the US-PRC strategic partnership to initiate a new round of regional and multilateral institutional building.

The record of most of the personnel in the new Republican administration gave little cause for believing this opportunity would be seized. By mid-2001, indeed, the opportunity appeared to be lost. In the relationship between the two dominant powers in Asia, the US and the PRC were once again becoming more like competitors than partners.

REFERENCES

Agence France Presse (2001) 30 April.

Babington, Charles, and Dana Milbank (2001) 'Bush Advisers to Limit Damage'. *Washington Post* April 27.

Biden Jr., Joseph R. (2001) 'Not So Deft on Taiwan'. *Washington Post* May 2.

Business Week Online (2001) 'Sea Change on China: The Bush Team Takes a Hard Line'. May 21.

Buzo, A. (1999) *The Guerilla Dynasty: Politics and Leadership in North Korea.* Boulder, Colorado: Westview Press.

Catley, B. (1999) 'The Arrogance of Power'. *Contemporary Southeast Asia* August.

—— (2001) *Waltzing with Matilda; Should New Zealand Join Au*stralia? Wellington: Dark Horse Publishing.

Catley, B., and Makmur Keliat (1997) *Spratlys, The Crisis in the South China Sea.* UK: Ashgate.

Catley, B., and V. Dugis (1998) *Australian Indonesian Relations Since 1945.* UK: Ashgate.

China Times (2001a) April 25.

—— (2001b) April 27.

—— (2001c) April 29.

—— (2001d) May 7.

—— (2001e) May 14.

CNN (2001) April 24.

Emmerson, D. (2000) 'Will Indonesia Survive?' *Foreign Affairs* May-June.

Helweg, M.D. (2000) 'Japan: A Rising Sun?' *Foreign Affairs* July-August.

Ji, You (1999) *The Armed Forces of China.* Sydney: Allen and Unwin.

Lloyd, Grayson (2000) 'Indonesia's Future Prospects: Separatism, Decentralisation and the Survival of the Unitary State'. *Australian Commonwealth Parliamentary Library,* Current Issues Brief 17 1999-2000, Foreign Affairs, Defence and Trade Group, 27 June.

Mosler, D., and B. Catley (2000) *Global America: Imposing Liberalism on a Recalcitrant World.* New York: Praeger.

Mufson, Steven (2000) 'In GOP, a Simmering Struggle on China Policy'. *Washington Post* August 22.

—— (2001) 'President Pledges Defense of Taiwan'. *Washington Post* April 26.

Mulgan, A.G. (2000) 'Japan: A Setting Sun?' *Foreign Affairs* July-August.

Nathan, Melina (1999) 'Vietnam: Is Globalisation a Friend or a Foe?' *Southeast Asian Affairs.* Singapore: ISEAS.

New York Times (2000) 'Man in the News: A Pentagon Veteran – Donald Henry Rumsfeld'. December 29.

New York Times (2001a) January 21.

New York Times (2001b) April 24.

Standish, Dr. Bill (1999) Parliament of Australia, Parliamentary Library, Research Paper 4 1999-2000, 'Papua New Guinea 1999: Crisis of Governance', Foreign Affairs, Defence and Trade Group, September 21.

Rice, C. (2000) 'Promoting the National Interest'. *Foreign Affairs* January-February.

Taipei Times (2001a) April 25.

—— (2001b) May 2.

Taiwan Headlines (2001) March 9.

US Department of Defense (1999) *The Security Situation in the Taiwan Strait.* Report to Congress, February 26. http://usinfo.org/usia/usinfo.state.gov/regional/ea/uschina/twnst. htm

—— (2000a) *Annual Report on Military Power of People's Republic of China.* Report to Congress, June 22. http://usinfo.org/usia/usinfo.state.gov/regional/ea/uschina/dodrpt 00.htm

—— (2000b) *Report to Congress on Implementation of Taiwan Relations Act,* December 19. http://usinfo.org/usia/usinfo.state.gov/regional/ea/uschina/taisec.htm

Washington Post (1999) December 6.

—— (2000a) March 2.

—— (2000b) November 21.

—— (2001a) April 25.

—— (2001b) April 27.

Weeks, S.B., and C.A. Meconis (1999) *The Armed Forces of the USA in the Asia-Pacific Region.* Sydney: Allen and Unwin.

ENDNOTES

[1] See Emmerson 2000; and Lloyd 2000, which concludes similarly, 'the Indonesian nation state is unlikely to disintegrate at the moment'.

[2] US Senator Joseph R. Biden Jr criticised Bush's remarks as a policy of 'ambiguous strategic ambiguity'. See Biden 2001.

Chapter 9

THE DIFFERENTIAL IMPACT OF THE ECONOMIC CRISIS ON THAILAND, INDONESIA AND SOUTH KOREA

Chung Sang-Hwa
Institute of East and West Studies
Yonsei University
Korea

INTRODUCTION

Korea began the process of industrialisation in the late 1960s, followed by Thailand and Indonesia in the mid-1970s. Despite variations in resource endowments, all three countries had recorded such impressive records of industrialisation[1] that international society loudly applauded their economic successes. In the late 1990s, however, the Asian economic crisis had entered a totally new phase, spawned by the July 1997 foreign currency crisis in Thailand. 'Currency crisis', defined as a large drop in the value of currency in a short period of time, had spread to Southeast Asia, and eventually reached Korea. Among the victims, Thailand, Indonesia and South Korea (hereafter Korea) asked the International Monetary Fund (IMF) for rescue loans, but Malaysia, which also had been hard hit by the crisis, closed its foreign exchange market instead of requesting the IMF for help.

The three Greater East Asian countries had several characteristics in common when they encountered economic crisis: they relied on trade in the process of economic development; enjoyed high levels of liquidity; had recently introduced financial liberalisation; and had opaque corporate and banking systems.[2] After they accepted the IMF stabilisation programs, they also faced such problems together as the precipitate decline of currency value, the instability of financial sectors, market contractions, decreases in investment, and increases in unemployment. As of early 2001, the economic crisis appears to be contained in Korea, but it still scratches Indonesia with its fingernails, and Thailand is located somewhere between the two.

Although there has been much research on the Asian economic crises, many issues still remain unclear and unanswered. Were the crises unavoidable? What was the decisive cause(s) of the foreign exchange crises? Were the IMF interventions adequate? What were the political and economic consequences of the crises? Should and can Asian countries reform their political and economic management styles? Which international political economy approach, for example, the interdependence school, neomercantilism, or structuralism, more adequately explains the crises?

This analysis examines the economic crises of Indonesia, Thailand and Korea in order to understand better their causes, processes and consequences. A comparative study has an advantage in that it clarifies the issue by contrasting similarities and differences. In the next section, the pre-crisis political and economic developments are compared. The following section explores the causes of the three countries' economic crises. Then, IMF programs and each country's reform efforts, and the consequences of the economic crises, are surveyed. The last section critically assesses the nature of the Asian economic crises based on the discussions of the previous parts, and presents theoretical and policy implications.

BEFORE THE ECONOMIC CRISES

1. Politics and Economics

Thailand had recorded spectacular economic growth rates since it implemented export-led industrialisation policies in the mid-1970s. Annual growth rates had been over 8 per cent and new buildings had changed the skyline of Bangkok (Table 1). In the early 1990s, the Anand and the first Chuan Governments had pushed on deregulation and liberalisation in order to attract more foreign investment. In 1996, however, an economic slowdown was expected and the Bank of Thailand revised its estimation of GDP growth rates from 8 per cent at the end of 1995 to 6.7 per cent. Exports were inactive and the current deficit was rising (Table 2). The Banharn Government in 1995 and the new Chavalit Government in 1996 could not handle the situation appropriately. Deregulation and financial liberalisation, along with political reforms, had weakened these governments' discretion and power. The fixed exchange rate system could not respond swiftly to the fast-growing trade deficit.

The Thai economy started to show signs of fading in 1996, and by early 1997 GDP growth rates were not as robust as previously. The GDP growth was sluggish in the third quarter of 1996, and recorded a minus growth rate in the first quarter of 1997. While inflation had been modest (between 4.2 per cent and 7.4 per cent) (www.nso.go.kr/cgi-bin/sws_999.cgi 2001),[3] external debt reached at the end of 1996 was US$108.7 billion (about 60 per cent of GDP) where short-term debts accounted for US$47.7 billion (43.9 per cent of the total external debt) (www.bot.or.th/bothomepage/databank/EconData 2001). In 1997, Thai external debt increased further, and so did the proportion of private debt. The government and the central bank failed to control the excessive borrowings of private financial institutions (Punyaratabandhu 1998, 162).[4] In July, the Thai government adopted a floating exchange system, but foreign investors competed to withdraw their money from the Thai market. The popularity of the Chavalit Government had dropped considerably. In the same month the cornered government asked for a Stand-by Credit Arrangement from IMF.

Table 1 Gross Domestic Product, Q1 1996 - Q3 2000

Year and Quarter	Thailand (mil. of baht)	Indonesia (bil. of Rp)	S. Korea (bil. of won)
1996			
Q1	1,120,089	122,530	94,533
Q2	1,151,915	128,846	102,169
Q3	1,154,597	136,940	104,870
Q4	1,196,231	144,253	116,907
1997			
Q1	1,159,123	145,801	101,061
Q2	1,168,765	149,406	110,337
Q3	1,181,739	163,252	113,227
Q4	1,230,622	169,252	112,865
1998			
Q1	1,211,955	217,654	107,674
Q2	1,118,301	232,387	107,992
Q3	1,112,595	273,463	108,357
Q4	1,185,580	266,108	120,344
1999			
Q1	1,162,112	281,052	107,797
Q2	1,095,676	279,712	116,412
Q3	1,144,423	277,583	121,847
Q4	1,213,177	281,095	137,722
2000			
Q1	1,229,472	301,929	121,240
Q2	1,197,668	317,604	126,123
Q3	1,226,205	329,279	130,426

Data: Indonesia - www.bi.go.id/bank_indonesia2 (2001);
    Thailand – www.bot.or.th /bothomepage/databank/EconData (2001);
    S. Korea – www.nso.go.kr/cgi-bin/sws_999.cgi (2001).

Until mid-1997, Indonesia under Suharto had healthier macroeconomic indicators than Thailand and Korea. GDP had grown steadily (Table 1) and inflation had been contained under 10 per cent (www.nso.go.kr/cgi-bin/sws_999.cgi 2001). Although current account was in deficit, the trade balance was positive (Table 2). Also, Indonesian external debt had been slightly decreasing in 1996 and in early 1997, from US$64 billion to US$56 billion (about 25 per cent of GDP) (www.bi.go.id/bank_indonesia2 2001). However, the New Order had been eroding the soundness of the Indonesian economy. Mostly Chinese private banks had been spawned by the 1988 deregulation, and many of them had connections with Suharto's family and friends. Foreign investments were wasted in support of prestige national projects such as the construction of a bridge to Malaysia and the tallest building in Jakarta (Bird 1998, 172).

Before the crisis, Bank Indonesia had set the rupiah's exchange rates to be depreciated 4-5 per cent annually. This 'managed' floating foreign exchange system was doomed to collapse when international funds massively flowed out, as occurred in Thailand, and the rupiah was depreciated by 9 per cent in August. The government further eased the 49 per cent limitation of foreign investors' stakes in corporations for holding foreign capital, but even this could not compensate for the short-term borrowings amounting to US$33 billion. In November, the Indonesian government and the IMF agreed on a US$38 billion package loan.

Table 2 National Account Balance / Trade Balance (millions of US$), Q1 1996 - Q2 2000

Year/Quarter	Thailand	Indonesia	S. Korea
1996			
Q1	-3,420 / -2,741	-2,034 / 1,166	-4,358 / -2,383
Q2	-4,888 / -3,032	-2,564 / 910	-5,127 / -3,125
Q3	-3,628 / -2,154	-2,111 / 1,343	-7,249 / -5,528
Q4	-2,756 / -1,561	-954 / 2,529	-6,272 / -3,931
1997			
Q1	-2,098 / -1,492	-2,192 / 1,438	-7,353 / -5,402
Q2	-3,134 / -1,413	-1,103 / 3,482	-2,723 / -806
Q3	-696 / 705	-1,393 / 2,176	-2,053 / -27
Q4	2,907 / 3,773	-201 / 2,979	3,962 / 3,055
1998			
Q1	4,183 / 4,100	1,001 / 4,821	10,712 / 9,717
Q2	2,799 / 3,633	669 / 4,971	11,007 / 11,458
Q3	3,406 / 4,148	1,682 / 5,100	9,745 / 10,596
Q4	3,854 / 4,357	744 / 3,537	8,901 / 9,856
1999			
Q1	3,954 / 3,671	1,512 / 4,039	6,057 / 6,770
Q2	2,220 / 3,274	852 / 4,457	6,146 / 7,902
Q3	3,003 / 3,597	1,886 / 6,344	6,597 / 6,923
Q4	3,251 / 3,471	1,535 / 5,804	5,676 / 6,776
2000			
Q1	3,188 / 3,350	1,898 / 6,264	-
Q2	1,484 / 2,408	-	-

Data: www.nso.go.kr/cgi-bin/sws_999.cgi (2001).

Korea was economically different from Indonesia and Thailand.[5] It was a member of the OECD and the eleventh largest economy in the world, and its per capita income was US$13,269 in 1995.[6] The history of Korea's economic development also had been considerably more seasoned than those of Thailand and Indonesia. Moreover, the country's development was mainly owing to the internal savings gained from export, although foreign capital had had its share. Korean GDP growth was set back in early 1997 (Table 1), but not many seriously worried about it because macroeconomic indicators such as inflation, the unemployment rate, and fiscal balance appeared to be sound.[7] The foreign currency market had maintained stability until October 1997, despite the Southeast Asian countries' foreign currency crises.

However, several interrelated factors had eroded the robustness of the Korean economy. First of all, trade had been under continuous stress in the 1990s. The US, suspecting Korea to be another Japan, had pressed heavily on the Korean government to reduce its trade surplus. In 1992, Korea started to record a trade deficit with the US.[8] Meanwhile, other East Asian countries, notably China, had emerged as competitors in international markets. Thanks to the democratisation in the latter half of the 1980s, labour unions and strikes had appeared, and wages had increased at unprecedented levels. In the presence of deteriorating businesses, Korean corporate owners tried in 1996 to trim their sizes by legalising lay-offs. However, the relevant bill could not pass the legislature because of strong opposition from both the unions and the opposition party. Korean companies were obliged to rely on borrowing to cope with decreasing profits.[9] Taking advantage of the recently introduced liberalisation and deregulation,[10] financial institutions, especially the newly established secondary (non-bank) financial institutions, competitively invited short-term loans from foreign financial institutions.[11] The result was growing national debt; external debt had increased from US$127.5 billion in 1995 to US$163.5 billion (about 32 per cent of GDP) in 1996.

Making things worse, the ratio of short-term borrowing in total foreign debt had been increasing and rose to 59 per cent at the end of 1997, while the foreign exchange reserves usable during this period had been reduced to approximately US$33 billion (www.nso.go.kr/cgi-bin/sws_999.cgi 2001). In addition to this, business accounts of major firms and banks were deteriorating due both to the bankruptcies of some big companies like Hanbo and to the foreign exchange crises in Southeast Asian countries.[12] Foreign creditors refused to roll over their loans, and the lame duck of the Kim Young Sam Government prevented Korea from steering clear of economic instability. In December 1997, the won slumped and foreign currency reserves dropped from US$22.5 billion in October to the value of US$3.9 billion. The Korean government, afraid of a moratorium, urgently requested help from the IMF, and a relief loan of US$55 billion was agreed between the IMF and Korean government on 3 December.

To summarise, macroeconomic statistics reveal that the Thai economy was the worst among the three countries before their crises. Its production looked worse than that of Korea, and, above all, its debt was too heavy compared to its GDP. If we look at just macroeconomic data, it is not easy to understand why Indonesia had fallen into an economic crisis.[13] Above all, the political leaderships of Indonesia and Korea had been without serious threats, although Thai governments had been short-term as usual. However, all three countries' governments could not effectively control their economies because of recent deregulation and liberalisation.

2. International Perspectives

It is not difficult to explain an event after it took place; more illuminating is an examination of what the international society had in mind when the crisis was in progress. The IMF claimed that it had given the Thai government continuous warnings for the 18 months preceding the foreign exchange crisis. However, according to Gohama (1999, 128), it was nothing but an *ex post facto* excuse. Although the Thai financial industry had shown signs of unhealthiness, there is little evidence indicating that the IMF as well as individual governments did in fact realise the formidable seriousness of the problem. On the contrary, the IMF and the World Bank reports continuously praised Thailand as a model country of sound macroeconomic management and open economy. Even foreign debt, the lion's share of which belonged in private hands instead of being the direct responsibility of the government, was regarded as a sign of Thailand's favorable business environment for foreign investors

(Focus on the Global South and CAFOD 1998, 12-16). Thailand's 1996 economic inactivity was regarded by the other East Asian governments and international institutions as a sign of tuning up its overheated growth (*Joongang Ilbo* 1997). It is not surprising that Thai governments and financial institutions failed to respond accordingly. Like Thailand, Indonesia was also praised by international financial institutions as a country of successful macroeconomic management, deregulation and liberalisation, as was Korea. Korean president Kim Young Sam argued just several days before his country's asking for rescue that Korea was different from Southeast Asian countries.

In short, it would be reasonable to say that Asian countries and international agents, with the exception of speculative investors, did not take the situation seriously before the crises became apparent.

CAUSES OF THE ECONOMIC CRISES

There are many analyses that address the causes of the Asian crises (see Goldstein 1998; Delhaise 1998, 11-32; Yoo and Moon 1999; Warne 1998; Demetriades and Fattough 1999). The causes presented range widely from a simple liquidity bottleneck, a US conspiracy, and so on, to the defects of Confucian state and corporate governances.[14] Now there seems a general agreement that all of these factors are interwoven.

1. Internal Factors

Among the explanations focusing on internal factors, the negativity (or out-of-datedness) of the East Asian development model or Confucian capitalism are prominent. The so-called East Asian development model[15] is characterised by the close formal and informal relationship between government, business and finance sectors. It sometimes means the patriarchal character of governmental leadership and the protection of domestic industries, and, in an extreme expression, crony capitalism where human networks play a much more important role than institutional provisions. Of the three countries, Korea seems to fit the first type, and Suharto's Indonesia can be labelled as the last type. Thailand is located somewhere between the two.

According to critics, the East Asian model of development has produced moral hazards and market inefficiency, and eventually hurt the soundness of the market economy, resulting in the crises (Delhaise 1998, 33-35). The crony relations among governments, banks and corporations have developed weaknesses in financial institutions and inadequacies in bank regulation and supervision (Fischer 1998). Large corporations had relied on lending to fuel their expansions. It is also true that capital for investments had been inefficiently used in real estate and money games leading to bubble economies (Corsetti, et al. 1999; Bird and Milne 1999). However, there is evidence that modifies this argument. First, it is not clear why the problem bulged out at that time. The government-led development strategy had been long embedded in East Asia, and many developmentalists had praised it when the regional economy looked good.[16] Also, the argument *per se* cannot explain why China, where the government was heavily involved in economic management, was immune from crisis when the others were not.

It is not clear, moreover, what proportion of bankers' and businessmen's moral hazards can be explained by the East Asian development model. Their moral hazards may simply be the result of protracted economic growth and generous investment. East Asian business and financial actors with limited experience could be too optimistic about their futures to respect risks. In fact, most East Asian countries except Hong Kong and, controversially, Singapore, have adopted state-led developmental strategies, and the countries devastated by the crises were ironically the model students of deregulation and liberalisation.[17] As we will see later, especially in the case of Indonesia, the negativity of politico-economic coalitions is prominent in the process of coping with the crises, not in the introductory phase of the crises.

Another explanation focusing on internal factors is the argument of governmental failure. It cannot be denied that Thailand, Indonesia and Korea had liberalised and deregulated their financial industries without adequate provision of supervisory and auditing institutions.[18] Although contemporary international financial transactions are very speedy and grow at rates well over those of objective economies, the governments can not avoid being blamed for their negligence. However, as mentioned before, the exchange rate crises and the economic crises should be distinguished from each other. Governmental agents were surely responsible for the occurrences of the exchange rate crises, but the ensuing economic crises included many other factors beyond that.

2. International Factors

If we turn to the explanations focusing on external causes, a series of factors can be named. Firstly, the conspiracy hypothesis claims that the crises were intended by Western economic powers that were feeling threats from the rising Asian economies. According to this argument, the Western interests concerned had agreed to discipline Asian countries to follow 'international' market principles. It is true that the essence of the so-called Washington consensus in the early 1990s was liberalisation and deregulation. Accordingly, one of the major objectives of IMF programs is the realisation of transparent and freer business activities. It is in a sense a compulsory program for making recipient countries assimilate into the US-led global market system. Although this argument seems persuasive, it might be implying a more complicated reasoning than is actually the case.

According to Sachs (1998, 17), the IMF's imposing of conditionality on troubled economies had made the international financial market aware of the looming crises. The IMF had encouraged rather than subdued the crises in East Asia. To normalise the foreign exchange crisis, investors' confidence needed to be restored as soon as possible. However, the investors equipped with electronic transaction instruments respected uncertainty above other indicators. Hedge funds and credit rating companies have also been blamed for contributing to the situation. Although hedge funds did not account for great volumes, they could have played the role of pilot in the international financial market. In Thailand, hedge funds sold baht in May and strengthened the confidence of those concerned about the Thai economic crisis (*Economist* 1998a). In a similar vein, the downgrading of country and corporation credits by such international credit rating companies as Moody's Investor's Service and Standard and Poor had driven foreign investors to retreat from risky businesses. Although the empirical causality between the prophecy effect and the economic crisis is not easy to trace, this argument seems logically robust.

Thirdly, some argue that the Asian crises were rooted in the changed international politico-business environment. In the post-Cold War era the US was not sufficiently concerned with protecting its strategic partners. Its hegemony had more interest in maintaining system-level stability than in helping individual needs. When the shocks shattered Asian economies, the victims were individual countries, not the international financial system itself.[19] Since the 1980s, China, with plenty of cheap labour, has risen as a competitor of the other Asian countries in export markets. The growth rates of Chinese exports of goods and services in GDP were 17.5 per cent in 1990 and 24.0 per cent in 1995 respectively, while its GDP growth rates during the equivalent years were each 4.0 per cent and 10.5 per cent (World Bank 2001). What these statistics show is that Chinese exports had grown at a very fast rate. Behind this development lay the 40 per cent depreciation of Chinese currency in 1994. Thai and Indonesian goods, therefore, lost their competitiveness in the presence of cheap Chinese products. Moreover, wages in manufacturing had risen rapidly in Thailand and Indonesia because of an insufficient pool of experienced workers.

The Japanese economic slump has been also blamed. When real estate and stock prices fell after the bursting of the bubble, Japanese financial institutions began to look for new international markets. They had increased their investments in Southeast Asia to a great degree; in 1994, Japan's investment in that region was US$40 billion, but by 1996 it was US$260 billion (*Businesshankyung* 1998, 52). The massive inflow of capital into Southeast Asian countries had raised real estate prices, encouraging speculative investment in real estate that eventually led to the bubble economies. Moreover, the low yen since the mid-1990s had weakened the competitive powers of the other East Asian countries, especially Korea, which had entered a technological upgrading process.[20] In addition to this, the Japanese trade surplus could not efficiently provide liquidity to East Asian countries because of the troubles and backwardness of its own financial institutions. Most trade surplus had been either kept inside Japan or invested in US Treasury bonds.

The boom of the US economy has also been named as a cause of the Asian economic crises. When the exchange rate crises took place, opportunistic international investors were not obliged to remain on risky East Asian capital markets. They regarded the US capital market that had prospered for nearly 10 years as a safe refuge. The economic boom of the US in the latter 1990s has sucked in considerable foreign direct investment (FDI), providing a shelter for the capital flowing from Asia. The total amount of the world FDI had been US$320.4 billion in 1995, and increased to US$884.5 billion in 1999, but during this period the FDI flowing into the US amounted to US$57.8 billion and US$275.5 billion, respectively (World Bank 2001). While the world FDI grew 2.8 times, the US equivalent increased 4.8 times, accounting for 31.1 per cent of the total world FDI in 1999. These international factors can partially, although not completely, explain the occurrence of the crises.

Lastly, the 'contagion effect' needs to be mentioned. When the Thai crisis had become apparent, international investors suspected the soundness of the other East Asian countries' economies. A country's vulnerability to the contagion of economic crisis is conditioned by both the visible similarities of economic behaviour and the proximity of geographical location between the country under crisis and the other countries (Pavan 2000). The strategic behaviour of foreign investors is understandable in two senses. One is rooted in the nature of money games. When selling is the common strategy of players, the faster player is less damaged in stock markets. Even banks competitively collect their lendings to make sure they receive their money back. The other driving factor is uncertainty and risk. If a country's business operations lack transparency, foreign investors cannot secure sufficient information in making decisions and generally choose safety over risk (as was claimed to be the case in East Asia). However, this argument refers to a catalyst factor and cannot explain the crises *per se*.

In brief, there were numerous factors in the Asian economic crises. If we concentrate on actors for the convenience of discussion, three groups seem prominent. The first is the group of international investors who made speculative or strategic choices of withdrawal. The second is the IMF that amplified the exchange crises. The third is the group of Asian governmental officials who neglected their roles in supervising dangerous financial games, and businessmen who engage in them. It was possible to cope with some changes in the international business environment in advance, but not all. The crisis-hit countries could have prepared for the intensification of international competition, but a shock like the sudden depreciation of the Chinese currency was purely, at least in the short run, external. Above all, it is noteworthy that the contemporary international financial market is not a perfect market in that, while demand exists everywhere, supply rests with the limited number of wealthy countries' financial institutions and funds (see Radelet and Sachs 1998, 70-71). This oligopolistic supplier market can be unstable in the short run and the occasional instability can hurt individual economies seriously, although it may seek an equilibrium in the long run.

COPING WITH THE ECONOMIC CRISES

1. IMF Conditionalities

IMF conditionality prescribes in general fiscal balance, price stability, restructuring of corporate governance, and free trade and capital/foreign exchange transactions. While these neoliberal prescriptions have positive effects in augmenting the transparency of economic activities and market efficiency, they may bring about unemployment, tax increases, and high interest rates (Choi 1999). However, the recipient countries that desperately need IMF money usually cannot make their own voices heard in arranging the loan conditions.

In Thailand, the Chavalit Government was replaced in early November 1997 by the Chuan-led coalition government on the excuse of its failure to handle economic disturbances. Although the new cabinet was not a cohesive body, Thai economic ministers could devote themselves to implementing IMF-recommended programs. Indonesia under Suharto admitted the IMF's assistance reluctantly, unlike Thailand and Korea. To this old dictator, Indonesia was a regional hegemony and a big country in terms of population and natural resources. The conflict between the IMF and Suharto, however, had caused enormous pain to the Indonesian people. Post-IMF Indonesia had fallen into confusion; Suharto's health was in doubt; his family and ministers had continued their old-style practices; and the IMF was embarrassed in the presence of the discrepancies between governmental announcements and actions. Later on, Indonesia had to negotiate with the IMF twice to gain the relief loans.

Although President Kim Dae Jung's party was not the first major party in the National Assembly, he could concentrate on rebuilding Korea's economy thanks to his coalition with the third party. The opposition party, the former government party responsible for the economic crisis, could not influence the new government at its disposal. Kim, who was elected just before the occurrence of the crisis, managed to implement the IMF package consistently.

The total amount of the rescue loans agreed to be given to Thailand was US$17.2 billion, and the equivalents to Indonesia and Korea were US$42.3 and US$58.4 billion, respectively (Gohama 1999, 122). Although the IMF was the main donor, the World Bank, the Asian Development Bank, and individual countries also contributed to these funds. Despite the IMF's announcements of rescue, there had been a continuous exodus of foreign investment from all three countries. As the Fund later painfully admitted, Thai, Indonesian and Korean markets failed to regain foreign investors' confidence.

It has been said that the IMF committed some critical mistakes in the early phase of the crises (Madrick 1998). The first was tight monetary policy, that is, maintaining high interest rates in the framework of a floating exchange system. In the three countries, the sharp increases in interest rates were associated with the flight, not holding or invitation, of foreign investments. Investors suspected that higher levels of interest rates would bring about the bankruptcy of companies. As a result, risk levels in these countries had increased, and speculative investors had turned their faces away (Basurto and Ghosh 2000).[21] Moreover, even if interest rates were set at high levels, they could not invite foreign investments if the levels were not high enough to compensate the decrease in exchange rate.[22]

It is conventionally believed that an external impact or shock is absorbed in the exchange rate regime under a floating exchange system. However, it did not happen in any of these three countries.[23] The depreciation of their currencies had failed not only to restore market confidence, but also to boost exports. The economies of the three countries, especially Thailand and Korea, are heavily dependent on their exports (about 30 per cent). In the presence of the contracted domestic markets, exports should have led their economic recoveries. Exports, however, were sluggish, at least in the early phase of the crises. The Thai baht, Indonesian rupiah, and Korean won dropped by about half their value after the crises, but these countries' exports had recorded only one digit rates of increase, unlike that of Mexico in the mid-1990s that recorded over 30 per cent. The currency values of the other competing exporters also dropped, while the prices of imported raw materials and parts increased. Moreover, following the IMF guidelines, the banks of these countries sharply raised interest rates (about 20-30 per cent) and became more prudent in their lending activities in order to meet the international Bank for International Settlements (BIS) standard.[24] One of the main outcomes was a kind of liquidity trap and severe credit crunch. The three Asian countries could not secure the raw materials and parts necessary for their exports because of their foreign currency shortage and domestic credit crunch. What made things worse was that the Asian market had shrunk[25] because of the member countries' tight fiscal policies and high interest rates, and Japan's economic stagnation. The IMF's prescription for recovering trade balance worked in the end, but it owed more to import contraction than to export growth, and above all it led to the costly extension of the economic disaster.

The IMF also made strong requests for the restructuring of corporate governance and bank activities. Many of the Thai, Indonesian and Korean business and financial sectors had high levels of moral hazard from their long associations with the financial and business conglomerates, *chaebols*,[26] which had dominated markets. As mentioned earlier, the IMF imposed the BIS capital ratio on banks, and, in order to maintain their reserve and capital adequacy ratios, banks were very prudential in their lending. As governments guaranteed deposits and investors did not have other viable alternatives, banks could accumulate deposits. However, the high interest rates resulted in a credit crunch, which in turn led to the contraction of business and to the increase in non-performing loans. Although the IMF programs have positively contributed to the transparency of business activities and to the decrease in moral hazards, they had led to business contraction and a tightening of liquidity. After this early post-IMF period, the East Asian governments lowered interest rates but their economies already had deep scars.

What were urgently needed in troubled Thailand, Indonesia and Korea were not austerity programs but agreeable expansionist policies that would have made up for the decreases in foreign investment. The government finances of the three countries had been healthy before the crises. The tight fiscal policies 'recommended' by the IMF in the early stage of the foreign exchange crises had driven these countries near to a state of economic depression. The fiscal adjustment requested by the IMF was 3 per cent of GDP for Thailand, 1 per cent for Indonesia, and 1.5 per cent for Korea, reflecting the sizes of their current account deficits (Fischer 1998). The IMF later agreed to ease the tightness of the targets but they had badly hurt the economies already.

2. Post-IMF Intervention Development

Since the first half of 1999 the three East Asian countries have shown healthier economic indicators than right after the crises. However, the improvements of these indicators are mainly due to such Keynesian credit creations as the expansion of fiscal expenditure, generous monetary policies, and international rescue funds. Their real economies have not recovered fully to the pre-crises level. Although the trade balances of the three countries have been positive (Table 2), such surpluses were, as previously mentioned, owed more to the decrease in imports than to the increases in export.

The Thai GDP has recovered since the latter half of 1999 (Table 1). Inflation also has been reduced from the mid-1998 double digits to lower one-digit levels since early 1999. The exchange rate, which plunged by 77 per cent in December 1997, has become stable in the range of around Bt40 per US$1 since the latter half of 1998. As the Thai economy has become healthy, so has its stock market. The Stock Market Exchange of Thailand (SET) increased by 29.8 per cent in mid-June 1999 (*Hanguk Ilbo* 1999). In 1999, the Bank of Thailand, the Ministry of Finance, the National Economic and Social Development Board, and international agencies such as the World Bank and the IMF agreed that the Thai economy has recovered steadily, although slowly (Bowornwathana 2000, 88-89). Although Thai businesses have shown clear signs of recovery since the latter half of 1999, thanks to the improvements in consumption, manufacturing output, export (cars and electronics), and construction, the country still has a huge sum of bad loans. The ratio of non-performing loans to the total bank loans was over 46 per cent in the first half of 1999 (*Far Eastern Economic Review* 1999, 63). Thus, the clearance of bank debts has become an urgent agenda for the Thai government.

Unlike the situation in Thailand, the Indonesian economy has taken a jagged way. It was only since late 1999 that Indonesia has shown signs of the restoration of economic stability. Indonesia was hit worse by the crisis than Korea or Thailand. Right after the crisis of 1997, the Indonesian rupiah plunged to Rp5,000 per US$1; the stock market index dropped from 734 to 335; inflation recorded double digits; and numerous small companies in Java closed their doors (Bird 1998, 175). In November 1997, Indonesia closed 16 private banks by the direction of the IMF,[27] but the closure of banks made people rush to withdraw their deposits, and Chinese capital started flying out to Singapore and Hong Kong looking for safe refuge. The Indonesian financial crisis had deepened, and the internal and international confidence in the Indonesian economy had weakened. Thus, in January 1998, the value of the rupiah dropped further to Rp11,200 per US$1. Of the 282 companies listed in the stock market, 260 were put into a state of default. The inconsistent attitudes of Suharto towards reform had made things worse. Sometimes he cooperated with, but sometimes resisted, the IMF. The Fund detailed the dismantling of the cartel, monopoly, and preferential treatment, and the cancellation of national projects where Suharto and his family had their vested interests (*Economist* 1998b).

In early 1998, unlike its Thai and Korean equivalents, the Indonesian financial system had not yet restored stability. As living expenses went up (inflation had increased by 250-500 per cent since July 1997),[28] attacks on ethnic Chinese and other social disturbances proliferated. In May, riots and violent demonstrations by not only students, but also by the middle class, took place. The sudden rise in food prices further led to the paralysis of food trading because many decided to secure foodstuffs at home. Importers could not fulfil their jobs because foreign banks refused to issue letters of credit, and the prices of importing goods were doubled or trebled. The exchange rate plunged beyond Rp10,000 per US$1, even lower than that of the foreign exchange crisis period in 1997. The central bank raised interest rates by 58 per cent making it impossible for many borrowers to pay back their interest. The number of unemployed reached around 8 million in May. Eventually the government dispatched soldiers to control the social disturbances. The then president Habibi and the IMF, realising the seriousness of the Indonesian economic situation, agreed with the third revision of the original IMF program. As a result, fiscal tightness was eased and macroeconomic targets were rearranged.[29]

The Indonesian GDP has shown signs of recovery since the end of 1999 (Table 1). From that time on, official inflation also declined considerably to less than 2 per cent, but it has increased again to more than 5 per cent since August 2000 (www.nso.go.kr/cgi-bin/sws_999.cgi 2001). The exchange rate had become stable since October 1998 at less than Rp9,000 per US$1, but has slightly increased again since May 2000 (www.nso.go.kr/cgi-bin/sws-999.cgi 2001). Also, the Indonesian composite stock price index rebounded in the latter half of 1999 but has dropped again since May 2000 (www.bi.go.id/bank_indonesia2 2001). Indonesian macroeconomic indicators such as inflation, exchange rate, and stock index, have deteriorated since the latter half of 2000, albeit not as seriously as before. The leadership crisis of Wahid is named as one of the main reasons.[30]

The recovery of the Korean economy has been relatively smooth compared to those of Thailand and Indonesia. The foreign currency reserve increased to US$30 billion in May 1998, US$64.3 billion in October 1999, and to over US$90 billion in 2000. International investors have started to reinvest in Korea since 1998. Exchange rates have been stable from the end of 1998 at under 1,300 won per US$1. GDP, National Account and the Balance of Trade all have shown robust signs of improvement (Tables 1 and 2). In 1999, some even worried about the possibility of business overheating. The recovery was owed largely to the increase in exports, thanks to the robust US economy and to the government's pump-priming policies. Consumption and major internal businesses like construction, however, were not yet so active. In 1999, the investments in manufacturing machines and equipment reached only

77 per cent of the pre-crisis level. Korea then encountered, in the latter half of 2000, another, although less serious, economic setback when the stock market deteriorated and the Daewoo, the then third greatest *chaebol*, became insolvent. As a result, the exchange rate increased to about 1,300 won per US$1 in early 2001 but there have been no apparent signs of serious economic setback.

Although Thailand and Korea have suffered from the crises, Indonesia has been most damaged of the three. In Indonesia, politics and economics have amplified each other's negativities. Political leadership has been unstable, and Indonesian business activities, which have long been explained by human networks rather than market principles, have been in turmoil. The Indonesian government also traditionally has been involved in the country's resource allocation to a greater degree than Thai and Korean governments. Indonesian society experienced much greater social disintegration than the other two countries. These factors together have aggravated the country's efforts to restore economic stability, and distorted the effects of reform programs (*Far Eastern Economic Review* 1999).

CONSEQUENCES OF THE ECONOMIC CRISES

1. Political Aspects

Thai, Indonesian and Korean governments all launched campaigns against corruption, clientism and cronyism in order to enhance efficiency and invite foreign investment. It has been said that their crises in part had stemmed from the opaque relationship between political and business sectors. As a byproduct of the economic crises, these countries could in some degree promote political development.

However, behind this façade, the political developments of individual countries show divergent paths. While the Korean political situation has been relatively stable compared to Thailand and Indonesia, the latter two countries' political situations have not settled down. The Thai general election of 6 January 2001, the first small-district election in Thai history, and the re-election of 26 January (held because 109 of those elected were nullified on the accusation of dishonest campaigns by the newly established Election Commission), showed enormous evidence of electoral irregularities, as did the 1998 Senate election. Apparent vote-buying and even bloody shootings contaminated the elections. The leader of the Thai Rak Thai (TRT, Thai Love Thai) party and a telecommunications tycoon, Thaksin Shinawatra, could secure the support of more than half of the 500-member Lower House. However, Thaksin himself is still under the investigation of the National Anti-Corruption Commission because of his intentional omission of millions of US dollars worth of stocks when he was inaugurated as deputy Prime Minister in 1997. His commitment to writing off farmers' and banks' debts would also be a political burden in the future. Further, one major reason for the defeat of the Chuan-led Democratic Party was the popular criticism of his government's selling-off of national banks and companies to foreigners. In order to perform economic reform successfully, Thaksin needs to convert the Thai people's nationalism to positive means of economic recovery. If he fails to handle it (and returns to protectionism), Thailand may invite further trouble.

Indonesia has experienced political instability ever since the crisis. Because of this political, and thus social, instability, Indonesia could not attract its previous levels of tourism, despite its depreciation of currency, although traditionally it has been a famous sightseeing country. In 1997, the number of tourists to Indonesia was 5.2 million, but it dropped to 4.6 million in 1998 and to 4.7 million in 1999 (www.bps.go.is/statbysector/tourism 2001). Suharto, whose 32 years' dictatorship[31] had been blamed for the economic crisis, stepped down on 21 May 1998, leaving his country near a state of default. Habibi, the then Vice-President, replaced Suharto, but gave his position to Wahid in October 1999. Wahid's democratisation programs (such as the legalisation of the communist party) have provoked internal disputes in his government. As a coalition, Wahid's government could not exert its power effectively, and, as a byproduct of democratisation, some Indonesian provinces have asked for their independence. Moreover, Wahid himself has been suspected of embezzlement, and the powerful military and students still have strong voices in Indonesian politics. In early 2001, street demonstrations both for and against Wahid have covered the front pages of the press, and Wahid's cabinet has continued to experience internal disputes.

Korea has been under the leadership of President Kim Dae Jung from the crisis until now. Although there was a general election in 2000, the political landscape of Korea has changed little. What has been lucky for Korea is its relative political stability compared to the other two countries after their crises.

In brief, the crisis has changed government in Thailand, and a more nationalistic and, in a sense, populist Thaksin and his party replaced the old coalition government. Indonesian politics has been beleaguered by government change and instability, troubling its economics and shaking its role as the leader of ASEAN. The present Korean government that took its power right after the crisis has managed to get along with economic difficulty.

2. Economic Aspects

The three countries have partially trimmed their economies. In Thailand, 56 of the total of 89 financial companies closed permanently because of bad loans. In Indonesia and Korea, 16 and 5 commercial banks were closed, respectively. In Thailand and Korea, corporate restructuring has proceeded in some degree, and parts of non-core businesses have been sold off through asset auctions aimed at lowering debt. Also, many Chinese family business networks in Thailand have disintegrated.

In Korea, many *chaebols*, such as Daewoo, Kia, Donga and Hanla, have disappeared. Although some bigger *chaebols* regarded their groups as too big (and thus too important to the economy) to be discarded, the Daewoo Group, the then third biggest conglomerate, could not continue its existence. The Daewoo case appeared to show that, if *chaebols* refuse to change their old-style business practices, they would, without exception, be restructured.[32] In August 1999 President Kim reconfirmed his government's will to reform corporate governance in order to enhance transparency. Regulations imposed on *chaebols* include the prohibition of cross-share holding, unfair internal transactions, and mutual assurance of payment. Mandatory framing of combined (consolidated) balance sheets has been codified also. As a result, the transparency of business has been enhanced considerably, and the financial soundness of the *chaebols* has become robust at the level of an approximately 200 per cent debt-equity ratio. However, this record of Korean restructuring should not be exaggerated. Many corporations had been marginal before their bankruptcy, and restructuring has been more successful in promise than in action.

The ratio of short-term loans in the total debt has significantly fallen in all three countries. In Thailand, it dropped from US$44.1 billion in 1995 to US$23.4 billion in 1999 (World Bank 2001). The equivalent figures for Indonesia and Korea are each from US$26.0 billion to US$20.0 billion, and from US$46.6 billion to US$34.7 billion (World Bank 2001). All countries have introduced safeguard systems and early warning systems. For example, in Korea, the Fair Trade Commission and the Financial Supervisory Service were established in 1999 for the supervision, examination and enforcement of the business activities of financial institutions.

Among the three East Asian countries, the Thai FDI had fallen from US$2.4 billion in 1990 to US$2.1 billion in 1995, but recovered to US$6.2 billion in 1999 (World Bank 2001). Korea has shown a continuous increase in inviting FDI after its foreign exchange crisis; from US$0.8 billion in 1990, to US$1.8 billion in 1995, and to US$9.3 billion in 1999 (World Bank 2001). Unlike these two countries, Indonesian FDI has dropped from US$4.3 billion in 1995 to US$2.8 billion in 1999 (World Bank 2001). This difference in inviting FDI is the reflection of the country's difference in economic recovery.

Certainly there have been negative effects of the crises. Public debt has increased in the East Asian countries because their governments have pursued expansionist fiscal policies during the last two or so years for the purpose of stimulating their economies. While tax collection, which may contract business again, cannot be activated, governmental expenditures either for bailing out troubled major corporations (Korea) or for supporting public corporations and activities (Thailand and Indonesia) have increased considerably.

In addition to this, the Thai external debt recorded in 1999 was US$94.3 billion, and it still cast a murky prospect on Thai economic recovery considering its GDP (US$124.4 billion in 1999) (World Bank 2001). The external debt is also too great considering its GDP. As of 1999, the external debt is US$149.7 billion, whereas that of GDP is US$142.5 billion (World Bank 2001). Korean external debt in 1999 was US$124.3 billion, a little over one fourth of its GDP (US$406.9 billion) (World Bank 2001). This external debt is a considerable amount, even if it indicates a much better performance than exists in Thailand and Indonesia, and the country can avoid foreign exchange crisis thanks to its provision of over US$90 billion foreign reserve.

There have been growing numbers of foreign investors in the economies of these countries, especially in their stock markets. After the crises foreign investors could increase their shares in many business and financial institutions when entry restrictions were lifted. Foreign hands took over some of the major banking and finance industries.[33] Also, much real estate has been sold to foreign investors.

The ratios of trade in national production have increased in all three countries, helping the recovery of their economies (World Bank 2001). The world averages of the trade ratio to GDP have been 19.4 per cent in 1990, 21.4 per cent in 1995, and 26.0 per cent in 1999 (World Bank 2001). However, the equivalent ratios of Thailand's trade are 37.9 per cent in 1990, 45.2 per cent in 1995, and 51.1 per cent in 1999, and those of Korea, 29.7 per cent in 1990, 31.0 per cent in 1995, and 38.7 per cent in 1999, respectively (World Bank 2001). Indonesian trade ratios in GDP have shown relatively sluggish growth rates (24.5 per cent in 1990, 27.0 per cent in 1995, and 30.9 per cent in 1999) compared to those of Thailand and Korea, reflecting its economic instability. Although trade *per se* can not be assumed to have negative effects on the economy, and it is true that trade growth is an international phenomenon, these figures imply that the three countries' economies have become increasingly sensitive to outside influences, and other outer shocks could interfere with policy efforts to revive their troubled economies. For firm economic restoration, domestic consumption needs to be revived.

There have been resistances and delays in reforming as well.[34] In Thailand, where many cabinet members are former businessmen, politicians and other vested interests have slowed the pace of restructuring (*Far Eastern Economic Review* 2000, 76-79). One typical example is Siam Cement, the largest Thai business group which is also partially owned by the royal family. The company was funded in the early crisis period by international investors who believed the announcement of restructuring. Many believed that the group could play a role as the model for Thailand's corporate restructuring. However, the group's selling-off of non-core branch companies and slashing of debt seem to have failed to show any progress (*Far Eastern Economic Review* 2000, 81). According to a foreign entrepreneur in Bangkok, Thai companies do not yet quite understand why they should change their managerial practices, which traditionally have stressed total assets and gross outputs, into those emphasising net assets and profits (*Far Eastern Economic Review* 2000, 82). Lack of legal provisions, as well as political interventions, mean that punishment of economic criminals has not been very visible. Moreover, the estimated non-performing loans as of July 1999 are still 46.1 per cent of the total loans (Limskull 2000).

In Indonesia, financial scandals have been more frequent than restructuring stories. The Bank Indonesia, the Ministry of Finance, and even the Indonesian Bank Restructuring Agency (IBRA), which was established after the 1998 banking collapse to assume the function of financial restructuring, have been riddled with scandals (Liddle 2000, 40-41). Also, populist styles of policy have continued, for example, bus fares were frozen and the rice and sugar industries have been protected. Politicians have resumed their interventions in market functioning, too. President Wahid claimed that four large, but financially troubled, Indonesian business groups, the Texmaco Group, Barito Pacific, the Gajah Tungal Group, and the Slaim Group, must be saved in order to keep up their exports (*Far Eastern Economic Review* 2000, 76).[35] Many major companies are still under the influence of a small group of Chinese families who have intimate relationships with politicians. Moreover, Indonesian restructuring has been focused on debt-to-equity swaps, loan extensions, and debt discounts rather than the introduction of new accounting and management systems and corporate culture. In Indonesia corporate restructuring has failed to show visible outcomes.

In Korea, lay-off has turned out to be the first and highest hurdle in the restructuring process. While the cosmetic accounting practice of corporations is finally being wiped out thanks to strengthened auditing, many public corporations are still believed to have excess labour (*Digital Chosunilbo* 2001). The resistance of workers and labour unions against layoff have intensified also. As the term of President Kim Dae Jung will end in 2002, the government will encounter increasingly difficult obstacles.

In brief, the signs of economic recovery vary across countries. While Korea has shown the most robust outcomes of recovery, Indonesia has fared worst, reflecting its political and social instability. What the restructuring efforts in the three countries have revealed in common is that old practices stubbornly remain in place. Moreover, as economic liberalisation proceeds, governments are losing their policy leverages *vis-à-vis* private financial institutions and corporations. Restructuring has a trade-off nature; while the benefit may be given to the society in general, the immediate cost is likely to be borne by certain social groups, especially workers and small investors; and the government enthusiasm for driving restructuring may hurt either democratic or market values. Although restructuring is a worthy pursuit, its structural complexity requires strenuous policy efforts and time.

3. Social Aspects

The crises have yielded enormous impacts on Thai, Indonesian and Korean societies. Because of restructuring and bankruptcy many people had fallen into a state of poverty. In all three countries a considerable proportion of the middle classes has disappeared. In the absence of social safety nets for the unemployed, and of flexible labour markets, lay-offs have brought serious social problems.[36]

The unemployment rates of these countries, however, have shown different patterns. In Thailand, the official unemployment rate at one time reached 10 per cent (3 million), and many unemployed had to go to the countryside where the situation was by no means better than in the cities. However, the unemployment rate has fallen from 4.6 per cent in February 1998 to 3.7 per cent in November 2000 (www.bot.or.th/bothomepage/databank/EconData 2001). In Indonesia, the unemployment rate increased to 10 per cent (20 million) and over 40 per cent of 220 million had been put into a state of absolute poverty (*Chosun Ilbo* 1998a). Even after the initial stage of the crisis, the situation has not improved significantly; even the official data reveals the rise of unemployment from 4.7 per cent in 1997, 5.5 per cent in 1998, to 6.4 per cent in 1999 (www.bps.go.id/statbysector/employ 2001). Thailand and Indonesia have numerous unofficial and provisional labourers, and the official statistics may not represent adequately their abject situations.

In Korea, the income of the middle class (those between the upper 20 per cent and lower 20 per cent) decreased on average by 5.5-5.8 per cent in 1998, and, as of June 1998, 64.9 per cent of Koreans thought they belonged to the lower class while only 34.8 per cent responded that they belong to the middle class (*Chosun Ilbo* 1998b).[37] A year ago those figures were 44.5 per cent and 53.1 per cent, respectively. The unemployment rate reached 6.8 per cent in 1998, and, moreover, among the unemployed, the ratio of the structural unemployed had increased to 20 per cent. In 1998, the real wage considering inflation dropped by 9.3 per cent, while the upper 10 per cent of urban households raised their annual income by 4 per cent thanks to their increased banking and portfolio incomes. But, in the same year, the lower 20 per cent, mainly relying on wage income, had experienced a 17.2 per cent decrease in their incomes.[38] However, the recent data shows an improvement; the unemployment rate has dropped to 6.3 per cent in 1999 and to 4.1 per cent in 2000 (www.nso.go.kr/eindex 2001).

The resistance of the workers in these three countries has been stronger and more effective than before thanks to the rise of their union powers and activities. Korean trade unions, which have developed through the democratisation movements in the 1980s, seem to be much stronger than their Thai and Indonesian counterparts. In Thailand two factors have suppressed labour union movements; one is the segregation of labour by region, gender, age, skill, and the like, and the other, submissive attitudes owing to the Buddhist culture (Yoon 1997, 83-84). Thai civil organisations have initiated many protests and demonstrations for the poor, and union strikes also have increased since the crisis. In Indonesia, thanks to the democratisation pursued by Wahid, trade unions have been spawned and labour movements have expanded since early 1998. Before that, Indonesian trade union movements had been heavily suppressed by the strong authoritarian state. According to a foreign businessman in

Indonesia, the lack of experience with labour movements has encouraged the unorganised labour campaigns by workers (*Digital Chosunilbo* 1998b).

Another social issue stemming from the crises is racial conflict. Although Chinese hold economic power both in Thailand and Indonesia, Thai Chinese have had good relationships with the indigenous Thai. Their immigration history can be traced farther than that of Indonesian Chinese, and many of them have been incorporated into the Thai nation. In Indonesia, however, the indigenous Indonesians often have attacked Chinese in the presence of economic difficulties.

Since the economic crises, all three countries have curtailed expenditure on health, education, social development and welfare. Social vices gain secondary consideration in relation to economic recovery in these countries. Poverty, disease, crime and child abuse, all of which have long-term negative effects, have increased enormously. The neglect of these issues may cost them dearly in the future.

4. International Aspects

The East Asian crises reminded the international society of the predominance of the US in the region. Although Japan contributed significant funds to help the three Asian countries, its role has not been so conspicuous.[39] The United States sponsored, either directly or via international organisations, the post-crisis economic management.

While the crises have proceeded, the need for regional cooperation has gained attention. The Asian Monetary Fund (AMF) was proposed by Japan at the annual meeting of the IMF, in September 1997, to prevent another crisis and to enhance the region's financial stability.[40] At first the US and China, afraid of lowering their voices and concerned by the rise of Japan's influence,[41] opposed the proposal; later, at the APEC Conference in November 1998, they indicated positive attitudes towards its institutionalisation. In a separate arrangement, Korea, China, Japan and ten ASEAN countries agreed in May 1998 to establish a collective foreign exchange swap system. Already Korea-Japan and Japan-Malaysia had organised reciprocal foreign currency swap systems after the crises.

CONCLUSIONS - SUMMARY AND POLICY IMPLICATIONS

The East Asian crises, originating in Thailand, spread quickly to other countries. Not many predicted the occurrence of the crises. Among those countries affected by the crises, Thailand, Indonesia and Korea requested IMF rescue loans. These countries had open economic systems heavily reliant on export and foreign investment, and all three countries had weak, underdeveloped financial sectors. Numerous factors, which are to some degree or another inter-related, explain the crises. Although the three countries' foreign exchange crises are unlikely to be repeated (except, perhaps, in Indonesia), the economic crises are not over yet, especially if one considers consumption, investment, and the normalisation of the banking system.

From a theoretical perspective, the development of the Asian crises strongly supports the argument of structuralism rather than liberal or realism traditions. US hegemony fails to provide regional stability, or, at best, it could contain the spread of economic instability beyond the region. Mutual transactions between Western investors and East Asian countries turn out to be structured for the interests of the former. The deeply vulnerable position of the borrowers casts doubt on the universal application of the interdependence thesis. The economic philosophy of neoliberalism and its practical program of globalism appear to downplay the difference in size and strength of transaction partners. Moreover, the beneficiaries of the crises have not been national entities, as the argument of neomercantilism would have it. Although the US Treasury and the IMF have initiated the post-crisis treatments, capital interests, not the states in general, have benefited most. Such structural approaches as Wallerstein's world-system argument (Wallerstein 1974; 1989) and Galtung's international structuralism (Galtung 1971) provide robust explanations of the Asian economic crises.[42] While Western investors, who had long enjoyed lucrative businesses in Asia, were exempted from paying the cost, the socially disadvantaged in the victim countries encountered most of the backwash. Foreign investors could successfully collect their shares from the crises, while many East Asian citizens paid the prices and donor countries' citizens contributed to the funds through their taxes.[43]

The conditionality of the IMF propelled the damaged economies into a vicious chain reaction of economic troubles that eventually led to economic contraction. In order to be flexible, the IMF should consider both the particular conditions of individual countries and the long-term stability of the regional economy. Thanks to the effects of the crises themselves as well as the policy prescriptions of the IMF, the three countries could somehow or other tune up their economies to varying degrees. However, the old practices have strongly resisted reform. The crises have had great impact on political and social fields, too. While democratisation has been enhanced to some extent, social problems have been generated by the crises. The most conspicuous costs of reform and restructuring have been the sharp increase in the number of the unemployed and the poor, and the contraction of the middle class. Along with economic difficulties, both class and ethnic conflicts have intensified. The shadow of the crises will long linger in the three countries.

The policy prescriptions of the IMF have centred on securing investment and institutionalising neoliberal economic order, rather than promoting healthy and smooth economic development. The general feature of the Asian economic crises clearly shows that the present international financial system is of advantage to investors rather than to investment recipients.

International financial institutions should take responsibility for their imprudent investments. The amount of international money transacted overnight is known to be more than US$1 trillion. If financial big hands play a game of 'casino' capitalism, small open countries are easily exposed to economic turmoil. Although individual investors and traders are rational, the contemporary international economic system is neither perfect nor rational in nature, considering both the imbalance of power between participants and the high mobility of information and transaction. Foreign exchange crisis can take place in any weak economy, especially in fast developing countries where capital is short, generating serious negative externalities that are very likely to develop into serious financial and economic crises. In order to prevent this inhumane misfortune, both national and international safeguarding arrangements should be introduced.

REFERENCES

Basurto, Gabriela and Atish Ghosh (2000) 'The Interest Rate-Exchange Rate Nexus in the Asian Crisis Countries'. *IMF Working Paper WP/00/19*.

Bird, Judith (1998) 'Indonesia in 1997: The Tinderbox Year'. *Asian Survey* 38: 2.

Bird, Graham and Alistair Milne (1999) 'Miracle to Meltdown: A Pathology of the East Asian Financial Crisis'. *Third World Quarterly* 20: 2.

Bowornwathana, Bidhya (2000) 'Thailand in 1999: A Royal Jubilee, Economic Recovery, and Political Reform'. *Asian Survey* 40: 1.

Businesshankyung (1998) 'Special Report: Asian Economic Crisis (Korean)'. March 3.

Chosun Ilbo (Korean Newspaper) (1998a) August 14.

—— (1998b) September 26.

Choi, Kwang (1999) 'Korean Financial Crisis and Fiscal Policy'. *International Area Review* 2: 2.

Chun, Jin-Hwan (2000) 'East Asian Economic Development and Confucian Tradition'. A Paper at the 8th International Regional Cooperation in Northeast Asia, Cheju, Korea.

Corsetti, Giancarlo, Paolo Pesenti and Nouriel Roubini (1999) 'Paper Tigers? A Model of the Asian Crisis'. *European Economic Review* 43.

Delhaise, Philippe F. (1998) *Asia in Crisis: The Implication of the Banking and Finance Systems*. Singapore: John Wiley and Sons.

Demetriades, O. Panicos, and Bassam A. Fattough (1999) 'The Korean Financial Crisis: Competing Explanations and Policy Lessons for Financial Liberalization'. *International Affairs* 75: 4.

Digital Chosunilbo (Korean Newspaper) (1997) October 1.

—— (1998a) April 3.

—— (1998b) April 10.

—— (2001) March 6.

Economist (1998a) June 13-19. 'A Hitchhiker's Guide to Hedge Funds'.

—— (1998b) January 17-23. 'And Now the Political Fall Out'.

—— (1999) August 21-27. 'On their Feet Again?'

Far Eastern Economic Review (1998) October 15.

—— (1999) August 19.

—— (2000) October 19.

Feng, Zhu and Jaewoo Choo (1998) 'Asian Financial Crisis and East Asian Economic Cooperation: A Chinese View'. *Global Economic Review* 27: 4.

Fischer, Stanley (1998) 'The Asian Crisis, the IMF, and the Japanese Economy'. *www.imf.org/external/np/speeches/1998/040898.htm*. April 8.

Focus on the Global South and CAFOD (1998) *IMF's Taming of Asian Tigers: The Economic Crises of Korea, Thailand, and Indonesia* (Korean). Seoul: Munhwagwagaksa.

Galtung, Johan (1971) 'A Structural Theory of Imperialism'. *Journal of Peace Research* 8: 1.

Gohama, Hirohisa (1999) 'The East Asian Economic Crises and Japan's Cooperation (Korean)'. *Wolganataejiyukdinghyang* 88.

Goldstein, Morris (1998) *International Policy Brief*. Washington, D.C.: Institute for International Economics.

Hanguk Ilbo (Korean Newspaper) (1999) June 9.

Joongang Ilbo (Korean Newspaper) (1997) March 10.

Kim, Gyu-ryun (1998) 'Financial Crises and Asian International Relations (Korean)'. *Sinasea* 5: 1.

Ko, Woo-sung (1998) 'The Influence of Southeast Asian Politico-Economic Instability on Korea (Korean)'. *Ataefocus* 9.

Kumar, Manmohan S., Paul Masson and Marcus Miller (2000) 'Global Financial Crises: Institutions and Incentives'. *IMF Working Paper WP/00/105.*

Lee, Kyung-Sook (1998) 'The Three Countries' Exports are Less Lively than Expected (Korean)'. *KIET Silmukyngje.*

Liddle, R. William (2000) 'Indonesia: Democracy Restored'. *Asian Survey* 40: 1.

Limskull, Kitti (2000) 'The Financial and Economic Crisis in Thailand: Dynamics of the Crisis-Root and Process'. *Economic Crisis in Southeast Asia and Korea: Its Economic, Social, Political and Cultural Impacts.* Seoul: Tradition and Modernity.

Madrick, Jeff (1998) 'The IMF Approach: The Half-Learned Lessons of History'. *World Policy Journal* 15: 3.

Park, Dae-Geun (2000) 'Looking for the Indicators of Overestimated Exchange Rate during the Asian Foreign Exchange Crisis (Korean)'. *Daedoekyungjejongchaekyongu* 4: 1.

Pavan, Ahluwalia (2000) 'Discriminating Contagion: An Alternative Explanation of Contagious Currency Crisis in Emerging Markets'. *IMF Working Paper WP/00/14.*

Punyaratabandhu, Suchitra (1998) 'Thailand in 1997: Financial Crisis and Constitutional Reform'. *Asian Survey* 38: 2.

Radelet, Steven and Jeffrey D. Sachs (1998) 'The East Asian Financial Crisis: Diagnosis, Remedies, Prospects'. *Brookings Papers on Economic Activity* 1.

Rosenstein-Rodan, Paul N. (1989) 'External Economies and Industrialization'. In Gerald M. Meier, ed., *Leading Issues in Economic Development.* New York: Oxford University Press.

Sachs, Jeffrey (1998) 'The IMF and the Asian Flu'. *The American Prospect* March-April.

Sikorski, Douglas (1999) 'The Financial Crisis in Southeast Asia and Korea: Issues of Political Economy. *Global Economic Review* 28: 1.

Wallerstein, Immanuel M. (1974) *The Modern World System I: Capitalist Agriculture and the Origin of the European World-Economy in the Sixteenth Century.* New York: Academy Press.

—— (1989) *The Modern World System III: The Second Era of Great Expansion of the Capitalist World-Economy, 1730-1840s.* New York: Academy Press.

Warne, W. Robert (1998) 'Washington's Perceptions on Korea's Financial Crisis'. *Korea Observer* 29: 3.

Wesley, Michael (1999) 'The Asian Crisis and the Adequacy of Regional Institutions'. *Contemporary Southeast Asia* 21: 1.

World Bank (2001) May 3. 'Country Data'. *www.worldbank.org/data/countrydata.*

Yoo, Jang-Hee and Chul Woo Moon. 'Korean Financial Crisis during the 1997-1998: Causes and Challenges'. *Journal of Asian Economics* 10: 2.

Yoon, Jin-ho (1998) 'IMF Regime and the Unemployment Crisis'. *Korea Focus* 6: 2.

Yoon, Jin-Pyo (1997) 'Changing State-Market Relations: The Case of Thailand (Korean)'. *Dongnamasiayongu* 5.

www.bi.go.id/bank_indonesia2 (2001) February 4.

www.bot.or.th/bothomepage/databank/EconData (2001) Feburuary 4.

www.bps.go.id/statbysector/employ (2001) May 3.
www.bps.go.is/statbysector/tourism (2001) May 3.
www.nso.go.kr/cgi-bin/sws_999.cgi (2001) February 7.
www.nso.go.kr/eindex (2001) May 5.
www.standardand poors.com/ratings/sovereigns/index.htm (2001) January 25.

ENDNOTES

[1] Korea had poor natural resources, but it could develop its economy thanks to skilled manpower and the effective governmental policies of the time. Indonesia and Thailand had rich natural endowments and could invite generous foreign investments to encourage speedy industrialisation.

[2] However, it is also true that each country had its own political and economic specificities as will be discussed later in detail.

[3] Developing economies usually have higher rates of inflation than those in developed economies.

[4] The Bangkok International Banking Facility, established in 1993 by the central bank, played an intermediary role between foreign lenders and private Thai corporations (Punyaratabandhu 1998, 163).

[5] Korea was a creditor and an investor in Southeast Asia.

[6] When the IMF prepared the draft of its conditionality, the IMF, the US Treasury, Wall Street and major European bankers, as well as the American Chamber of Commerce in Korea, acted in coordination. The IMF introduced a new loan system for Korea, the Supplemental Reserve Facility, in order to circumvent the quarter option. Korea received a rescue loan that was 20-fold larger than its quarter (Focus on the Global South and CAFOD 1998, 54-56).

[7] The issue of currencies seems tricky because there is no agreed standard for judging a currency's overvaluation. According to Park (2000), exchange rates of the three countries before the crises were not seriously overvalued if the currency value is analysed based on the evaluation of their purchasing powers. However, if the currency value is tested based on the equilibrium of real exchange rates considered in terms of trade, the difference of productivity between domestic and international industries, capital accounts, and the ratios of governmental expenditure on national product, all three countries had had considerably overvalued currencies for one or two years before the crises.

[8] The US asked for voluntary restrictions on exports such as cars and steel, and strongly protested along with the EU at the Korean government's boycott campaigns against importation of luxury goods.

[9] In early 1997, chaebols like Hanbo, Sammi, and Kia were on the verge of bankruptcy. It is also true that chaebols, the long-served engines of Korean economic development, had sunk into moral hazards; they had neglected efforts in R&D when their businesses were doing well. Many of them, instead, sought to make profits in real estate and portfolio investments.

[10] Korea was not prepared for the opening of its financial market. Without appropriate regulatory, supervisory, and legal provisions, Korea hastily permitted financial liberalisation in order to acquire OECD membership, which was encouraged by the US Treasury Department, on the basis that Korean financial liberalisation would serve US financial interests (*Joongang Ilbo* 1997).

[11] Korean financial institutions played a dangerous game; they borrowed short-term loans for long-term lending.

[12] In 1997 Korea had lent a total of US$173 million to Thailand, and 34 per cent of export was destined to Southeast Asian countries (*Digital Chosunilbo* 1997; 1998b).

[13] However, this judgement should be weighed against the consideration that there are no clear or agreed standards to judge a country's economic conditions based on statistical figures.

[14] If we talk about the cause of the 'exchange rate' crises, this can be understood simply as the combined force of the withdrawal of foreign funds and the shortages of an individual country's liquidity. According to a report of the McKinsey consulting company, the Thai exchange rate crisis was initiated by the loan collecting of Japanese, French, and German banks, not by either stock or foreign exchange withdrawing (*Digital Chosunilbo* 1998a). However, when we say the Asian 'economic' crises, we comprehend them in a broader conceptual framework comprising major macroeconomic instabilities.

[15] For discussion of the Asian model, see Chun (2000).

[16] Many developmentalists recommend developing countries appropriate governmental interventions for their economic development. They argue that it is necessary in the presence of, among other elements, capital shortage (Rosenstein-Rodan 1989).

[17] Some may argue that the East Asian developmental state is out of date because corporations now can access the global capital market. However, the Asian crises have shown that states still can exert their wills to tame corporations. Moreover, the crises had stemmed from the lack of governmental regulation, not from regulation. Thus, East Asian states require changes in regulation not the removal of regulation itself.

[18] In Korea the policy confusion had been partly due to the reorganisation of government. In December 1994 the Korean government had merged the Economic Planning Board and the Ministry of Finance into the Board of Finance and Economy, which later in February 1998 changed its name to the Department of Finance and Economy, transferring some rights to other governmental agencies.

[19] The socially disadvantaged in the victim countries were hurt most and the international capital investors fared best.

[20] Some argue that Japan should increase its imports from the troubled countries; the US already has trade deficits with East Asian countries, and Europe is busy both preparing for further economic integration and supporting former communist neighbours. Thus Japan, which has close production networks with Southeast Asia, should play a leading role as export market. However, we have to admit that Japan's economy itself has long been in recess.

[21] Although there were other factors that conditioned country risk, it cannot be said that this tight monetary policy was irrelevant to the decreasing country risk ratings of Thailand and Indonesia. The Thai foreign currency rating could not recover until early 1999, and that of Indonesia, in late 2000 (www.standardandpoors.com/ratings/sovereigns/index.htm 2001). Korea, however, has increased its equivalent rating ever since the occurrence of the foreign exchange crisis.

[22] If an interest rate increases by 10 per cent and an exchange rate decreases by 10 per cent, there are no offsetting effects from which foreign investors benefit.

[23] Indonesia and Korea had had floating foreign exchange systems before their crises, although the former had 'managed' the system. Thailand changed its foreign exchange system just before the crisis from a managed floating to a floating system.

[24] The Bank of International Settlements is located in Switzerland. Established after the First World War to take care of German reparation, the bank now mainly deals with European central banks' foreign currency exchanges. The bank proposed in 1988 an international standard of banks' capital ratio (the BIS standard) in order to cope with risk.

[25] The Asian market explains about 30-40 per cent of the total exports of Indonesia, Thailand and Korea (Lee 1998).

[26] The US and other developed countries worried about the Korean chaebols' aggressive building of semi-conductors, steel, and car producing facilities.

[27] Also, four national banks were merged into one.

[28] The IMF asked for the dismantling of the *Bulog*, a monopolistic importing organisation aided by the government and responsible for providing food such as rice, sugar, cooking oil, and the like at lower prices than international levels. This led to an abrupt rise in cost of basic necessities.

[29] They agreed to lower their expectations as follows: GDP growth rate, from -5 per cent to over -10 per cent; inflation, from 45 per cent to 80 per cent; and the end-year exchange rate, from Rp6,000 to Rp10,000 per US$1 (Ko 1998, 119).

[30] On Wahid's announcement in spring 2000 of the legalisation of the communist party, Islamic parties threatened to leave the coalition government. In spring, Indonesia also suffered from the independence movements of Sulawesi and Aceh.

[31] Suharto had made political parties powerless by the forcible merging of opposite parties and by organising a de facto ruling party, *Golkar* (a coalition of vocational representatives). Moreover, all parties had to adopt *Pancasila* (nationalism, democracy, internationalism, socialism, and monotheism) as their party ideology.

[32] However, the relief of the near bankrupt Hyundai construction company in spring 2001 shows that there can be an exception.

[33] For the Thai case, see Bowornwathana (2000, 18).

[34] For detail, see Sikorski (1999); *Economist* (1999).

[35] These groups have accounted about 41.6 per cent of the total amount owed to the Indonesian Bank Restructuring Agency (IBRA). Of major concern, however, is that, rather than being punished, the owners are still controlling their groups without inviting new management partners.

[36] Thailand and Indonesia still have traditional sectors. Fortunately, the effects of the crises in the modern sector did not reach into the more remote areas, which consequently avoided significant economic hardship.

[37] For the detailed discussion of the Korean unemployment issue, see Yoon (1998).

[38] Although the Korean job market recently has been generous, many of the jobs offered are part-time. It is not surprising that many workers, who have witnessed their discharged colleagues' tragedies, stubbornly resist being dismissed.

[39] Japan provided US$44 billion to help the three troubled Asian countries (Gohama 1999). Kim (1998) argues that Japan's role has been neither enough nor appropriate. Because of its lack of initiative, Japan seemed to fail to gain international respect. However, considering that the total amount given to the three countries was US$117.9 billion, Japan's monetary contribution should be appreciated.

[40] For a discussion of new international rescue systems, see Wesley (1999); Kumar *et al.* (2000).

[41] See Feng and Choo (1998).

[42] Although both macrohistoric approaches pay attention to the inequality of international and internal structures, Wallerstein emphasises the exchange structure, while Galtung stresses the actors.

[43] Unlike Latin American foreign currency crises in the early 1980s, foreign investors were exempted from accountability in the East Asian crises.

INDEX

HIEBERT LIBRARY

3 6877 00182 6824

HC
412
.A744
1998
v.5